littleDallas

THE DEFINITIVE GUIDE TO LIFE WITH LITTLE ONES IN THE DALLAS AREA

littleDallas

The Definitive Guide to Life With Little Ones in the Dallas Area

Kim Radtke Bannister
Kelli Strobel Chabria

photography by Kimberly Wylie

PUBLISHER'S NOTE

Except for Kim Radtke Bannister's listing of *little words, one-of-a-kind stories for children*, neither Three Little Monkeys, L.L.C., nor the authors have any interest, financial or personal, in the businesses listed in the book. No fees were paid or services rendered in exchange for inclusion in these pages. Please note that while every effort was made to ensure that the information regarding phone numbers, addresses, hours, admission fees, and prices was accurate at the time of publication, it is always best to call ahead and verify all information. Furthermore, readers should discuss all health-related issues with their medical practitioner before acting.

Manufactured in the United States of America.

For information, please contact:
Brown Books Publishing Group
16200 North Dallas Parkway, Suite 170
Dallas, Texas 75248
www.brownbooks.com
972-381-0009

ISBN 0-9753907-9-1
LCCN 2004114501
2 3 4 5 6 7 8 9 10

ACKNOWLEDGMENTS

A wise person once said, "You can't achieve great things on your own"—and we have found she is right! A copious amount of generosity, energy, breath, and insight from family and friends (old and new alike) took this book from conception to birth. We are forever thankful . . . to our husbands, Nevin Bannister (for his business savvy) and A.J. Chabria (for his literary touches); to our parents, Carol (editor extraordinaire) and Ken Radtke, and Carlene and Jack Strobel; to Laura and Larry Bannister, for their parental words of wisdom; and to our support group, talented friends, and confidants: Kimberly Wylie, Jessica Alexandersson, Ainsely Gordon, Stacy Bratton, Rachel Shope, Stephanie Bernal, Mary Beth Bland, Cristy Coltrin, Kelly Starns, Stephanie Rosuck, Jamie Gerard, Tish and Vito Scarola, Matt and Catherine Radtke, Alica Wood, Kalena Cook, Michelle Hertzog, Lisa Nelson, and Lauren Stanley.

We wish a lifetime of love and gratitude to all and to our children who inspired us to write this book . . . thank you, our three little monkeys . . . Sawyer and Ford Bannister and Joshua Chabria.

A special note of appreciation goes to our publisher, Brown Books Publishing Group, and especially Kathryn Grant and Erica Jennings, for their advice, guidance, and expertise.

TABLE OF CONTENTS

INTRODUCTION

I'm what?!" Finding out you're pregnant can take you on a "roller coaster" of emotions. While hormones and anticipation take over, remember to laugh, cry, and feel reassured it doesn't mean you have to go it alone. We met expectant parents, experienced and inexperienced, along our parenthood adventure . . . all filled with plans, questions, and ideas. That's why we wrote *littleDallas* . . . Learning and sharing was the best part.

How do you put in a car seat? Where can I take a prenatal yoga class? We've wondered and have felt overwhelmed about questions such as these, too, and now we know . . . but only after raising three Dallas babes. Kim moved to Dallas from Lake Forest, Illinois, and Kelli is a native of Orange County, California. We met during graduate school at Southern Methodist University—shortly before we met our husbands. Kim was one of the first of her friends to have a baby, and soon after she and her husband Nevin had their daughter Sawyer, Kelli and A.J. gave birth to their son, Joshua. We both considered ourselves very in-the-know about things to do, where to shop, eat, exercise, etc., in Dallas. But parenthood changed everything! Kim still felt overwhelmed two years later, when her son Ford was born, with all of the new resources and information. This is when we decided that it was time to pool resources, share our experiences, talk to others, and gather research.

We've done our best to include the most recent information, but services, policies, phone numbers, and prices do change. So forgive us. Now we have to go . . . the grocery deliveryman is ringing the bell or could it be the dry cleaner, the dog sitter, or the pharmacy? Sound easy? You too can find these helpful resources—just read on!

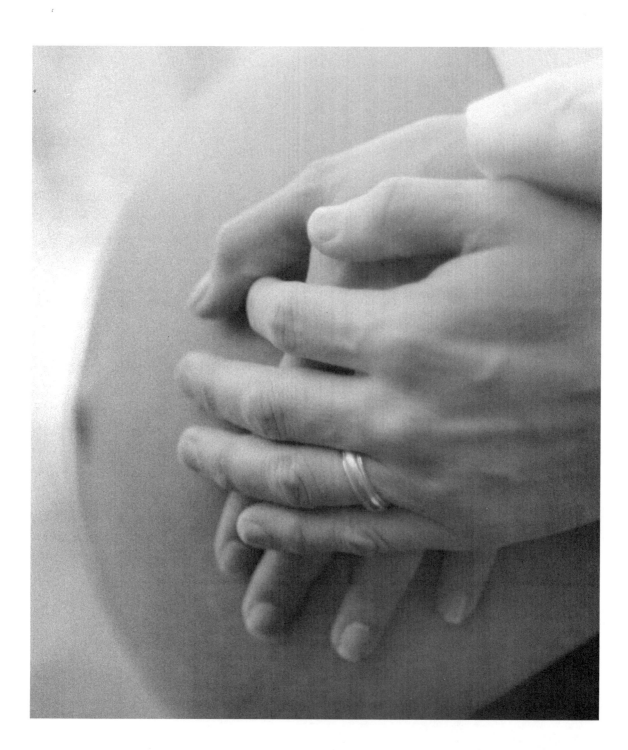

PART ONE:

GETTING READY FOR BABY

CHAPTER ONE:
HAVING YOUR BABY

BIRTHING LOCALES AND ATTENDANTS

WANTED: "A CHEERY STORK WHO FLIES OUT OF THE CLOUDS WITH A HEALTHY AND BEAUTIFUL BUNDLE OF JOY." Everyone wants a safe and comfortable delivery, and there are a multitude of options for having a positive birthing experience in the Dallas-Fort Worth area. It is up to you to look at the choices, exhaust all research methods (from safety issues to cost), and talk with your doctor or selected certified nurse midwife (CNM) about your findings, questions, and concerns.

If you have chosen to go more naturally and use a midwife, know that few hospitals allow them. In the hospital, the certified midwife (by the American College of Nurse Midwives, or ACNM) may administer medication and call an anesthesiologist at your request. Friends who used midwives after their experiences with RNs during their previous pregnancies told us that they went this route because of the one-on-one, personalized attention they received from the midwife throughout their entire pregnancy (same scheduled visits as your OB/GYN and similar exams, including blood pressure, weight, and baby heartbeat checks), during labor, and even after delivery. It was "a unique bond," completely unlike the relationships they had with hospital RN staff. Both of us had amazing physician relationships and RN support, but we value the insight and experience of birth with a midwife.

Another childbirth option is to enlist the support of a doula (Greek for "woman's servant"). In today's terminology, a doula is a professionally trained labor support companion who provides the mom-to-be physical and emotional support and encouragement. A "birth doula" is there to help from early pregnancy (nutrition, massage, birthing methods, and more) and throughout the entire laboring process (relaxation techniques, massage, and communication with partner and medical staff). There are also "postpartum doulas" who will take care of the new mom and family (breastfeeding and emotional support, household chores, and baby care). For high-risk pregnancies, an "antepartum doula" assists moms-to-be, who are on bed rest, with emotional and informative support and comforting strategies.

Expecting a baby today is individualized and personal and presents countless resources. Together, you and your partner should make the choices for a memorable birth experience.

HOSPITALS

Hospital options may not be the first thought that pops into a mom-to-be's head. Your OB/GYN will dictate your delivery hospital based on his or her privileges and affiliations. We have provided information on Dallas's main hospitals including visiting hours, NICU level, and classes. Talk openly with your doctor about the hospital and what you can expect after delivery. You can also check out www.healthgrades.com, which is an online resource solely dedicated to rating healthcare quality, including hospital and obstetric ratings. Don't just assume all of your questions will be answered by taking a hospital tour and a parenting class. You can't be too prepared when it comes to one of the biggest moments of your life—having a baby!

We also suggest creating a "birthing plan" and sharing it with your doctor. Compose a wish list that includes your preferences regarding pain relief, episiotomy, emergency C-section options, and other contingencies. You need to take ownership of your body and think about what you believe will be best for you. Do not wait until you are in labor to share these thoughts with your doctor. These important issues deserve a great deal of forethought, and be sure to give your doctor time to answer your questions and have a two-way discussion.

Before you know it, it's time for delivery. The nurses and assistants are about to be your best friends and advocates. Do not be afraid to rely on them—they have seen it all, and it is their job to share their knowledge with you. You will be spending far more time with them than even your OB/GYN, whom you will probably only see briefly during labor and the birth process. Take advantage of what the RNs have to offer, and ask for a Popsicle or two—forget the ice chips!

The average hospital stay is forty-eight hours unless you have a C-section, which usually increases your stay to seventy-two hours. Use your time in the hospital to get some rest! Don't feel guilty if you let your new baby sleep in the nursery, even if you are breastfeeding. Trust us, you will have plenty of time to bond with your baby once you get home. Rest is crucial to the healing process—physical, mental, and emotional.

Having said all of this, the best-laid plans will change. Count on it. The most important thing you can do is relax and go with the flow. Don't be distraught if you have to have a C-section and you were convinced that you would give birth vaginally. It may seem like the end of the world at the moment, but once you see and hold your precious baby, nothing else will matter.

- Pre-register for admitting and reserve a private room if desired.

- Sign up for a hospital tour and childbirth class.

- About one month prior to your due date, pack a labor bag with these items: a phone list of people you want to call, snacks (for dad and visitors), gum, a pillow from home, a camera with an extra roll of film, some change for the vending machine, a photo of the big sibling for the baby's bassinet, an outfit for the first photo op and ride home, your robe, nightgown, extra socks, slippers, nail clippers for your baby, blood cord preservation kit (See Resources in this chapter), supplemental newborn screening kit (See Resources in this chapter, available from the Baylor Institute of Metabolic Disease, www.baylorhealth.com), and baby book for footprints and visitor signatures.

- It is not "tacky" to take home everything the hospital has to offer! You have paid for it all—from pads to underwear, and baby necessities such as combs, lotion, onesies, the baby blanket, hats, and the thermometer. These items are for your use to help that first week go smoothly.

- Talk to relatives and friends about visiting you during labor and afterward. Suggest that they visit you at home, and if they want to give you a congratulatory gift, have them deliver it to you at home so you do not have to move anything but your labor bag and your bundle of joy.

- Bring a sibling gift for the new baby to give to your older child. This is a special touch and one Kim and others have found helpful in the introduction process. We also suggest that you bring a photo of the "big sibling" to place in the baby's hospital bassinet (goes over well with the "big sib" and makes him feel a part of the birth even though he wasn't there with you during the process).

- Feel confident in the safety procedures at the hospitals we have listed, but be vigilant when it comes to hospital security. If you are suspicious of anyone, don't hesitate to ask for photo identification.

- Do not keep money or valuables in your room.

- Most of all, ask questions of one and all.

HOSPITAL	CLASSES	DELIVERY
Baylor University Medical Center—Dallas 3500 Gaston Avenue Dallas 75246 214-820-0111 (Main) 800-422-9567 (Classes) 214-820-3103 (Simply Mom's, Breastfeeding Boutique) www.baylorhealth.com **Visiting Hours:** 8 a.m. to 9 p.m. **Father:** 24 Hours	• Prepared Childbirth • Breastfeeding • Cesarean • Infant/Child CPR • Nutrition and Pregnancy Class • Refresher Childbirth • Maternity Tour • Dads Only • Breathing and Relaxation • Basics of Baby Care • Vaginal Birth after Cesarean • Sibling • Safesitter • Moms on the Move	**MIDWIVES: Yes,** through Women's Health Alliance 214-824-3200 **NICU LEVEL: III** This is one of the top hospitals nationwide and provides obstetric, gynecologic, and infant and pediatric services with advanced technology for prenatal diagnostics and care, labor and delivery, high-risk infant care, genetic counseling, and family education. More than 4,400 babies are delivered at Baylor University Medical Center each year. The level III NICU has 72 beds. There are private rooms available. They also offer special treatment services for infants and children at the TINY TOT Clinic and Children's House.
Baylor All Saints Medical Center at Fort Worth 1400 Eighth Avenue Fort Worth 76104 817-926-2544 (General) www.baylorhealth.com **Visiting Hours:** 7:30 a.m. to 8:30 p.m. **Father:** 24 Hours	• Baby Basics • Breastfeeding • Infant/Child CPR • Prepared Childbirth • Refresher Childbirth • Siblings "Big Brother, Big Sister"	**MIDWIVES:** No **NICU:** III
Baylor Medical Center at Garland 2300 Marie Curie Garland 75042 972-487-5000 (General) 972-487-5154 (Simply Mom's, Breastfeeding Boutique) www.baylorhealth.com **Visiting Hours:** 9 a.m. to 9 p.m. **Father:** 24 hrs	A variety of classes are offered through Baylor Healthcare System. Call 800-422-9567.	**MIDWIVES:** No **NICU LEVEL:** III
Baylor Medical Center at Irving 1901 North MacArthur Irving 75061 972-579-8100 www.baylorhealth.com **Visiting Hours:** 10:30 a.m. to 9 p.m. **Father:** 24 hours	A variety of classes are offered through Baylor Healthcare System. Call 800-422-9567.	**MIDWIVES:** No **NICU LEVEL:** II
Baylor Regional Medical Center at Grapevine 1650 West College Grapevine 76051 817-481-1588 www.baylorhealth.com **Visiting Hours:** Noon to 8 p.m. **Father:** 24 hours	A variety of classes are offered through Baylor Healthcare System. Call 800-422-9567.	**MIDWIVES: Depends on doctor** **NICU LEVEL: III**

HOSPITAL	CLASSES	DELIVERY
Presbyterian Hospital of Dallas 8200 Walnut Lane Dallas 75231 214-345-6789 (General) www.texashealth.org **Visiting Hours:** 7 a.m. to 9 p.m. **Father:** 24 Hours	**Childbirth and Family Education Classes:** • Early Pregnancy • Breastfeeding • Basics of Baby Care/CPR • Lamaze Preparation for Childbirth • Lamaze Preparation for Multiples • Lamaze Natural Childbirth • Refresher • Anesthesia Class • Sibling Class **Postpartum Classes:** • Newborn Group • Graduate Group • Employed Moms • Baby Sign Language • Raising Sexually Healthy Kids **Parenting Series:** • Growing up Again • Infant Massage • Perinatal Bereavement Support Group **Call 1-800-4-PRESBY (1-800-477-3729)**	**MIDWIVES:** No **NICU LEVEL:** III The labor and delivery nurses and the postpartum nurses are attentive. The nurse that takes care of you also brings you your baby and can answer any questions. The labor and delivery rooms at the Margot Perot Center at Presbyterian Hospital are large and have everything you will need, from a private bath to a TV. Presbyterian is the first hospital in North Texas dedicated exclusively to caring for women and their babies, and it has more than 100 OB/GYNs and over 100 pediatricians on staff.
Presbyterian Hospital of Plano 6200 West Parker Road Plano 75093 972-981-8000 (General) 972-981-3788 (A Mother's Gift for Lactation) www.texashealth.org **Visiting Hours:** 9:30 a.m. to 9:30 p.m. **Father:** 24 Hours	• A Grandparent Is Born • Anesthesia Lecture • Babycare/CPR • Breastfeeding • C-Section • Infant CPR & Safety **Call 1-800-4-PRESBY (1-800-477-3729) for more classes offered by Presbyterian Hospitals.**	**MIDWIVES:** No **NICU LEVEL:** III All rooms are private. While they do not allow midwives, friends and a labor and delivery staff member have told us that doulas are okay as long as you call them a "friend." This is one of the first hospitals in the Metroplex to open a lactation boutique and resource center, called A Mother's Gift. It is on the third floor next to the nursery and offers in-house and out-patient consultations.
Medical City Hospital 7777 Forest Lane Dallas 75230 972-566-7000 (General) 972-566-7153 (Parent Education) www.medicalcityhospital.com **Visiting Hours:** 10 a.m. to 8:30 p.m. **Father:** 7 a.m. to 10:30 p.m.; 24 hours in a private room	• Preparation for Childbirth • Breastfeeding • Daddy Boot Camp • Pediatric Basic Life Support and Safety • Maternity Tour • Sibling Class • Refresher Childbirth **Call 972-566-7153 for Parent Education.**	**MIDWIVES:** No **NICU LEVEL:** III Medical City is the only hospital in the area that has neonatologists and pediatric anesthesiologists on-site 24 hours a day, 7 days a week. It's also the only hospital in North Texas where a mother facing a high-risk pregnancy can deliver her baby in the same facility that can treat and attend to the needs of both the mother and baby. The birthing rooms are spacious and have a couch, TV, and private bathroom. They also have in-house lactation consultants to help with any breastfeeding issues, and the hospital has a bereavement care team. Medical City is also the home of North Texas Hospital for Children.

HOSPITAL	CLASSES	DELIVERY
Harris Methodist—Fort Worth 1301 Pennsylvania Avenue Fort Worth 76104 817-882-2000 (General) 817-882-BABY (Breastfeeding Resource Center) 888-4-HARRIS (Classes) www.texashealth.org **Visiting Hours:** No set hours before 9 p.m. **Father:** 24 Hours	• Lamaze • Newborn 101 • Touch Points for Toddlers • Safe Sitter • Car Seat Safety • Grandparents • Breastfeeding • CPR • Baby Signs, and many more **Call 888-4-HARRIS for more information.**	**MIDWIVES: Yes** **NICU LEVEL: III** In 1997, this hospital merged with Dallas-based Presbyterian Healthcare Resources, and later it merged again with Arlington Memorial Hospital, which is now a part of Texas Health Resources. There are 27 rooms, all of which are private and equipped with a crib. Lactation consultants are available.
Methodist Dallas Medical Center 1441 North Beckley Avenue Dallas 75203 214-947-8181 (General) 214-947-3000 (Maternity) www.methodisthealthsystem.org **Visiting Hours:** 9 a.m. to 9 p.m. **Father:** 24 Hours	• Preparation for Labor and Childbirth • First Born for First-time Parents • Breastfeeding • Sibling Classes • Baby Care • Parenting Skills	**MIDWIVES: No** **NICU: III** There are 9 private labor/delivery/recovery suites and 38 postpartum rooms, which are designed for the baby to "room-in" with the new mother. Three Neonatologists provide 24-hour support for babies born at Methodist Dallas, and perinatology services are offered.
Methodist Charlton Medical Center 3500 West Wheatland Road Dallas 75237 214-947-7777 (General) 214-947-7199 (Labor and Delivery) www.methodisthealthsystem.org **Visiting Hours:** 9 a.m. to 9 p.m. **Father:** 24 Hours	• Childbirth Preparation • Breastfeeding, Baby Care • Infant CPR • Babysitting • Sibling Classes	**MIDWIVES: No** **NICU LEVEL: II** There are 11 private labor/delivery/recovery rooms and 35 private postpartum rooms. You have the option to have your baby "room-in" with you. Lactation consultants and bereavement support services are available.
Medical Center of Plano 3901 West 15th Street Plano 75075 972-596-6800 (General) 972-519-1251 (Classes) www.medicalcenterofplano.com **Visiting Hours:** 10:30 a.m. to 8:30 p.m. **Father:** 24 Hours	• Hospital Orientation Class and Tour • Cesarean Section Pre-Op Program • Refresher Class • Breastfeeding Classes • Prenatal/Postnatal Water Aerobics Class • SIBS (Special Ideas for Brothers and Sisters) • Infant CPR • Grandparent CPR • Baby Care Class During Pregnancy • Bootcamp for New Dads	**MIDWIVES: No** **NICU LEVEL: III** There are 23 labor/delivery/recovery suites, 44 postpartum rooms, and 40 NICU beds. Unique to this hospital is the Oral-Motor Feeding Clinic, which deals with unique nutritional or feeding concerns, such as sucking or swallowing. In-house lactation consultants are available, as is a Grief Support Group.
Las Colinas Medical Center 6800 North MacArthur Boulevard Irving 75039 972-969-2000 (General) www.lascolinasmedical.com **Visiting Hours:** 10 a.m. to 9 p.m. **Father:** 24 Hours	• Preparing for Childbirth • Preparing for Parenthood • Infant Care, Breastfeeding • Infant CPR • Sibling Class	**MIDWIVES: Per Doctor Approval** **NICU: II** All 12 postpartum rooms are private. Nurses offer lactation consulting during the day.

HOSPITAL	CLASSES	DELIVERY
Parkland Memorial Hospital 5201 Harry Hines Boulevard Dallas 75235 214-590-8000 (General) 214-631-BABY (University Neonatal Services) www.pmh.org **Visiting Hours:** Noon to 8 p.m. **Father:** 24 Hours	A variety of classes are available, from childbirth and infant safety to lactation.	**MIDWIVES: No** **NICU LEVEL: III** This is the only public hospital in the county and it is the primary teaching institution of the University of Texas Southwestern Medical School. It is often rated among the best hospitals in the United States. Parkland delivers over 13,000 babies a year. Low-risk pregnancies are delivered by in-house certified nurse midwives, with a physician's assistance. The university's neonatal services for the seriously ill has 102 beds, 24 ICU beds, and a 6-bed neonatal surgical area. Children's Medical Center is located adjacent to Parkland.
Denton Community Hospital 207 North Bonnie Brae Denton 76201 940-898-7000 www.dentonhospital.com **Visiting Hours:** 7 a.m. to 9 p.m. **Father:** 24 Hours	Prenatal and sibling classes. More classes will be offered beginning in spring 2005.	**MIDWIVES: Yes, and waterbirth services are available as well.** **NICU LEVEL: I** Denton Community Hospital will become a $100 million facility—Presbyterian Hospital of Denton—in spring 2005. The Birth Place at Denton Community Hospital currently has 6 labor and delivery rooms and 17 private postpartum rooms. Goodmoms, a program for expectant mothers planning to deliver at Denton Community Hospital, includes a monthly newsletter, a take-home kit with a keepsake footprint certificate, and a CD of lullabies. Look for changes and upgrades after the renovation is complete.
Medical Center of Lewisville 500 West Main Street Lewisville 75057 972-420-1000 (General) 972-420-1036 (Classes) www.lewisvillemedical.com **Visiting Hours:** 9 a.m. to 9 p.m. **Father:** 24 Hours	• Maternity Orientation • Breastfeeding • Infant/Child Safety and CPR • Hysterectomy • Prepared Childbirth • Sibling • Baby Care Basics	**MIDWIVES: No** **NICU LEVEL: III** Every expectant mother stays in one of the 28 private labor/delivery/recovery obstetrical suites. Lactation consultants are available.
Arlington Memorial Hospital 800 West Randol Mill Road Arlington 76012 817-548-6100 (General) 817-548-6500 (Classes) www.texashealth.org **Visiting Hours:** 9 a.m. to 9 p.m. **Father:** 24 hours	• Infant CPR • No-Nonsense Nutrition for Pregnancy • Breastfeeding • Baby Care Basics • Sibling	**Midwives: No** **NICU: III** There are 13 private labor and delivery rooms and 35 postpartum rooms. Lactation consultants are available.

BIRTHING CENTERS

If you are committed to natural childbirth and looking for a home-like setting, a birthing center offers this and more. Friends and family are welcome to wait or be with you at all times. You can also find comfort from walking around, sipping tea, getting a massage, using Jacuzzi tubs, or sitting on a birth ball and showers—all without being confined to a hospital bed. There is no use of drugs (Demerol or epidural). Waterbirth (giving birth in a tub) is also an option at some of the centers listed below.

A midwife is with you throughout your birth. The birthing center is typically run by a midwife (or two) who will attend the birth. Ask to meet the midwives personally, view the center, interview them, check for compatibility (it takes a certain rapport or chemistry to feel comfortable and confident with someone), and ask about their training and experience and/or certification (not all midwives are a CNM). Other helpful tips and suggestions are to ask for three referrals before choosing a birth center and/or midwife, check the proximity to the nearest hospital in case of an emergency, inquire about their transfer rate and C-section rate, and ask if they take health insurance (some will call to check benefits and make the claims for you). The birthing centers we have listed below offer tours. Call for information and ask to speak with the director personally.

Last, only a few hospitals (such as Baylor University Medical Center–Dallas and Parkland Memorial Hospital) in the area that we have listed allow or use midwives. If you are interested in midwife services for a hospital birth, or even a home birth, a birthing center is a great resource for finding a midwife or doula, birthing classes, and well-woman care. You may also see our Resource listing.

Allen Birthing Center
406 West Main Street
Allen 75013
214-495-9911
www.allenbirthingcenter.com

Birth and Women's Center
3100 Swiss Avenue
Dallas 75204
214-821-8190
www.birthcenter.net

Lovers Lane Birth Center
4309 West Lovers Lane
Dallas 75209
214-366-3579
www.dallasmidwife.com

Women's Health Alliance
3600 Gaston Avenue
Dallas 75246
214-824-3200
www.wha-docs.com
*Susan W. Akins, CNM, is on staff with Baylor University Medical Center–Dallas.

BIRTHING METHODS

THE BRADLEY METHOD

This method, developed by obstetrician and gynecologist Robert A. Bradley, focuses on deep relaxation and breathing, along with a close-working partnership and coaching by the father-to-be. The parents-to-be are to view the pregnancy as preparing for the birth. Dr. Bradley believed in a healthy, natural approach with a goal of not using medications or drugs during pregnancy and labor. Courses are usually taught in twelve sessions and discuss topics, such as health and nutritional needs; growth of the baby; changes in the mom-to-be's body; the father's role before, during, and after birth; the stages of labor; adjusting to your new baby; and breastfeeding. You may visit www.bradleybirth.com to find an instructor or see our listing in Childbirth Educators.

HYPNOBIRTHING

Since ancient times, methods of hypnobirthing have been used to transfer mom into a relaxed state in order to prepare and nurture the body through the natural process of birth. In 1989, Marie Mongan founded the HypnoBirthing Institute to offer training and certification for this childbirth method. The logic behind hypnobirthing is to self-hypnotize to prevent the body from going into the fight-or-flight mode, which happens when we are frightened or extremely nervous. It is when the body goes into this mode—or reflex—that studies have shown certain organs shut down (the nonessential ones to fight-or-flight), such as the uterus—thus restricting the flow of blood, causing cramps and pain. Believers and some experts feel that self-hypnosis can prevent this reflex and even shorten labor. Mongan's method of hypnobirthing is offered through group or private instruction. You may visit www.hypnobirthing.com to find an instructor, or see our listing in Childbirth Educators.

LAMAZE

The majority of hospitals we have listed offer Lamaze courses and reinforce its use with the aid of nurses in the labor and delivery room. Thought by many as "just breathing techniques" that were developed in the early 1950s by French obstetrician Ferdinand Lamaze, the technique has evolved to include other ways of coping during labor such as positioning, hydrotherapy, walking, visualization, and relaxation techniques. Most classes are taught for couples. The method does not dictate the use of drugs; having an epidural is a personal choice. The classes, typically done in a series totaling twelve hours, often discuss options and offer other tips and facts helpful to the process of labor and your hospital stay. You may visit www.lamaze-childbirth.com to find an instructor outside area hospitals or see our listing in Childbirth Educators.

WATERBIRTH

Some have told us that this is a soothing and safe way to welcome your baby into the world. Experts say that waterbirth can lessen pain during labor, thus possibly creating a better birth experience. Some women choose to use portions of this method for labor only, while others actually deliver their baby in the tub. Since babies do not breathe until they are brought out of the water (similar to their experience in the womb), many studies and experts say this is a safe birthing option. With the help of a midwife, waterbirth can take place in your own home (depending on your tub size and other resources).

CHILDBIRTH EDUCATORS AND COURSES

Confident Beginnings
Jill Walpole, RN, LCCE
972-390-0812 or 972-814-7556

Jill Walpole, a registered nurse with the state of Texas, offers childbirth classes that are intimate in size, and arrangements can be made for independent courses. Classes are taught by Lamaze Certified Childbirth Educators, like Jill. Discussions range from health care to trusting your inner wisdom while giving birth. Breastfeeding classes and postpartum doula services are also available.

Gentle Birth Companions
Nadine Romain, PhD, CHt
972-237-1626

Nadine Romain is a well-known name for certified HypnoBirthing instruction and for her classes. She offers several series of courses throughout the year. Classes are for couples, meet once a week for five weeks, and last for two hours. Some of the valuable topics Nadine will address are the background and philosophy of hypnobirthing, nutrition for you and the baby, stretching inner thighs, how to release emotions and fears, breathing techniques, the dad's role, how labor proceeds, and ways to adjust if progress is slow. She also offers private instruction.

Janet Miller, ICCE, CD (DONA)
972-475-6556
www.yourpregnancymatters.com

For over eight years, this mother of three has been teaching childbirth courses both at Presbyterian Hospital of Dallas and privately. If you are on bed rest or have a busy schedule, Janet can come to your home to teach her three and one-half hour Prepared Childbirth Class for $125. Topics include signs and phases of labor, medications, hospital routines, cesarean birth, and relaxation techniques. Janet does not believe that there is one set method for birthing and therefore integrates the best of several methods such as Lamaze, the Bradley Method, and HypnoBirthing. She also offers breastfeeding and basics of baby care courses—all in the privacy of your home. Janet is also available for groups.

Natural Beginnings
Sharon Mattes, RLC, IBCLC, LLLL, AAHCC
972-495-2805

Linda Worzer, BMEd, IBCLC, AAHCC, CD (DONA)
972-699-3921

www.naturalbeginningsonline.com

Anyone who uses Natural Beginnings is in good hands. Sharon and Linda have over fifty years of combined professional and mothering experience. Their eight-week course (certified Bradley Method childbirth instructors) on the processes of pregnancy, labor, and parenting will make you feel more comfortable and knowledgeable about your upcoming birth and your choices. There is "homework" such as practicing relaxation and breathing with your partner. Sharon and Linda also offer individualized childbirth preparation courses, and Sharon teaches early parenting courses.

The Nesting Place
Kay Willis, RN
877-625-6803
www.thenestingplace.net

Since they will come to your home to teach one-on-one, the Nesting Place is a great resource for women who are on bed rest, or for people who are too busy with their careers. They also offer group courses in childbirth for you, your pregnant friends, and all partners. All of the educators are RNs and can help with questions on pregnancy and childbirth. They also offer classes in lactation consulting, infant safety and CPR, breastfeeding, and baby basics.

Jill Stillwell, CCCE, CD, BFE
817-563-1007

Jill Stillwell is a certified childbirth educator and certified doula whose goal is to teach the expectant mother and the family how the body works during the last stages of pregnancy and to teach coping methods for labor. She doesn't teach a certain set childbirth method, but rather focuses on taking the fear out of giving birth by instilling knowledge of your body. Jill recommends scheduling your private childbirth class (six hours, tailored to your needs and schedule, in your home) in the middle of your seventh month or at the eighth month. She works with high-risk and multiple pregnancies and is a tremendous resource for those on bed rest. Jill also serves as a postpartum doula.

CALL YOUR INSURANCE COMPANY FOR INFORMATION ON REIMBURSEMENT OF A PORTION OF YOUR SELECTED CHILDBIRTH COURSE FEES.

RESOURCES

The following list of organizations and individual services will help you locate and learn more about midwives, doulas, childbirth methods, educators, newborn blood cord preservation, and lifesaving metabolic disease testing.

ALACE (Association of Labor Assistants and Childbirth Educators)
888-222-5223
www.alace.org

Association of Texas Midwives
903-592-4220
www.texasmidwives.com

Baylor Institute of Metabolic Disease
800-4BAYLOR
www.BaylorHealth.com

Baylor Medical Center Dallas offers a kit ($35) that you can order and take to the hospital with you at the time of delivery. The kit requires blood samples to be placed on a specific card, and we highly suggest that you ask your nurse to coordinate this when the hospital does its blood testing (required by the state). Texas hospitals only check for five metabolic disorders, but the kit tests for more. If the hospital staff gives you any problems or tells you that you don't need the kit since the hospital conducts its own tests, ask your pediatrician to take care of taking your baby's blood for the test when he or she makes a hospital visit.

The Bradley Method of Natural Childbirth
800-4-A-BIRTH
www.bradleybirth.com

Childbirth & Postpartum Professional Association (CAPPA)
888-MY-CAPPA
www.childbirthprofessional.com

Cryo-Cell International, Inc.
800-786-7235
www.cryo-cell.com

Kim and Nevin have used Cryo-Cell for both Sawyer's and Ford's umbilical cord blood preservation. The service is professional and very informative.

Doulas of North America
888-788-DONA
www.DONA.org

HypnoBirthing
www.hypnobirthing.com

Intuitive Birth: The Amazing, Life Changing Benefits of Natural Birth
www.IntuitiveBirth.com

A book by Kalena Cook, with Margaret Christensen, MD

MANA (Midwives Alliance of North America)
888-923-MANA
www.mana.org

Natural Beginnings
www.naturalbeginningsonline.com

Pregnancy Matters
www.yourpregnancymatters.com

Sidelines
888-447-4754
www.sidelines.org

An online resource for moms-to-be who are on bed rest

ViaCord

866-668-4895

www.viacord.com

Preserves and stores your baby's umbilical cord blood

Waterbirth International

800-641-2229

www.waterbirth.org

Women's Health Alliance

3600 Gaston Avenue
Dallas 75246
214-824-3200
www.wha-docs.com

*Susan W. Akins, CNM, is on staff with Baylor University Medical Center–Dallas.

Women to Women Health Associates

214-823-6500
www.wwha.yourmd.com

CHAPTER TWO:
BABYING YOU

FIT MOMMIES

Many of us would rather eat a pint of cookie dough ice cream or enjoy a long nap instead of finding the time to exercise. We continued to exercise throughout our pregnancies and resumed shortly after we gave birth because it gave us the extra boost of energy we needed—not to mention, it helped fight the bloating! For many women, it can be difficult to find the time and energy to exercise, but trust us, the benefits are worth it. Appropriate measures of exercise during pregnancy can ease labor, reduce pregnancy discomfort, increase overall energy, and decrease your recovery time after delivery. Postnatal exercise helps you lose those pregnancy pounds while releasing stress. Several postnatal classes incorporate your baby in the exercise routine.

If you already belong to a gym, check the schedule or talk to the fitness director to see if they offer prenatal or postnatal classes. We have not mentioned most "big" gyms like 24-Hour Fitness or Bally's. However, we did list two we felt have superb and specialized amenities and services for women. If you don't already have an exercise plan, there are structured classes or individual trainers to raise that heartbeat. Most locations we have listed have experienced and certified instructors and trainers who have experience working with prenatal and postnatal women. It is crucial to check with your physician before you begin or alter an exercise regimen. Be aware that many studios and fitness centers ask for a doctor's consent. Wearing a heart monitor while exercising throughout your pregnancy is a must! So grab your baby and water bottle . . . and get ready to move! Just make sure your heart rate (when pregnant) does not exceed the recommended rate of 140.

EXERCISE PROGRAMS AND STUDIOS

Arlington Memorial Hospital
800 West Randol Mill Road
Arlington 76012
817-548-6575
www.texashealth.org

Easy Does It is especially for moms-to-be. The class is 45 minutes of low impact cardiovascular and strength training. It's a wonderful way to take care of your baby and yourself.

Fees: A once-a-week class costs $25 a month.

Baby Boot Camp

Allen, Dallas, Grapevine, McKinney, and Plano
Megan Keele
214-402-1130

McKinney
Jennifer Murray
214-448-6994

www.babybootcamp.com

Baby Boot Camp is the fitness class that won't allow a new mother an excuse not to work out. All you need to bring is water, a towel, a stroller, and your baby! Offered both indoors and outdoors, depending on the location, these classes are designed for new mothers and their babies between the ages of six months and two years. Classes highlight both cardiovascular and strength training, as they make you work hard to get back into shape. Kelli and Josh hit the Katy Trail and it was challenging—my, how quickly time flies! It's a great opportunity to get to know other new moms in your area. You can register by filling out an online form or by calling your local instructor to reserve your spot. If you are afraid to sign up without trying the class, you can sign up for a complimentary session.

Fees: Prices range from $84 for six classes to $256 for an unlimited pass. Sessions run eight weeks, and unused classes cannot be carried over into the next session.

Baylor Tom Landry Fitness Center

411 North Washington
Dallas 75246
214-820-7870
www.baylortomlandryfitnesscenter.com

Moms on the Move is an aquatic prenatal class that is designed to help you get in shape or maintain your current level of fitness. You learn how to manage common problems associated with pregnancy and how to prepare for childbirth. Goals of the class are to maintain recommended weight gain, improve emotional health, relieve back pain, and minimize water retention. You do not need to be a member of the fitness center in order to take advantage of this class.

Fees: Twelve classes are $60, and the session expires 90 days after date of purchase. You may try your first class at no cost.

Bend Studio

5014 McKinney Avenue
Dallas 75205
214-841-9642
www.bendstudio.com

The YamaMama Prenatal Yoga and Mommy and Me Yoga classes are offered at owner Ally David's uptown area studio. See YamaMama Prenatal Yoga on page 23.

Fees: Prices range from $250 for a twenty-class pass to $150 for an unlimited monthly membership, to $1,350 for a yearly membership.

Dallas Yoga Center

4525 Lemmon Avenue, Suite 305
Dallas 75219
214-443-9642
www.dallasyogacenter.com

Serving Dallas for the past fifteen years, Dallas Yoga Center is owned by David Sunshine and offers both Prenatal and Mommy and Me yoga classes. Prenatal Yoga is for women of all fitness levels and stages of pregnancy. Mommy and Me Yoga, for mothers and infants from six to twenty months of age, encourages the moms to use the time with baby to strengthen and tone their bodies. Infant massage and baby yoga are also part of the class.

Fees: The eight-week Prenatal Yoga series is $108, and six months of unlimited classes are $576.

Future Mommy Fitness

Steve Trentham, BS, CPT
972-985-0363
www.futuremommy.com

Steve Trentham is a father and personal trainer and has developed a comprehensive program for prenatal women called Future Mommy and a postnatal program appropriately named Lean Mean Mommy Machine. After Steve's wife became pregnant, he saw the lack of information available to pregnant women and was disappointed that most fitness programs are not set up to work with the assistance of an OB/GYN. He decided to collaborate with doctors, nutritionists, and counselors to develop a specialized program. He combines the efforts of a fitness specialist, a nutritionist, a chiropractor, a child development specialist, and a psychotherapist into a program that helps women have a healthy, happy pregnancy and postpartum experience.

Fees: The six-week course is $175 and is held at Plano Health Club. You don't have to be a member of the club to participate in Steve's programs. The course includes a coupon for 60 percent off massage therapy. Steve offers a 100 percent money back guarantee if you are not satisfied.

Goodbody's Yoga Center

5401 West Lovers Lane at Inwood Road
Dallas 75209
214-351-9931
www.goodbodysyoga.com

Goodbody's Yoga Center offers a couple of options for expectant mothers. Prenatal teachers are on staff for private instruction—perfect for you and your pregnant friends. While half of the classes offered are "power yoga" (not recommended during pregnancy), many expectant mothers take Iyengar yoga, which includes assistance in adjusting positions and teaches movements for pregnant women, if needed.

Fees: Drop-in rates are $15 per class. Private lesson rates depend on the number of people taking the class.

Hart's Military Fitness Training

214-826-1466
www.hmftdallas.com

After the baby, moms and dads can get into shape with the help of Bobby Hart. Bobby is a former Marine and has used his experiences to create a challenging fitness program. Classes are conducted at local parks where there is plenty of room to run, participate in team relays, and perform static exercises. Beginners are welcome, and exercising with a group is a great motivator.

Fee: The session (about one month) is $395 for five days a week or $325 for three days a week, and only $175 for returning students.

Joe Farmer Recreation Center

1201 East Bethany
Allen 75002
214-509-4810
www.cityofallen.org/parks/jfreccenter.htm

This recreation center offers a wide range of exercise classes. Prenatal Mamaste Yoga and aqua classes are offered to expectant mothers; both are an hour long and designed to be relaxing.

Postnatal classes include Mommy and Me Fitness, Aqua Fitness, and Strollerfit! Mommy and Me Fitness. These are great, fun classes to get back into shape while beginning to develop your baby's motor skills. Strength training, stretching, and baby massage are also a part of some classes. (See a detailed description of Strollerfit! below).

Fees: Mommy and Me Fitness is $60 for twelve classes, Prenatal Yoga is $60 for six classes, Strollerfit! costs $54 for six classes, and prenatal and postnatal Aqua Fitness runs $30 for eight classes.

Kokopelli's Wellness Spa and Yoga Center
4760 Preston Road, Suite 208
Frisco 75034
972-225-2623
www.kokopellispa.com

Kokopelli's offers a few classes aimed at mothers-to-be. Prenatal women are welcome to attend both beginner and gentle yoga classes, and a Prenatal Yoga / Water Exercise class. In the Water Exercise class, gentle stretching and breathing exercises help the expectant mother release stress accumulated in the body. "This is a special class for that special time in a woman's life as she becomes in touch with her inner self and the developing baby within." The expectant mother needs to be at least thirteen weeks pregnant and have a doctor's release to participate.

Fees: $125 per month for unlimited yoga, Pilates, and water aerobics at Kokopelli's.

Life Time Fitness
7100 Preston Road
Plano 75024
214-202-8100
www.lifetimefitness.com
Other locations scheduled to open are Garland, Flower Mound, North Dallas, and Colleyville.

This 150,000-square-foot facility has everything you could ever want and really tries to cater to families. Their superb child-care center, for children three months to eleven years, is 8,000 square feet of fun and education. There are ten computers that teach children about nutrition and fitness. The play areas and the security system to check in and check out your child are excellent. There are indoor and outdoor swimming pools with beach entry so you can wade with your little ones and get them comfortable with the water (See chapter 11, Birthday Cheer). Mamaste prenatal yoga is taught here, along with postnatal Mommy and Me yoga classes for mothers and their babies six weeks to six months (babies must not be crawling). Other amenities include a full service spa, five outdoor tennis courts, and a restaurant.

Fees: Prenatal Yoga for a six-week session: $54 for members, $72 for nonmembers.

Mommy and Me for a six-week session: $54 for members, $72 for nonmembers.

Child care is available for nonmembers for $5 per child, per class, with a two-hour limit per day.

Mamaste Prenatal Yoga
www.MamasteYoga.com

Karen Prior has spent the past ten years developing and teaching Mamaste Yoga. Karen, a mother herself, realized the importance of yoga for pregnant women because of the special connection that develops between the mothers-to-be with each other and with their babies during class. Karen's brand of yoga focuses on soothing aches and pains, reducing stress with relaxation techniques and breathing, improving flexibility, and opening the joints and hips to prepare the body for childbirth. This class is not to be taken until after the first trimester and you must have a doctor's release. For more information about the studios where Mamaste Yoga is offered, look under Joe Farmer Recreation Center, Life Time Fitness, Oak Point Recreation Center, the Pilates and Yoga Center, and Natural Trends or check the Mamaste Yoga Web site for new locations.

Medical Center of Plano

3901 West 15th Street
Plano 75075
972-519-1206
www.medicalcenterofplano.com

Moms in Motion conditions your body in a warm pool during this prenatal/postpartum aquatic fitness class. Classes last forty-five minutes, three days a week, and are a gentle way to improve your strength and breathing.

Fees: Classes are limited to twelve women and cost $40 per month. The first class is free.

Medical City Hospital

7777 Forest Lane, Building C, Suite 240
Dallas 75230
972-566-BEAT
www.medicalcityhospital.com

MOMentum is for expectant or new mothers and consists of cardiovascular and strength training, information on adjusting exercises throughout pregnancy, and nutrition advice. It also provides a chance for moms or moms-to-be to socialize and find support from others.

Fees: The first session is free, and then the cost is $45 per month.

MyTime Women's Fitness & Spa

5964 West Parker Road at the Tollway
Plano 75093
972-781-2244
www.mytimeplaytime.com

MyTime specializes in the fitness and pampering of women. The fitness center also has a spa and is located next door to PlayTime, the children's fitness and learning center that has child-sitting services during mom's workout or spa use.

Fees: Membership at MyTime is $65 per month for a one-year agreement, or $75 for a month-to-month agreement. There is a $100 initiation fee.

Natural Trends
The Shops at Legacy
7202 Bishop Road, Suite D4
Plano 75024
972-546-3600
www.naturaltrends.biz

Ronit Mor opened her studio in 2003 and offers not only prenatal Mamaste yoga, but prenatal massage, reflexology, and a gift shop. Throughout the year, Natural Trends presents special workshops in prenatal couples yoga, postnatal mommy and me yoga, and family yoga (children must be three and up).

Fees: A wide range of pricing options are offered. Two selections are eight classes for $92 and unlimited membership for morning classes for $99 per month.

Oak Point Recreation Center
6000 Jupiter Road
Plano 75074
972-941-7540
www.planoparks.org

Oak Point Recreation Center offers Mamaste prenatal yoga throughout the year as well as several aerobics, strength training, tennis, and golf classes.

Fees: For a series of five classes, Mamaste prenatal yoga is $40 for residents and $44 for nonresidents. Fees for other courses vary.

The Pilates and Yoga Center
966 North Garden Ridge Boulevard, Suite 550
Lewisville 75067
972-353-9642
www.pilatesyogacenter.com

This center services Lewisville, Flower Mound, and Southlake. Sixty- to seventy-five-minute Mamaste yoga classes are offered for moms-to-be who are in their second or third trimester. Baby and Me workout, infant massage, and private training is also available. Couples yoga workshops are offered. You may enroll at any time, but since class size is limited, call to register.

Fees: Registration is $20. Prenatal yoga is $90 for a series of six classes.

Priya Yoga Studio
6337 Prospect Avenue
Dallas 75214
214-328-9642 (Studio)
214-327-8863 (Pregnancy yoga)
www.priyayoga.net

This Lakewood yoga studio offers YamaMama prenatal yoga as well several other yoga courses throughout the day. Several friends can't get enough of their classes and they have met other pregnant and new moms.

Fees: Prices range from four classes for $56 to twenty-four classes for $240.

Rhythm & Moves
2008 Highway 114
Southlake 76092
817-251-MOVE
www.rhythmmoves.com

Bridget Boland began studying yoga in 1998 and now shares her knowledge by helping women maintain their fitness while pregnant. Her class will help with relaxation and breathing and increase flexibility, strength, circulation, and balance.

Fees: $60 for a four-week series, one day a week, and $105 for two days a week.

Rockin' Mamas
Contact: Rachel Kim
rockin_mamas@yahoo.com

If you love to run—besides just after the kiddos—then Rockin' Mamas is the running group to join! Open to moms, dads, grandparents, and caregivers, the group meets the first and third Sunday of every month at 8 a.m. in front of the Boat House at White Rock Lake. New and experienced runners and walkers are welcome. Rockin' Mamas wants to add a weekday run, so e-mail Rachel for more information.

Strollerfit!
Allen, Dallas, and Frisco
Darlene Davis
214-394-5101

Plano and Richardson
Victoria Patel
469-633-1151

www.strollerfit.com

If you are a new mom, dad, grandparent, or nanny, all you need is a stroller and a baby (typically between ten weeks and two and a half years of age) to enroll in Strollerfit! This fitness program is designed to take advantage of your stroller's movement, resistance, and stability by building cardiovascular endurance, improving flexibility, and toning muscles—all while bonding with baby. These classes are done both indoors and outdoors, last approximately fifty minutes, and are open to all fitness levels. It's a great way to meet other new moms, and the first class is free so you can try it out before committing yourself.

Fees: The cost for ten sessions (two-month expiration) is $90, twenty-five sessions (five-month expiration) is $200, and fifty sessions (one-year expiration) is $350.

YamaMama Prenatal Yoga
214-327-8863

Created and taught by Mara Black, YamaMama yoga is enhanced by Mara's twenty-nine years of experience with pre- and postnatal women as a doula who is now working in children's education. This style of yoga strengthens the body and focuses on breathing techniques. You must be at least twelve weeks pregnant to attend class, and previous yoga experience is not required. To see more information about the studios where Mara teaches, see Bend Studio, Priya Yoga Studio, and Yoga for Life.

YMCA Downtown Dallas
601 North Akard Street
Dallas 75201
214-954-0500
www.downtowndallasymca.org

Yogababies is a parent and child postnatal fitness class offered to all Dallas-Fort Worth YMCA members. The class is open to parents of all fitness levels who have babies between six weeks and eighteen months. New, exhausted, or underactive parents can get in shape and learn to relax while bonding with their babies.

Fees: Check your local YMCA, as prices may vary.

Yoga for Life
972-392-9642
12835 Preston Road at LBJ Freeway, Suite 427
Dallas 75230
www.yfldallas.com

YamaMama Prenatal Yoga class for all fitness levels is taught at this studio. Postnatal yoga classes are offered periodically.

Fees: Prices range from four classes for $56 to twenty-four classes for $240.

PERSONAL TRAINERS

Delivering Fitness
Owner: Erinn Mikeska
214-679-7871
www.deliveringfitness.com

If looking at trainer and owner Erinn Mikeska's physique doesn't motivate you to stay in shape, pregnant or not, most likely nothing will. Catering to the Dallas-Fort Worth area, Delivering Fitness provides personal fitness training, pregnancy yoga, and nutritional guidance to expectant moms. They also have a postnatal workout and weight loss program to get you into shape after the baby arrives. Erinn and the other trainers who work for her are certified in Personal Fitness Training with additional certification in Prenatal and Postnatal Fitness and Nutrition.

Fees: Each session costs between $40 and $65, depending on the package you choose, and sessions last forty-five minutes to one hour.

Executive Personal Training
Chad Krisher
214-581-5299

A father of two boys and one girl, Chad has twelve years of fitness experience and provides in-home training for those of us who can't always find the motivation to make it to the gym. Chad views pregnancy as an athletic event and concentrates on three phases: becoming pregnant, being pregnant, and recovering during postpartum. The first and foremost precaution Chad takes is to work with your OB/GYN. He lets your doctor set your parameters as guidelines (i.e., heart rate, etc.). He incorporates the client's and doctor's goals into a fitness regimen. He is also a personal trainer at Preston Gym in Dallas (214-739-2266).

Fees: A one-hour in-home session and consultation is $100. At Preston Gym, a private session with Chad is $75 per session plus membership fees.

Future Mommy Fitness
Steve Trentham, BS, CPT
972-985-0363
www.futuremommy.com

See Future Mommy Fitness in the Exercise Programs and Studios section of this chapter for information on Steve's background and his pregnancy and postpartum fitness program.

Fees: One-hour in-home session in the Dallas area: $95.

Muscle Moms
Laurie Stein
214-340-2199

An exercise enthusiast and mother, Laurie understands what a balancing act it can be for mothers to manage taking care of the kids and finding time to exercise. Certified by the Cooper Institute, she developed Muscle Moms for anyone who can't find the time to make it to the gym or who wants to break up a monotonous exercise routine. Laurie customizes a fitness program designed for your home and individualize your program so you will be motivated to stick with it. Your program consists of cardiovascular and strength training focusing on your fitness goals, and she will bring equipment, such as bands and balls, or use your own equipment. Best of all, Laurie is so much fun, you will feel like you are working out with your best friend.

Fees: Medical assessment: $40. In-home training: $60 an hour. If you have two or more people who want to train, the rate is on a sliding scale.

Muscle Moms will design an eight-week program to specifically fit your needs. Cost for the program design is $75.

NUTRITION

Besides exercise, nutrition is the other component to having a healthy baby and a healthy you. Your OB/GYN should be a great resource to get information on what foods you should be eating or eliminating from your diet. The nutritional choices you make prior to and during pregnancy are one of the few factors you actually have complete control over—so choose wisely. The following Web site can assist you with finding a nutritionist. You may also want to ask your OB/GYN for a recommendation.

American Dietetic Association
800-877-1600
www.eatright.org

The American Dietetic Association can provide you with a nutritionist who specializes in prenatal nutrition and practices in the Dallas-Fort Worth area.

PAMPERING THE BODY, MIND, AND SPIRIT

Do you feel swollen, exhausted, and achy in your lower back? Pregnancy can cause all of these symptoms, but it doesn't have to. Massage, during pregnancy and after, is a wonderful way to relieve excess bloating, back and neck aches, leg pain, and digestive distress. During labor, massage can help you emotionally, ease your pain, and help shorten labor. We have found massage to be an essential part of the entire nine months and after for its rejuvenating elements of the mind, body, and spirit. Massage brought us an elevated closeness with our babies in utero. Perhaps they felt our worries and anxieties melt away, too!

There are several independent massage therapists and spas that offer pre- and postnatal massage, along with other pampering treats such as pedicures and facials. Some therapists are also trained in infant massage—a wonderful way not only to bond with your newborn, but also to help reduce colic and digestive discomforts. Kim found massage extremely helpful with both of her gassy babies.

We have also included massage therapists who will come to your home if desired—a great gift or necessity if on bed rest. We have provided a small listing of spas we have personally tried and those who have come highly recommended to us as a result of their Texas-registered and knowledgeable therapists, quality of customer service, and clean facility.

WHAT TO REMEMBER AND WHAT TO AVOID

- Get your doctor's approval for a massage or any spa treatment.

- Be sure to schedule an appointment with a Texas registered massage therapist who has extensive training in prenatal massage.

- Drink lots of water and be sure not to overheat. Your core body temperature shouldn't be above 102.2 F for more than ten minutes, according to the American College of Obstetrics and Gynecology.

- Don't lie flat on your back for extended periods of time, as it restricts the blood flow to the fetus.

- Some reports say that lying on your stomach with a pregnancy belly hole pillow can stretch uterine ligaments. Check with your doctor and ask for a left-side lying massage.

- Ask for unscented massage oils and lotions, because some scented formulas may be considered unsafe during pregnancy.

- When having a massage or a pedicure, some therapists recommend steering clear of certain pressure points on your ankles and feet that correspond to uterine pressure points (reflexology) and could cause contractions and possibly labor.

PRE- AND POSTNATAL MASSAGE AND INFANT MASSAGE

Baylor Tom Landry Fitness Center
411 North Washington
Dallas 75246
214-820-7870
www.baylortomlandryfitnesscenter.com

This fitness center has more than twelve Texas registered massage therapists who do pre- and postnatal massages. A friend of ours had great massages throughout her pregnancy by Victoria Zac, who has been with the Fitness Center for over ten years. Victoria even went to the hospital at 10 p.m. the night our friend's daughter was born, to give a massage. Her massages are strong and relaxing and she is "knowledgeable at what she is doing." You may choose what is comfortable for you—either the Body Support pregnancy pillows for the belly and chest or the side-lying position. Gift certificates are available. It is $65 for a fifty-five-minute massage or $90 for an eighty-five-minute massage. If you only have twenty-five minutes to spare, it is $38.

Body Essentials
1600 Coit Road, Suite 201
Plano 75075
972-596-2470

This "medical spa" owned by Plano Women's Health Care provides great services especially designed for prenatal and postpartum clients. From facials, hand and foot treatments, waxing, and massage, you will find yourself feeling rested and relaxed. They use the Prego Pillow and other support pillows for massages. Body Essentials also sells a line of wonderful products such as bath soaks, lotions, and creams that are safe for moms-to-be. Gift certificates are available, and you do not have to be a patient of this OB/GYN practice. Prices are $35 per half hour and $70 per full hour.

Sue Brown's massages are out of this world! **—Jamie Gerard, mother of two, Dallas.**

The Greenhouse
817-640-4000
www.thegreenhousespa.net

For the ultimate new-mommy pampering package, the Greenhouse in Arlington offers a Baby and Me Week twice a year for moms and babies eleven months and under. There are discussions about children's health and development, healthy eating, and sleeping issues with Maria Trozzi, an associate of the famed Dr. T. Berry Brazelton; the editor-in-chief of *Child Magazine*; and a nutritionist. Also included are yoga and Pilates classes, massages, facials, a fitness consultation, a professional nanny for your child, all baby needs (high chair to diapers), a deluxe room, food, and airport transportation—all of this for $3,850. Take us away!

Rhonda Grubb, RMT, NCTMB
214-327-1013
RGSportfit@aol.com

Rhonda Grubb is a Texas-registered massage therapist and a nationally certified bodywork therapist with over twelve years of experience. An Ironman triathlete and mother of two, she knows the tolls everyday life and pregnancy can take on the body. Kim's scoliosis made her pregnancies painful at times and even her everyday mommy pick up and carry was uncomfortable. Rhonda's knowledge, expertise, and caring personality have provided her with unbelievable relief—Kim has even been able to resume her running regime. Rhonda's massages are good and strong, but it is her "Bodywork" technique and Cranial Sacral Therapy that will make you melt. She works out of her home and appointments fill fast, so it is best to make a standing appointment! Her hourly rate is $70, and she offers packages and gift certificates.

Monica Hamer
214-642-0242
www.monicahamer.com

Monica Hamer offers massage for before, during, and after birth, as well as for infants. A mother of three, she knows how to work with you and your needs at any stage. She is a Texas-registered massage therapist, certified in Bodywork for the childbearing year, and a Reiki practitioner. She also has her certification in infant massage and teaches infant massage classes. Her relaxing and therapeutic prenatal massage starts at $80 for one hour. Gift certificates are available.

Lori Larsen-Hart, RMT
5749 Vickery, Suite 1
Dallas 75206
214-213-5111

Lori Larsen-Hart has a relaxing therapeutic touch. While you are in the side-lying position and supported by pillows, the quiet atmosphere and peaceful music will take you away. Being a young mother herself, people have said that Lori is in tune with the body, providing instrumental relief for lower back pain and neck and shoulder stress. Lori will also teach you how to massage your infant, or you can bring her in for some pampering! She works by appointment only, and a one-hour massage is $65. Lori will come to your home for an extra charge. Gift certificates are also available.

Sandra Honea
717 Lingco, Suite 203
Richardson 75081
469-358-8960

Sandra Honea has been teaching specialized courses in pregnancy massage for over six years and is a Texas-registered massage therapist with over twelve years of experience. She does a good, firm massage and takes the time to work with her clients finding their likes and needs. She may incorporate pressure points, Myofascial work, and hot stones. She uses a body cushion and supportive pillows in either the side-lying or belly down position, depending on the client's preferences and stage of pregnancy. Her one-hour massage is $65, and it includes an extra thirty minutes for bathroom breaks and getting on and off the table. Sandra also encourages clients to bring in their partners, starting at the seventh month, to teach them helpful massage techniques to use during labor. Sandra loves to teach new parents infant massage.

The Riviera Spa
4445 Travis Street, Suite 102
Dallas 75205
214-521-2112
www.rivieraspadallas.com

This upscale day spa is energizing, yet peaceful, and services are good. Be sure to ask for Jennifer for your prenatal massage that is "pampering for both mommy and baby!" Our friends say that Jennifer is particularly good at working on the stress areas of the lower back. They use pregnancy pillows with a hole in the middle for the growing belly. Prices are $80 for a fifty-minute massage or $95 for eighty minutes.

This is a great day spa that you can run in and out of fast without it being a big affair, and the most wonderful thing ever was lying on my stomach at nine months! —**Tara Price, mother of one, Dallas**

The Spa at the Cooper Aerobics Center
12100 Preston Road
Dallas 75230
972-392-7729
www.cooperaerobics.com

A great thing about this full-service day spa is the hours. Sunday afternoon massages are a treat! The nationally known Cooper Aerobics Center's Mediterranean spa offers both pregnancy and postpartum massage by certified therapists. They use specially contoured body pillows, soft music, and aromatherapy, but they suggest you discuss your preferences with the therapist before your treatment. Close friends have told us that they have had great relief from their massages and returned for more after their babes were born. Two pieces of advice: book appointments at least one week in advance, and request a massage room away from the front area of the spa. The most peaceful rooms are downstairs. Prices are $45 for twenty-five minutes, $85 for fifty minutes, and $115 for eighty minutes.

The Spa at the Crescent
Hotel Crescent Court
400 Crescent Court
Dallas 75201
214-871-3232
www.crescentcourt.com

The Spa at the Crescent has several therapists who are certified in prenatal massage and are happy to accommodate your needs. Their therapists use the special support of pregnancy pillows while they work to "calm the body, mind, and spirit." You may choose from the fifty-minute massage for $90, or an eighty-minute massage for $120. If you are in need of a predelivery bikini wax and are bold enough, be sure to book Izam. She makes it as painless as it can be. This is a great place to have a friend join you for a mini retreat or to have your husband meet you for a light lunch at the juice bar.

FRONT DOOR DELIVERY SERVICES
FOR BED REST AND BEYOND

Whether you are on bed rest or are simply sleep-deprived parents trying to cut down that "to do" list, we have found that there are several services that can be true lifesavers. Included in our listing are dry cleaners, grocers, beauty services, diaper delivery services, a pharmacy, and even pet services. After all, who wants to walk a dog late at night while you are alone with a newborn or the kiddos? And if you can order diapers and formula for the same price as the grocery store, then you'll save the juggling act for the delivery guy! Give a service a try. We have, and our lives have been simplified without sacrificing our family time and budget.

BABY GEAR RENTAL

Baby's Away
www.babysaway.com

Baby's Away takes the hassle out of traveling by renting baby and child supplies such as cribs, high chairs, strollers, car seats, safety gates, room monitors, toys, rocking chairs, and more (the products are certified by the JPMA). They have over fifty locations in the US and are located in most major resort and metropolitan destinations. All you have to do is call or e-mail the location you are traveling to; pay by credit card, cash, or check; and they will have everything set up for you when you arrive. Prices vary but for example, to rent a crib, including a sheet, mattress pad, and bumper, in Orlando, Florida, costs $9 a day/$50 a week. A tub of toys costs $6 a day/$36 a week. There is a $15 delivery and set-up charge. For us germaphobes, rest assured that they clean and sanitize every item before it is delivered. A friend of ours says it has made her life simpler when traveling, and she couldn't be happier with Baby's Away's constant quality service and products—now if they only had a sitter too! This is also a great resource for friends and family visiting with children.

DRY CLEANING

Avon Cleaners
469-621-2656

This full-service cleaners specializes in "hand-finishing," whether the item is a shirt or a tablecloth. Avon's work is pretty incredible and costly, but worth it—as we've been told by several parents. A laundered shirt runs about $1.79 when pressed in a machine. The same shirt is $6 and up if it is hand pressed. This Park Cities luxury delivers to the Preston Hollow, Plano, and Frisco areas. There is about a three- to four-day turnaround.

Avon is fantastic! They noticed we weren't home once and made sure our cleaning was out of view and put it in a safe place. **—Dallas mom of two and wife of a dress shirt kind of guy.**

Bibbentucker's
Multiple locations
www.bibbentuckers.com

If you can't make it to Bibbentucker's drive-up window, then free home delivery is a great option. They will pick up laundry and dry cleaning and return it to you the next day, or as scheduled. Bibbentucker's doesn't mind last-minute orders; just call! They offer automatic button repair, linen service, repairs, and American Airlines miles for each dollar you spend. On a day when you have the time, be sure to visit them for a free window wash, coffee or lemonade, candy for the kids, and a treat for your favorite pet.

In two years, we've never had anything missing or a shirt returned with a broken button. **—Kay Giesecke, mother of two, Dallas.**

FOOD DELIVERY

Albertson's
www.albertsons.com

"Making life a little easier," the company's food delivery motto is so true! For only $9.95 for delivery service, you can get everything you find at the store. Kim, who uses them on a regular basis, ordered flowers one Friday afternoon, along with numerous packages of diapers, heavy soda packs, formula cans, produce, frozen food . . . and the roses lasted a week. What a treat for yourself! Be sure to take the extra time to initially fill out your grocery list online and go through each category. This will make the next time a breeze. Prices are competitive with other grocery stores. And you can put your tip money away because the delivery persons don't accept them. Orders must be in by midnight the day prior to delivery, and all orders come to you in a climate-controlled truck—especially useful for keeping those crab legs cool! Deliveries are scheduled with about a two- to three-hour window. If you prefer to pick up your goods, for $4.95 they will be chosen, bagged, and loaded in your car.

Central Market
5750 East Lovers Lane
Dallas 75206
214-361-2169

320 Coit Road
Plano 75075
469-241-8386

www.centralmarket.com

This "by referral only" program is great if you don't mind paying for Central Market's personal shopper to gather your fine products and have them delivered to your door. From chef-prepared meals to hard-to-find organic delights; from fresh bakery items to grand produce; from wine and beer to staples like milk, coffee, bottled water, and juice, Central Market carries almost everything you need except diapers, formula, and economy packages of paper towels. Cental Market's wonderful natural health department stocks vitamins, lotions, and baby care products. All you need is to be referred by a personal shopper member, like Kim, and then arrange for an escorted shopping tour, during which you show the store's personal shopper what you like and dislike, your regulars, and your staples. From this meeting, the personal shopper creates a master list from which you will order. You may place your order by phone, fax, or e-mail. Orders in by 10 a.m. can be delivered or picked up the same day. There is a shopping fee of $12.50 per order, and delivery fees range from $12.50 to over $20, depending on how many miles you live from the store. If you want to save the delivery charge, you can arrange to pick up.

The Chefmeister
972-539-1887
www.thechefmeister.com

Nutritious and great-tasting food cooked in your home, packaged, and labeled for the rest of the week—complete with reheating instructions—what more could a tired new parent want? Kristin Lyon, chef/owner, has been servicing families throughout the Metroplex for over fifteen years. Her belief is that dinnertime should be family time. All meals are tailored to your likes, dislikes, and nutritional needs and are prepared in your kitchen on a scheduled cook date and time. The Chefmeister does the grocery shopping and the dishes! There are several packages to choose from, with prices starting at $200 for the "3/4" weekly plan, plus the cost of food. This plan includes three complete meals (four portions) and side dishes. Gift certificates are available.

Diet Gourmet
972-934-0900
www.dietgourmet.com

Diet Gourmet specializes in freshly prepared meals, handmade and brought to you. Whether it is breakfast, lunch, and/or dinner, each meal is "designed to conform to or exceed the nutritional guidelines established by the American Heart Association, the American Cancer Association, and the American Dietetic Association." Some of our friends swear by Diet Gourmet's taste and quality of service. Some sample entrees include roasted pork, three cheese ravioli, BBQ cornish hen, and various sides and desserts. Their meals are kept to a 1,100 to 1,700 calorie level, so make sure to follow your doctor's guidelines. Diet Gourmet will adjust the calories through portion size. You can order online, over the phone, or via fax.

Feastivities, Gourmet-to-Go
5724 Locke Avenue
Fort Worth 76107
817-377-3011
www.feastivitiesinc.com

The selection of gourmet items is endless. Choose from homemade soups, fresh salads, entrees, sides, and desserts to stock your fridge or for a "welcome home" gift. New parents will not only be appreciative, but they will love the breakfast choices as well. The adorable store is located off Camp Bowie and is worth the visit to pick up frozen entrees, fresh salads, and sandwiches. Feastivities asks that you place your order three days in advance. Trays to feed a crowd and catering services are also available.

Rehoboth Ranch
2238 County Road, 1081
Greenville 75401
903-450-8145
www.rehobothranch.com

Do you want to feed your family beef, chicken, turkey, and lamb that are free of pesticides, fertilizer residue, and synthetic hormones? Look no further than this Greenville family farm. For over ten years, the Hutchins family's Rehoboth Ranch has been raising animals in clean pastures—additive, steroid, and chemical free. Their USDA inspected facility offers the ultimate in quality, and the Hutchins invite you to come visit—or they can deliver your meat to your door once a month. You must be home and prices vary. They also offer pick-up service throughout the area on Tuesdays. New in 2004 is their State of Texas certification for Grade A raw goat milk. This is a great alternative for children with milk sensitivities or allergies. The milk comes fresh or frozen, $3 for a quart or $12 for a gallon, and must be picked up at the farm.

BEAUTY SERVICES

Alice Hughes
214-343-7021

For over forty years, Miss Alice has been maintaining and polishing the nails of Dallas women and men and massaging away their aches and pains. A strong hand and spirit are enough to make this a delightful experience. Have her visit you at home, in the hospital, or book her for one of her "pamper parties" in which she comes to your home. Alice can book you, your friends, or your husband for neck and shoulder rubs, reflexology, pedicures, and manicures. Pedicures take about one and a half hours and cost $60. A manicure is one hour at $30, and a thirty-minute neck and shoulder massage is $2 a minute.

NLook
469-241-9744

For over ten years, Johnny Rodriguez, recommended by D Magazine, has been cutting and styling hair in Dallas. His group includes two colorists who are not only talented, but professional and personable. They are sure to make you feel your best even if you're swollen or sleep-deprived. They will cater to your schedule, but remember to try and book them at least two weeks in advance. Haircuts start at $95, which includes a small travel fee. Hospital visits are possible.

PET SERVICES

Is your first "baby," your beloved dog or cat, in need of some extra attention? From emptying cat litter boxes to daily dog walks to watering your plants, a pet care giver can offer numerous services to help make life better for you and Fido. While we can't offer to come and walk your dog, we can offer you some names of services that can, and that are bonded and insured for the safety of you and your pet. Walks or visits are usually about thirty minutes, and pricing is typically for one to two animals, increasing for each additional pet. Be sure to ask your pet sitters of choice if they have emergency backup systems in place, are bonded and insured, and are pet first aid certified. The ones we list here all fit the bill.

Marsha's Pampered Pet Sitting

214-341-4350

www.marshaspets.com

Whether you need only one or two visits a day, or you need someone to help watch your pets and home while you are away, Marsha has to be one of the friendliest people around. This retired school teacher and mother of three loves to pamper your pets. She services Lake Highlands, Lakewood, Park Cities, Uptown, and Preston Hollow. All of Kelli's neighbors who have pets use Marsha and feel like she's more a part of the family than just a pet sitter. Her fee is $12 to $15 a visit and most importantly, you can rest assured that you will know your walker and/or sitter, for she is the owner/operator.

Park Cities Pet Sitter

214-828-0192

www.parkcitiespetsitter.com

Owner Joette White, who started out as a sitter for Park Cities Pet Sitter, bought the company from the founder in 2000. She has professionally worked with pets for over seven years and couldn't be friendlier. Voted number one among pet services by *D Magazine*, Park Cities Pet Sitter is not so big of a service that you have to worry about a different sitter each visit. They ensure that you meet with a sitter who lives in your area, and that your pets get to know the sitter first. Once a sitter is mutually agreed upon and only in case of an emergency when your sitter is unavailable, White will make the rounds herself. Whether it is a walk, a litter box change, or a game of dog tennis, each individual visit is $16 and Park Cities Pet Sitter services all over Dallas and Plano. There are discounts for more than four scheduled visits each week, every week. There is a "pet taxi" service for trips to the vet or groomer, for an additional $25 per thirty minutes. Park Cities Pet Sitters is bonded and insured and is a member of the National Association of Professional Pet Sitters, Pet Sitters International, and the National Association of Professional Dog Walkers. Park Cities has a pet first aid certification by the American Red Cross.

PHARMACIES

Dougherty's Pharmacy

515 Preston Royal Village

Dallas 75230

214-363-4318

Hours: Monday-Saturday, 8 a.m. to 9 p.m.; Sunday, 10 a.m. to 5 p.m.

Serving Dallas since 1929, Dougherty's will deliver almost everywhere in the area. We have found that they are the best place to get hard-to-find prescriptions and prescription formula outside of the hospitals. The friendly staff will be sure to figure out a way to help you get your prescription as soon as possible. They also supply and deliver medical equipment.

We needed a breathing machine for our toddler and the children's hospitals were out, but Dougherty's had it! —**Mom of two, Preston Hollow**

Drugstore.com
800-378-4786
www.drugstore.com

Drugstore.com is an online pharmacy where you can get your prescriptions mailed to you on a regular basis and buy baby products and everything you need, from lotions, toothpaste, and parenting magazines, to environmentally friendly cleaning products. Ordering is easy and delivery is reliable. Some of our favorite product lines they carry are Avent bottles, Mother Nature Diapers, Burt's Bees, Little Remedies, Hylands teething tablets, and Seventh Generation diaper wipes.

DIAPER DELIVERY SERVICES

For those of us who use disposable diapers, we owe a debt of gratitude to housewife Marion Donovan, who created the disposable diaper in 1950. Yet not everyone is thankful for the invention of disposable diapers. The great debate between cloth vs. disposable diapers continues to this day. While the majority of people in this country choose to use disposable diapers, advocates of cloth diapers argue that they are more economical and environmentally friendly, and that they help prevent diaper rash since they are breathable.

The American Academy of Pediatrics says there are some health aspects to consider when choosing cloth or disposable diapers. Because cloth diapers can't keep wetness away from your baby's skin as effectively as disposables, it is important that cloth diapers are changed immediately after they become wet or soiled. Cloth diapers are less likely to prevent leakage of urine and stool than disposable diapers—a crucial fact in a group child-care setting where intestinal diseases can be easily transmitted among children. Whatever you decide your needs and concerns are, it is best to plan which type of diaper you want to use before your baby arrives, so you can stock up or arrange for delivery.

Albertson's
www.albertsons.com

Choose from Baby Basics, Huggies, Pampers, and Luvs diapers. Delivery to your front door in the Dallas, Fort Worth, and Arlington areas is $9.95. They also deliver groceries (See Food Delivery).

The Baby Outlet
877-693-BABY
www.babyoutlet.com
Customer Service: 8 a.m. to 5 p.m.

One-stop shopping! This online store carries everything for parents and parents-to-be, including Pampers and Huggies diapers and Diaper Genie refills. Their prices are competitive or sometimes less than the bigger retail and grocery chains. Shipping is free on orders over $99.

DFW Grocer
972-267-4440
www.dfwgrocer.com

Stay in your pajamas, skip the shower, and shop from home using this online service. They carry Chicolor, Huggies, Luvs, and Pampers diapers. There is an $8 fee for same-day or next-day delivery.

Dry Bottoms
866-drybottoms
www.drybottoms.com

With the click of your mouse, diapers and wipes are delivered to your doorstep. Sign up for the automatic "TimeSaver" option, or place an order at your convenience. If you select the "TimeSaver" program, diapers and wipes are delivered every three weeks. The DryBottoms.com ultra-premium disposable diapers are comparable to Huggies or Pampers and have a patented wetness indicator that changes color when the diaper is wet. Dry Bottoms will also provide up to a 20 percent discount for parents of multiples. Prices vary, but for example, if you ordered 144 medium diapers and wipes on the "TimeSaver" program, you would pay $53.90 including delivery. They also deliver Bright Beginnings formula.

Metroplex Diaper Service
838 Gable Avenue
Duncanville 75137
972-780-9801
www.metroplexdiapers.com

This family-owned and operated service delivers prefolded 100 percent cotton diapers (also known as "prefolds") to your front door, and on a designated day and time. Each week, clean diapers are traded out for the soiled ones. The diapers are cleaned following a multiple-step process which ensures the cleanest diaper possible. The first diaper pail, deodorizers, and diaper bags are provided at no extra charge. Prices are eighty cotton diapers for $16.95, seventy cotton diapers for $15.95, and sixty cotton diapers for $14.95

CHAPTER THREE:
BEING A NEW PARENT

LEARNING TO BE PARENTS . . .
GRANDPARENTS, SIBLINGS, AND CAREGIVERS!

No matter how well prepared you think you are, expect the unexpected! While we tried to read everything we could to learn how our little creatures tick, we found that there are no set rights or wrongs and going with your mother's instinct is a good thing. However, we also found that taking courses and talking with others was extremely valuable. We continue to educate ourselves each day just by being around others.

Being a new parent can be demanding, exhausting, and even isolating. We have learned that you can't do it alone. Friends and family can offer comfort. Talk to them, as well as other new and veteran parents and available experts. Don't be afraid to ask how to "dry up" your milk, what bottles help prevent air, or if they felt sad at times. We have found that an open conversation can prove not only to be grounding, but life altering. After the premature birth and death of Kim's niece and nephew, and then her sister's miscarriage—all in one week—a mother at Sawyer's school who had lost her unborn son during her seventh month of pregnancy offered valuable insight and helpful suggestions for living with a loss. This insight proved to be tremendous support for Kim to share with her family. Support is something you can only get by opening up—a gift beyond words. Approach parenting with an open view. Take a course, join a support group, and encourage your child's grandparents and caregivers to do the same.

Dallas-Fort Worth has a wealth of resources. There are several trusted specialists who would love nothing more than to share what they know. Just remember that you and your spouse, as well as many others, are going through the same experience as fun, thrilling, and yes, exhausting as it is. Make a conscious effort to support each other—it is empowering.

HOSPITAL COURSES

Classes at the hospitals listed below will help you and members of your family get off to a healthy and educated start. Times, locations, and fees vary since there may be several locations for one hospital system. Enrollment is often limited so it is best to sign up early in your pregnancy (by the sixth month). Some courses offer registration online and are open to the public. You do not have to be delivering your baby at that particular health-care system to enroll. We have had friends take courses with other friends at Baylor and then deliver at Presbyterian Hospital. This is also true with the grandparent, sibling, and caregiver courses, but if your delivering hospital offers these special courses, register there so that siblings and grandparents will be familiar with the facilities.

Baylor Healthcare System
1-800-4-BAYLOR
www.bhcs.com

With locations all over the Metroplex, Baylor Healthcare System is a great resource when it comes to parenting classes. Basics of Babycare walks parents through sleep cycles, circumcision care, bathing, diapering, feeding, and immunizations—everything first-time parents need to know. Other classes include Breastfeeding, Siblings, Dads Only, Grandparents, Safe Sitter Babysitting, and Infant/Child CPR.

Harris Methodist Hospitals
817-261-BABY (2229)
www.HarrisMethodistHospitals.org

Serving Fort Worth and the surrounding area, Harris Methodist Hospitals offer a variety of classes. Just for Dads assists fathers with balancing family and work, maintaining a healthy marriage, and knowing what to expect beyond diapers. Incredible Infants is a discussion and support group that covers an array of topics concerning what parents and infants will experience over the first year. After this course, you can join the Terrific Toddlers group for speakers, outings, and new friends. Harris's Grandparenting Class teaches grandparents how to support the new parents, informs them of the changes in parenting since they had their own babies, teaches car and home safety, and more. They also offer sibling and breastfeeding support and classes.

Medical Center of Plano

3901 West 15th Street
Plano 75075
972-519-1251
www.medicalcenterofplano.com

Medical Center of Plano offers Boot Camp for New Dads, a seminar focusing on responsibilities as role models, caring for mom and baby, forming a new family, plus outings for fathers and babies to share. Grandparenting 101: Bragging Rights, helps grandparents learn about how things have changed since they were new parents. New products and baby-proofing techniques are some of the topics covered. There is also a segment with a psychologist who discusses what grandchildren need most from their grandparents. Methods of Mothering is a six-week course that tackles questions new moms have after the baby is born, and you get to bring the little one with you. The course covers safety, first aid, growth and development, and taking care of yourself while taking care of a new baby. Other classes offered are SIBS (siblings preparation course), Breastfeeding, and Infant CPR. There are also support groups and courses for complicated pregnancies.

Medical City Hospital

7777 Forest Lane
Dallas 75230
972-566-7153
www.medicalcityhospital.com

Medical City Dallas offers a variety of classes, such as an informational session with Dr. Baby Proofer (Thom Golden), called The ABCs of Child Safety. This former RN and BSN has coupled his emergency room experience with his studies in child safety to offer a service which evaluates the safety needs of your home and pool and offers car seat inspections. In this course, you will learn about the best products to buy, how to make your home and yard babysafe, and how to properly install a car seat. At Daddy Boot Camp, veteran fathers spend an hour orienting "rookie" dads on becoming fathers. Other classes offered are Breastfeeding, a Sibling Class, and a Refresher Childbirth class.

Presbyterian Healthcare System

800-477-3729
www.phscare.org

With hospitals in Dallas, Allen, and Plano, there is a wide range of courses. A Grandparent Is Born is a seven-hour class that looks at the bond between children and grandparents and offers information about CPR, changes in baby care, car seat issues, and feeding information. Other classes offered are BabySigns, Babycare/Infant CPR, Infant Massage, and aerobic and water exercise. There are also support and discussion groups that meet weekly for moms and babies (broken into groups by ages) and for employed moms (birth to twenty-four months). You can register online for a variety of courses.

GROUPS, OTHER CLASSES, AND SEMINARS

Equally as important as preparing you for the birth of your child is the peace you can gain from support groups. We have learned everything from easing baby gas and colic to where to take swim classes and what to seek in a preschool. Being in a group is also a great venue to raise questions or concerns, or to just make sure that your child isn't the only one to spontaneously hurl things across a room or avoid naps like the plague!

Baby and Me Week
The Greenhouse Spa
817-640-4000
www.thegreenhousespa.net

The Greenhouse Spa in Arlington offers a Baby and Me Week twice a year for moms and babies eleven months and under. There are discussions and informative seminars on children's health and development, healthy eating, and sleeping issues. Speakers include Maria Trozzi, an associate of the famed Dr. T. Berry Brazelton; the editor-in-chief of *Child* magazine; and a nutritionist. Beyond meeting other moms and sharing stories and tips, also included are yoga and Pilates classes, massages, facials, a fitness consultation, a professional nanny for your child, all baby needs (high chair to diapers), a deluxe room, food, and airport transportation—all of this for $3,850.

Cradle Roll at Temple Emanu-El
8500 Hillcrest Road
Dallas 75225
214-706-0000
www.tedallas.org

Cradle Roll is a free program for parents of children three months to one year and is offered every Friday from 9 a.m. to 11 a.m. You can meet with other families to share in Shabbat services and activities, and to discuss topics of interest to new parents.

Dallas Association for Parent Education
777 South Central, Building 1, Suite 1-T
Richardson 75080
972-699-0420
972-699-7742 (Warmline: Monday-Friday, 9 a.m. to 3 p.m.)
www.dallasparents.org

DAPE is a respected nonprofit organization founded in 1959 by a group of parents who wanted child preparation to be available for everyone. From prenatal topics to parenting throughout the years, their goal and commitment is building a strong bond between parent and child. "We want people to understand child development because it makes them better parents," says Melissa Ferrer of DAPE. They also sponsor "Warmline," a free, nonmedical phone service available to parents and caregivers, on which trained volunteers offer support and suggestions for everyday problems, developmental facts, and resource information. Other classes and workshops offered are Baby Care Basics; Breast-feeding Basics; Adult, Child, and Infant CPR and First Aid; Preschooler Development; Baby Massage; and Positive Parenting.

Dr. Jan Dunn, LPC, LMFT
8222 Douglas Avenue, Suite 777
Dallas 75225
214-890-6637
www.drjandunn.com

For over seventeen years, this mother of three has counseled couples, individuals, and families and has held discussions for groups on such issues as marital relationships, parent/child conflict, adoption, grief and loss, and personal growth. Dr. Dunn has her Doctorate of Philosophy in marriage and family therapy and a Master of Science in speech pathology. Kim has friends who have used her and say she is an "invaluable resource for parents."

Homebirth Association of North Dallas (HAND)
214-521-9310
www.homebirthdallas.org

HAND is a group of parents, expectant parents, childbirth educators, doulas, midwives, lactation consultants, and family members who support one another and promote midwifery and homebirth. The group meets the second Monday of each month and there are speakers every other month on topics ranging from fitness to cloth diapers. There are also family events at parks and holiday events.

Incredible Infants
Harris Methodist Southwest Education Center
701 5th Avenue
Fort Worth 76104
888-4-HARRIS
www.texashealth.org

Celebrate parenthood with other new parents at this ongoing group for new parents and infants! Parenting will become a little easier after you discuss a variety of issues such as baby massage and feeding your infant. You will also learn songs and games to encourage your baby's development. Groups meet once a week and you can enroll on a monthly basis.

Jewish Community Center

7900 Northhaven Road
Dallas 75230
214-739-2737
www.jccdallas.org

It is worth your time to periodically check the classes offered at the Jewish Community Center. They offer a variety of parenting classes throughout the year and classes are open to the public. Love and Logic (see Love and Logic below) is taught by Tara Ohayon, a JCC special needs director. The JCC is also a wonderful resource for activities and groups for children with special needs.

Love and Logic

2207 Jackson Street, Suite 102
Golden, Colorado 80401
800-338-4065
www.loveandlogic.com

For over twenty-five years, the Love and Logic Institute in Golden, Colorado, has been providing parents, educators, and counselors support with research-driven methods for promoting a healthy and respectful relationship with children. Founded by Jim Fay, a former teacher and father of three, Love and Logic gives parents powerful skills all with something delightful to make you giggle. Through seminars and products, Love and Logic's unique and practical parenting methods have been rewarding to several of our friends. Kim asked a mother of three, all under the age of five, how she kept so calm through the toddler tantrums and power struggles. The mom told Kim about a Love and Logic seminar she had attended at her parent association meeting and some of the "quite effective methods and reasoning" she learned. Another mom praises the effectiveness of their books (available on audiocassettes, CDs, and videos). Seminars are regularly scheduled in our area, and speakers are available for parenting groups. Check their Web site for more information.

Moms and Babies Newborn and Crawler Groups

Contact: Jeannette Crenshaw
Family Education Coordinator at Presbyterian Hospital of Dallas
214-345-8568
www.phscare.org

The Newborn and Crawler groups, sponsored and held at Presbyterian Hospital of Dallas, offer weekly meetings and support in an informal setting. You have the chance to bond with your baby and other families. Topics include communication with your partner, balancing work and home, sleeping issues, updates on infant health and development, and baby proofing. There is also fun time for singing, playing games, and reading stories. The group is a great way to learn survival tips while making new friends and is intended for mothers and their infants from birth to six months (newborns) and six to twelve months (crawlers).

MOMS Club
www.MOMSClub.org

MOMS is a support group designed for stay-at-home mothers of children of all ages. There are over one hundred chapters across Texas, and a few of our friends can't say enough about how much this organization has helped them with the transition to becoming a mom. They have book and cooking clubs, MOMS' night out, babysitting co-ops, park days with children, charity events (MOMS is a non-profit organization), and exercise groups. Dues range from $15 to $30 a year and there is no registration fee. E-mail MOMS Club to find the chapter closest to you. There are chapters in Allen, Arlington, Coppell, Dallas, Denton, Flower Mound, Grapevine, Hurst/Euless, Lewisville, and McKinney.

MOPS (Mothers of Preschoolers)
www.gospelcom.net/mops

MOPS exists to meet the needs of all mothers. Whether you work, stay at home, live in the city or suburbs, or are married or single, MOPS wants to help mothers be the best they can be. The group is designed for moms with children between newborn and age five. To find a chapter near you, visit the Web site and type in your zip code.

Mothers and More
Plano
972-994-1118
www.mothersandmoreplano.org

Lewisville
www.greaterlewisvillemothersandmore.org

Hurst/Euless/Bedford
817-424-8858
www.ahconnect.com/mothersandmore

National Headquarters
630-941-3553
www.mothersandmore.org

This nonprofit organization is designed to give support and educate caregivers. Mothers and More is open to any woman, whether she works full time, part time, or is a stay-at-home mother. Some of the events the chapters have include monthly meetings, playgroups, couples' night out, bunko night, movie night, speakers, and special events for children.

Natural Beginnings
Sharon Mattes
972-495-2805

Linda Worzer
972-699-3921

www.naturalbeginningsonline.com

Founders Sharon and Linda have over fifty years of professional and mothering experience between them. Together, they provide a variety of classes such as the Newborn Care Class, which is much more than just how to hold, bathe, and diaper a baby (although those topics are included too)! Discussions include self-esteem, nutrition for the new mom, new roles in the marriage, and different parenting styles. Helping Your Child Welcome the New Baby and Breastfeeding for Mothers Preparing to Return to Work or School are two more classes offered.

The Nesting Place
Kay Willis, RN
877-625-6803
www.thenestingplace.net

The Nesting Place is a great resource for all family members, not just the expectant mom. The Siblings Class is designed for children to have fun while learning what a new baby in the house is all about. For grandparents, they offer open discussion groups and courses all designed to teach the latest sleeping recommendations, safety issues, and more.

New Dad Group
Contact: Jeannette Crenshaw
Family Education Coordinator at Presbyterian Hospital of Dallas
214-345-8568
www.phscare.org

Calling all dads . . . this is a fantastic opportunity to bond with your newborn (to six months) one Saturday morning each month and meet other new fathers, all while giving moms a break! In a laid-back atmosphere, new dads will discuss parenting skills, share any concerns, and have questions answered.

New Moms and Babies Support Group
Highland Park United Methodist Church
3300 Mockingbird Lane
Dallas 75225
214-523-2202

This is a chance for new moms to meet others and to be a part of a discussion group lead by Kathryn

Quest, a licensed family counselor. For over five weeks, moms will get to talk openly with others about finding time for themselves, returning to work, fertility issues, the birth story, helpful tips, local resources, and postpartum depression. The group is open to the public and is offered four times throughout the year for $50. Scholarships are available.

New Moms Support Group
Contact: Monica Hamer
214-642-0242
www.monicahamer.com

Meet other moms with children ranging in age from newborn to eighteen months. Meetings are held at Lovers Lane Birth Center the third Tuesday of the month from 7 p.m. to 8:30 p.m. This is a great opportunity to ask questions and discuss topics such as sleeping, nutrition, soothing, and relationships. Siblings are welcome to attend.

Parents of Little Ones (POLO)
Church of the Incarnation
3966 McKinney Avenue
Dallas 75204
214-522-0160

This group of moms meets at the Church of the Incarnation every Thursday during the fall, from 9:30 a.m. to 11:30 a.m., for informal coffee followed by a speaker. Topics in the past have included nursing, discipline, and helpful parenting tips. This is a great way to meet local moms with children from birth to preschool, and it is open to the public. Child care is free (twenty-four-hour notice required). There are activities with children during the summer (Summer Surviving) and there are quarterly Project Days for finishing your scrapbooking, knitting, and holiday cards—lunch and child care is provided. This group is open to the public; you do not have to be a member of the church.

St. Alcuin Montessori School
6144 Churchill Way
Dallas 75230
972-239-1745
www.saintalcuin.org

St. Alcuin Montessori School is a highly regarded Montessori school in Dallas offering classes for new parents. An adult/infant series for infants from birth to sixteen months and their primary caregivers is based on one of the observations made by Maria Montessori: children can teach themselves if they are free to interact within an environment designed to meet their developmental needs. Parents, grandparents, and nannies are welcome to attend. The class meets for two hours, twice weekly, for eight weeks. The first two-hour class focuses on the adult and infant working together and is assisted by a trained St. Alcuin faculty member. The second two-hour class is a discussion group.

They also offer a twelve-week discussion series aimed at newborn to three-year-olds. Whether you are expecting, are a grandparent, or just want to understand more about child development, you are welcome to attend. The class meets for two hours weekly and is led by a trained St. Alcuin faculty member. Topics include sleeping, exercising the will, labor and delivery, the development of movement and language, and toilet training.

Touch Points for Toddlers
888-4-HARRIS

Sometimes parenting seems to intensify as your child gets older when there are more challenges to face. Touch Points is a free, parents-only group that meets four times a year at Harris Methodist Fort Worth Hospital. This is a time to discuss toilet training, discipline, temperament, and personality issues, and to compare notes on any other areas of interest or concern.

HELPFUL BOOKS

We feel that you don't learn to parent by reading a book, but we do feel that they are helpful and can be a great resource for various issues, from stages of pregnancy to disciplining your preschooler. Here are some to add to your reading list and your bookshelves.

NEWBORN AND INFANCY

Baby Signs: How to Talk with Your Baby Before Your Baby Can Talk by Linda Acredolo, PhD, and Susan Goodwyn, PhD

On Becoming Baby Wise by Gary Ezzo and Robert Bucknam, MD

The Baby Book by William Sears, MD, and Martha Sears, RN

The Complete and Authoritative Guide to Caring for Your Baby and Young Child by the American Academy of Pediatrics

The Discipline Book by William Sears, MD, and Martha Sears, RN

The Happiest Baby on the Block: The New Way to Calm Crying and Help Your Newborn Baby Sleep Longer by Harvey Karp, MD

Secrets of the Baby Whisperer by Tracy Hogg with Melinda Blau

The Pregnancy Journal and *The Toddler Journal* by A. Christine Harris, PhD

The Strong-Willed Child by Dr. James Dobson

Touchpoints by T. Berry Brazelton, MD

What to Expect When You're Expecting and *What to Expect the First Year* by Arlene Eisenberg, Heidi E. Murkoff, and Sandee E. Hathaway

Your Child's Self-Esteem by Dorothy Corkille Briggs

THE TODDLER YEARS AND BEYOND

A Mind at a Time by Mel Levine, MD

How to Behave So Your Children Will, Too by Sal Severe, PhD

Is This Your Child? Discovering and Treating Unrecognized Allergies in Children and Adults by Doris Rapp, MD

Making the "Terrible" Twos Terrific! by John Rosemond

John Rosemond's Six-Point Plan for Raising Happy, Healthy Children by John Rosemond

What to Expect: the Toddler Years by Arlene Eisenberg, Heidi E. Murkoff, and Sandee E. Hathaway

Your Three-Year-Old: Friend or Enemy by Louise Bates Ames, PhD, and Frances L. Ilg, MD

VOLUNTEER GROUPS AND ORGANIZATIONS

Volunteering is a great way to help those less fortunate, to meet other parents, and to teach children to give back to the community. Since we can remember, our parents have volunteered, and often, we volunteered as a family. Today, as parents also, we find ourselves planning an annual calendar for our "giving time" and believe it is never too early to get the kiddos involved, especially by talking about the exchange of gifts and how important it is to share with others. Sawyer, at the age of four, has grasped the concept and asks Kim if she can bake items for her teachers to thank them for all they teach to her class.

So whether it is a local Early Childhood Parent Teacher Organization (ECPTA), a nonprofit, or your church, we hope that once you settle into parenthood, you will find the joy we have found by giving back to the community. Some organizations that we have been involved with, or that have come highly recommended by friends, family, and those surveyed, are listed below.

Early Childhood PTA

Typically ECPTA groups are for parents/caregivers of newborns. When children start kindergarten, parents can join the PTA. Many of the area elementary schools also offer Preschool Associations. Speakers and parent education programs, playgroups, fundraising, and monthly meetings are just a few of the ways someone can get involved with these organizations. Kelli and Kim both belong to their local ECPTA chapter and have found it to be an excellent way to meet other mothers, help raise money for worthwhile causes, and find playmates. Several of the associations below also have Dads' Clubs events and this is a great way for them to meet other neighborhood fathers. For further and/or updated information, you may call the Texas PTA at 800-TALKPTA. You may also visit www.myschoolonline.com and select "Texas" under "Find a Site." Select the city you want under "Find your community in Texas" and browse the listings for PTA/Community Web sites.

Allen ECPTA
www.aecpta.com

Bradfield Elementary Preschool Association
214-780-3200

Carrollton ECPTA
www.cecpta.org

North Carrollton ECTA
www.ncecpta.org

Collin County ECPTA
www.ccecpta.com

The Colony ECPTA
www.inthecolony.com

Coppell ECPTA
www.myschoolonline.com

North Dallas ECPTA
www.ndecpta.com

Far North Dallas ECPTA
972-732-6574

Farmers Branch ECPTA
www.myschoolonline.com

Garland ECPTA
www.earlychildhoodpta.com

Hyer Elementary School Preschool Association
214-361-9658

Lake Highlands ECPTA
www.lhaecpta.org

Lakewood ECPTA
www.lecpta.org

Greater Lewisville ECPTA
www.myschoolonline.com

Mesquite ECPTA
972-613-7607

Preston Hollow ECPTA
www.phecpta.org

Richardson ECPTA
www.town-mall.net/Education/ptsa.html

University Park Preschool Association
214-750-1233

NONPROFIT VOLUNTEER ORGANIZATIONS

There are countless organizations where you can volunteer time, help plan and organize fundraisers, or donate items, all while making new friends, touching the lives of others, and setting an example for your children. Here are a few worth checking into.

Boys and Girls Clubs of Greater Dallas
214-821-2950
www.bgcdallas.org

You can volunteer by being a mentor, tutoring, coaching, working at a club, or helping out with field trips. There are also fundraising event opportunities.

Bryan's House
214-559-3946
www.bryanshouse.org

Bryan's House is a twenty-four-hour, medically managed child-care and family support service for kids with HIV. The facility needs baby formula, bottles, toddler clothing, strollers, and store gift certificates. All items must be new.

ChildCareGroup
214-630-7911
www.ChildCareGroup.org

Every day, ChildCareGroup is responsible for providing and managing the care of more than 13,000 local children from low-income families. Their Annual Adolphus Tea is a special event that calls for volunteers and support. Kim and Sawyer and several friends have attended this event with special celebrity guests for the kids like Madeline and Jay Jay the Jet Plane. Kim is a fan of the Lecture Series, which provides an array of developmental research and information for parents, caregivers, and the community.

Dallas Children's Advocacy Center
Contact:Shari Markey
214-818-2600
www.dcac.org

The mission of the DCAC is "to break the cycle of child abuse through collaborative intervention in a child-sensitive environment." Anyone is welcome to assist children with play activities, serve as a speaker, work in the office, or help with special projects and fund-raising events. New toy and clothing donations are always needed.

The Family Place
214-559-2170
www.familyplace.org

By donating used clothing and household items, you can make a difference for local victims of family violence. If you have extra time, volunteer to work with children at the center, work in the office, or help out at the Family Place Thrift Shop.

Genesis Women's Shelter
214-559-2050
www.genesisshelter.org

This shelter is a safe place for battered women and their children, and it provides crisis intervention and therapy. You can volunteer to work with the children or in the Children's Store.

Junior League
Junior League of Arlington
817-277-9481
www.jlarlington.org

Junior League of Dallas
214-357-8822
www.jld.net

Junior League of Fort Worth
817-332-7500
www.juniorleaguefw.org

Junior League of Plano
972-769-0557
www.jlplano.org

Junior League of Richardson
972-644-5979
www.jlrtx.com

The Association of Junior League International is an organization of women who are committed to promoting volunteerism and supporting their community. Be forewarned that over sixty hours of community service are required during your provisional year. There are several local chapters:

Love for Children, Inc.
Contact: Monica Hinkle, 214-662-0130
www.love4children.org

Throughout the Metroplex, Love for Children, Inc. helps sick children and their families in crisis. Their annual Vintner's Dinner raises funds for a different charity each year (the Social Work Department of Children's Medical Center Dallas was the 2004 choice). This is a great venue to meet other moms while helping with public relations, decorations, auctions, and other committees.

Ronald McDonald House Charities of Greater North Texas
214-520-5614
www.rmhcntx.com

For over thirty years, Ronald McDonald houses across the country have been providing a "home away from home" for families of seriously ill and hospitalized children. Both Dallas and Fort Worth have a Ronald McDonald House and need volunteers to cook meals, answer phones, help celebrate birthdays, and raise funds.

Volunteers of America, Texas
817-529-7300
www.voatx.org

Use your parenting skills and volunteer to teach parent education programs, mentor and tutor at-risk children, or work in the senior facilities.

Volunteer Center of North Texas
Dallas County
214-826-6767

Collin County
972-422-1050

Tarrant County
817-926-9001

www.volunteernorthtexas.org

This is a great resource if you'd like more information on local volunteer opportunities or to speak to a volunteer counselor.

Women's Auxiliary of Children's Medical Center Dallas
214-456-8360
www.childrens.com

Since 1962, the Women's Auxiliary has supported Children's Medical Center Dallas "to make life better for kids." Even with a membership of 750, new members are needed to volunteer in The Children's Corner store and to join in annual fund-raising events such as the annual Breakfast with Santa. Membership is $30. Kim and Kelli have enjoyed working together for events and have made new friendships.

SUPPORT GROUPS

Allen/McKinney Area Mothers of Multiples
972-260-9330
www.amamom.org

American Cancer Society
800-ACS-2345
www.cancer.org

At-Home Dads of Greater Dallas
972-267-7699
www.slowlane.com/groups/ahddallas

At-Home Dads of Greater Fort Worth
817-475-9963
www.slowlane.com/groups/fwahd

Autism Society of America
Collin County
214-925-2722

Denton County
866-407-6593

Tarrant County
817-390-2829

www.autism-society.org

Bereaved Parents USA
North Texas
940-387-5767

National office
708-748-7866
www.bereavedparentsusa.org

Candlelighters Support Group
972-566-7367 or 972-566-4987

A support group for families with children who have cancer.

Caring Hearts
214-345-2613

This group is for parents and family members who have lost a child through miscarriage, fetal loss, or neonatal death.

Compassionate Friends of Carrollton-Farmers Branch
972-245-9773

They provide support for bereaved parents, siblings, and grandparents.

Dallas Epilepsy Foundation Support Group
214-823-8809

North Dallas Mothers of Twins Club
214-890-5965

Depression after Delivery
800-944-4773
www.depressionafterdelivery.com

DMOTTC (Dallas Mothers of Twins and Triplets Club)
www.dallastwins.org

Down Syndrome Guild
214-267-1374

Down Syndrome Partnership of Tarrant County
www.dsptc.org

Early Childhood Intervention
800-250-2246
www.eci.state.tx.us

ECI is the state agency that serves Texas families with infants and toddlers who have disabilities or developmental delays. Friends who are using this service can't rave enough about the positive effects ECI has had on their children and their families.

Easter Seals
Dallas
214-366-4201
www.dallas.easterseals.com

Fort Worth:
817-536-8693
www.easterseals-fw.org

Easter Seals offers help for families who have children with disabilities.

Infant and Toddler Intervention Program
972-599-7722
www.itipnt.org

A nonprofit agency that offers assistance to families whose children have disabilities or learning delays.

Leukemia Society of America: North Texas Chapter
972-239-0959 or 800-955-4572
www.leukemia.org

MEND (Mommies Enduring Neonatal Death)
972-459-2396

Muscular Dystrophy Association
800-572-1717
www.mdausa.org

National Down Syndrome Society
800-221-4602
www.ndss.org

New Moms Support Group
214-345-8568

Parents Without Partners
214-676-3553
www.parentswithoutpartners.com

Plano Area Mothers of Multiples
214-890-5966
www.pamom.org

Postpartum Depression Support Group
972-699-0420
www.dallasparents.org

Postpartum Resource Center of Texas
877-472-1002
www.texaspostpartum.org

Spina Bifida Association of Dallas
972-238-8755
www.sbad.gpcreative.com

WARM (What About Remembering Me) Place
817-870-2722

They provide support for children ages three to eighteen who have experienced a loss through death.

CHILDREN'S HEALTH AND RESOURCES

CHILDREN'S HOSPTIALS

When there is an emergency and your child needs acute care, most pediatricians will refer you to a children's hospital emergency room. Kim and Nevin discovered this when Ford needed emergency care. They were headed to a nationally recognized local hospital but were redirected by their pediatrician to a hospital that specializes in and deals exclusively with children. Makes sense. From stitches to trauma, calling your doctor can provide you with enough information to make the best choice for your situation, which may lead to faster service and attention at the hospital.

Children's Medical Center Dallas

1935 Motor Street
Dallas 75235
214-456-8360
www.childrens.com

For over ninety years, Children's Medical Center Dallas has been a facility for kids. Every year, this nonprofit hospital cares for approximately 270,000 children a year with a variety of diseases and disorders, and it has a state-of-the-art emergency center. Access to the most advanced medical research and treatments through its affiliation with UT Southwestern Medical Center of Dallas make Children's a leader in specialized care. There are 348 beds, including a fifty-two-bed pediatric intensive care. This is a referral hospital to which all patients come by recommendation from their pediatrician. For emergency situations, a referral is not required.

Cook Children's

801 Seventh Avenue
Fort Worth 76104
682-885-4000
www.cookchildrens.com

Cook Children's provides the highest level of care through its family-oriented and child-friendly environment. A new patient pavilion was built in 2002, and in that year, over 250,000 patients were treated at Cook Children's. They have a Pediatric ICU, a Newborn ICU, a Cardiac ICU, and an emergency room.

North Texas Hospital for Children at Medical City Dallas

7777 Forest Lane
Dallas 75230
972-566-8888
www.jacknjill.com

This pediatric hospital attracts children from all over the world because of its first-rate, specialized treatments for children. Emergency care, pediatric/neonatal support, level III neonatal ICU, hematology-oncology, and craniofacial surgery are a few of their areas of expertise.

Our Children's House

Baylor Health Care System
3301 Swiss Avenue
Dallas 75204
214-820-9850
www.baylorhealth.com
Satellite locations are located in Allen, Coppell, Irving, and Grapevine.

Our Children's House is dedicated to providing comprehensive care in a warm, family-oriented environment for children from birth to age eighteen. The House offers treatment for developmental or birth disorders, for traumatic injury, and for children suffering from severe illness. The goal is to make it easier for families to have access to specialists without having to visit multiple hospitals.

The Dallas location is a distinctive facility located in a Victorian home. Parents who have a child staying as a patient can offer twenty-four hours a day of love and support by staying with their child. Siblings are encouraged to participate. The other locations extend invaluable services on an outpatient basis, letting children remain in the comfort of their homes, while making treatment convenient.

The services at each location vary; some include some developmental screenings and equipment ·assessments, occupational therapy, speech/language therapy, parent education and support, physical therapy, and care coordination with a social worker who serves as a patient's advocate.

Texas Scottish Rite Hospital for Children
2222 Welborn Street
Dallas 75219
214-559-5000
www.tsrhc.org

This is one of the leading pediatric centers for treatments for orthopedic conditions, certain neurological disorders, dyslexia, and other learning disorders. For over eighty years, Texas Scottish Rite Hospital for Children has been helping children worldwide, through research and teaching programs. There is no charge for treatment at the hospital, and it is open to Texas children from birth to age eighteen.

SPECIALTY HEALTH RESOURCES

While some parents are often timid about voicing their concerns about their child's development, there are others who can't ask enough questions—both are okay. There is not a right or wrong concern or question when it comes to your child. If you feel that perhaps your child isn't talking enough for his age, is overly sensitive to certain textures in food or clothing, or lacks progression in her gross or fine motor skills, then ask your pediatrician's advice. For additional information, we also suggest contacting one of the resources we have listed below.

Please keep in mind that each clinic or center offers different therapies and techniques. One that is extremely fascinating is craniosacral therapy. This is "a light-touch manual therapy that addresses restrictions in the craniosacral system (the membranes and fluid that surround and protect the brain and spinal cord)" and directly impacts the central nervous system by opening up any restrictions or clearing imbalances. Founded by osteopath physician and researcher John E. Upledger, DO, OMM, craniosacral therapy has been used for over twenty-five years to improve conditions in newborns and children, such as colic, hearing problems, dyslexia, autism, cerebral palsy, motor skill delays, and much more.

Upledger, along with other researchers, suggests that the birthing process can take a toll on a baby's central nervous system and can cause brain dysfunctions as well as other problems that might not be noticeable until the toddler or preschool years. Since 1985, The Upledger Institute has worked to teach and certify physicians and therapists.

Remember that early intervention, evaluation, and help is best. You, the parent, have to take charge—do the research, never stop asking questions, and exhaust all efforts and resources.

Early Childhood Intervention
800-250-2246
www.eci.state.tx.us

ECI is the state agency that serves Texas families with infants and toddlers who have disabilities or developmental delays. Friends who are using this service can't rave enough about the positive effects it has had on their children and their families.

Lakewood Pediatric Therapy, Inc.
The Sensory Integration Center of Dallas
2122 Kidwell Street
Dallas 75214
214-821-9083

The Sensory Integration Center of Coppell
1203 Crestside Drive, Suite 150
Coppell 75109
972-745-8087

www.sensoryintegration.com

Specializing in therapy for sensory integration, Lakewood Pediatric Therapy offers one-on-one, private evaluation, therapy, and support for children with developmental delays and disabilities in such areas as speech and language, oral-motor skills, handwriting, and muscle tone. These well respected centers also offer craniosacral massage therapy, adult programs, nutritional consultations, and parent/teacher workshops. If you are going through an adoption process, they can help with an assessment of the child.

The Language, Speech, and Hearing Clinic
The Shelton School
15720 Hillcrest Road
Dallas 75248
972-774-1772
www.shelton.org
Hours: Monday-Friday, 8:30 a.m. to 5 p.m.

This clinic, a part of Shelton School and Evaluation Center (the largest private school for learning differences in the world), provides evaluation and therapy for both children and adults with difficulties in such areas as voice, language, articulation, auditory processing, and reading problems. They strive to identify and intervene with preschool and school-age children to not only help them achieve their potential, but also to foster their self-esteem. Their full-time staff, who are licensed and ASHA-certified speech pathologists, offer the utmost professionalism and care to the child and work with the parents, providing useful information and support. The clinic also offers craniosacral therapy.

COMPLEMENTARY MEDICINE

Several parents use complementary medicine, such as chiropractic or applied kinesiology, for their children and themselves, for overall well-being and to address a range of ailments like colic, ear infections, food allergies, asthma, and learning differences. "Applied kinesiology allows the doctor to assess the nervous system functions with a 'gentle touch' approach to address underlying causes of a condition such as colic, an ear infection, and even a common cold," explains Dr. Nancy Miller, who specializes in Chiro + Kinesiology (CPK). "The doctor learns from the nervous system what is going on physiologically and structurally and how to treat the individual through an adjustment, nutritional supplements, an acupuncture point, or an emotional release."

As with most innovative treatments, there are both positive research and controversial findings. Know that not all pediatricians might be open to "alternative" practitioners (and vice versa), but keep lines of communication open and use your best judgment. So whether you choose massage (See the Pampering the Body, Mind, and Spirit section of chapter 2, Babying You, for infant massage), chiropractic, applied kinesiology, CPK, or acupuncture, make sure all practitioners are licensed in the state of Texas. Since this is a new area of interest, we have listed only three licensed resources that have come highly recommended for their expertise, professionalism, knowledge, and care for their patients.

Greenville Avenue Chiropractic and Applied Kinesiology
Kristi Long, DC
David Thorne, DC
3404 Greenville Avenue
Dallas 75206
214-823-1323
By appointment only.

Kinesiology Clinic, Integrated Healing Sciences
Josh P. Huse, DC
3511 Hall Street, Suite 108
Dallas 75219
214-521-4873
By appointment only.

Nancy Miller, DC
2050 West Spring Creek Parkway
Plano 75023
214-473-8188
By appointment only.

RESOURCES

American Academy of Medical Acupuncture
www.medicalacupuncture.org

American Chiropractor Association
800-986-4636
www.amerchiro.org

International Chiropractic Pediatric Association
610-565-2360
www.icpa4kids.com

International College of Applied Kinesiology
www.icak.com

The International Dyslexia Association Dallas
972-233-9107
www.interdys.org

Learning Disabilities Association of Texas
800-604-7500
www.ldat.org

The National Center for Complementary and Alternative Medicine
www.nccam.nih.gov

The Upledger Institute, Inc.
561-622-4706
www.upledger.com

NOTE: Also see Support Groups in the section Learning to Be Parents . . . Grandparents, Siblings, and Caregivers! in this chapter.

LACTATION CONSULTANTS, ORGANIZATIONS, AND BREAST PUMP RENTAL

It has been said human milk is the best possible food for infants and breastfeeding provides psychological and emotional advantages . . . when it goes smoothly. One of the greatest sources of strain on a new mother (and everyone around her) is when the decision to breastfeed turns out to be frustrating, confusing, and unnatural. Shortly after Joshua's birth, Kelli had difficulty breastfeeding, which resulted in many tearful days and nights for both Joshua and Kelli. Thankfully, Kim found the name of a lactation consultant who came to the rescue. Kelli's only regret is that she waited so long! While we are led to believe that breastfeeding is completely natural and quite easy, that isn't the case for everyone. Don't be afraid to call on a lactation consultant, even if it's only for reassurance that everything is okay.

After deciding to call for help, things can get confusing. There are lactation nurses, lactation consultants, and then there are lactation consultants who have an International Board of Certified Lactation Consultant certification. The IBCLC designation signifies completion of coursework, hands-on experience, completion of an independent examination, and periodic recertification. Bottom line if you hire someone with the designation IBCLC, he or she will be a person who can provide substantive breastfeeding assistance. This doesn't mean someone who doesn't have this certification can't provide valuable assistance, but if you are unsure about who to call, start with a Certified Lactation Consultant (CLC).

You can expect to pay anywhere from $50–$125 per hour, depending on whether it's an in-home or an office consultation. The initial visit is about two hours, and a follow-up is typically less time and money. It's also useful to remember that many consultants are willing to provide documentation to be used in filing an insurance claim. Just remember, if you decide you need help, do not hesitate. Many of us have been just where you are.

CONTACT A LACTATION CONSULTANT FOR HELP WITH . . .

- Nipple or breast pain

- Latch-on difficulties

- Flat or inverted nipples

- Low milk supply

- Slow weight gain in baby

- A crying or colicky baby

- Breastfeeding a premature baby

- Breastfeeding twins and triplets

- Adoptive breastfeeding

- Breastfeeding and return to employment outside the home

- Pumping and storing breast milk

- Nursing a special needs baby

- Reassurance that breastfeeding is going well

The Breast Feeding Center and Boutique
Harris Methodist Fort Worth Hospital
1301 Pennsylvania Avenue
Fort Worth 76104
817-882-2000
www.harrisfw.org
Hours: Monday and Saturday, noon to 5 p.m.; Tuesday-Friday, 10 a.m. to 5 p.m.

The Breast Feeding Center and Boutique at Harris Methodist Fort Worth Hospital assists new mothers in the quest to successfully breastfeed. The center is staffed with registered nurses who are also certified lactation consultants. They also carry Medela nursing bras, pumps, and accessories; breastfeeding books; pillows and slings; and many other essentials.

Confident Beginnings
Jill Walpole, RN, Lamaze Breastfeeding Specialist
972-390-0812

Jill Walpole began Confident Beginnings in 2002, after years of experience as a high-risk labor and delivery nurse. She felt that new mothers needed more support and honesty than they received in the hospital, so Jill decided to fill that void and open a business that "mothers new mothers." Confident Beginnings offers private, in-home childbirth and baby-care basics classes, postpartum doulas, and breastfeeding support. Jill says, "Bottom line, I support your values, choices, and parenting style. I just help you put it all together." Jill is currently working toward her IBCLC certification. Confident Beginnings does not sell or rent breast pumps.

Lactation Consultant Services
Judy Eastburn, IBCLC
972-931-5578

Judy Eastburn is IBCLC certified and a highly regarded and well known consultant. Judy came to the rescue after Kelli called her when she had problems breastfeeding her son Joshua. Judy is wonderfully patient and has many helpful tips for a first-time mother. She's terrific about following up with you and answering any questions. Judy rents and sells Medela pumps and accessories; you can be certain that if you rent a pump from Judy, she will give you a thorough demonstration and be available to address any questions or problems you may have along the way.

La Leche League
Dallas County
972-669-5714

Tarrant County
817-588-1006

www.lllusa.org

La Leche League's main purpose is to help breastfeeding mothers. The league provides assistance, information, and ongoing education for women who want to breastfeed but may need extra encouragement and/or are having difficulty. There are monthly meetings to which mothers are welcome to bring their babies and receive support. Membership in La Leche League is $36 for one year. There are groups in Arlington, Allen, Lewisville, Garland, Dallas, Plano, McKinney, Richardson, and Fort Worth.

Medela
www.medela.com

The "Rolls-Royce" of breast pump manufacturers, Medela is the pump of choice for hospitals and lactation consultants listed here. Medela's Web site has breastfeeding information, online advice, the ability to locate Medela products in your area, and descriptions of their pumps.

Medical City Hospital
7777 Forrest Lane
Dallas 75230
972-566-4580 (Rental Station)
972-566-4811 (Warmline)
www.medicalcityhospital.com

If you decide to breastfeed, Medical City Dallas offers several services to help you get off to a positive start. There are lactation consultants to assist with feeding techniques and schedules, and they have Medela breast pump rentals and sales. They also have a "Warmline" on which a trained professional can assist you (over the phone) with any difficulties or concerns. Medical City Dallas is planning to open a breastfeeding boutique in the late spring of 2005.

A Mother's Gift
Presbyterian Hospital of Plano
6200 West Parker Road
Plano 75093
972-981-3788
Hours: Monday-Friday, 10 a.m. to 5 p.m.

A Mother's Gift is a comprehensive resource center and boutique for nursing mothers and their babies. Nursing attire, breast pump rental and sales, and replacement parts can all be found here. Board-certified lactation consultants and certified lactation educators are available to nursing mothers who are now at home.

Mother's Milk Bank at Austin
512-494-0800
www.mmbaustin.org

Mother's Milk Bank accepts the surplus of breast milk from healthy moms and passes it along to premature and sick babies. Since some mothers are unable to breastfeed because of medication, a chronic infection, or a delay in milk supply, Mother's Milk Bank makes breast milk available for these infants. Call or go to the Web site for more information or if you are interested in donating. A milk bank is scheduled to open in the Dallas-Fort Worth area in 2005.

Natural Beginnings
Sharon Mattes, IBCLC
972-495-2805

Linda Worzer, IBCLC
972-699-3921

www.naturalbeginningsonline.com

Both Sharon and Linda are IBCLC certified and have over fifty combined years of professional and personal experience. After talking to them, you will feel like you have known them for years, and you'll be reassured. Besides breastfeeding assistance, they offer a variety of services including breastfeeding classes and breast pump rental, phone counseling, and in-home or office visits. Sharon and Linda are available by phone to answer any basic breastfeeding question. Sharon and Linda sell and rent a variety of nursing products. Besides carrying Medela pumps and accessories, Natural Beginnings is the only distributor in this area of the popular Maya Wrap Baby Carriers.

The Nesting Place
Kay Willis, RN
877-625-6803
www.thenestingplace.net

Kay Willis is the founder of the Nesting Place and is dedicated to offering personalized education and care. She has a variety of classes, including breastfeeding, to provide instruction and support before delivery. There are also lactation consultants available to come to the hospital, to your home, or to speak to you over the phone in order to assist you with any problems or concerns. Kay travels anywhere in the Dallas-Fort Worth area. She sells and rents Medela breast pumps.

Simply Mom's, A Breastfeeding Boutique
Baylor University Medical Center at Dallas
3500 Gaston Avenue
Dallas 75246
214-820-3103
www.bhcs.com
Hours: Monday-Friday, 10 a.m. to 3 p.m.; Saturday, 9 a.m. to noon.

Baylor Medical Center at Garland
2300 Marie Curie Boulevard
Garland 75042
972-487-5154
www.bhcs.com
Hours: Monday-Friday, 9 a.m. to 3 p.m.

Simply Mom's gives extra attention to the women who come to their store. They provide breast pump sales and rental, a large selection of nursing bras, and layette items. Jennifer can help you with hard-to-find items and Medela parts. Outpatient certified lactation consultations are available by appointment.

PROTECTIVE PARENTS, CREATING A SAFE ENVIRONMENT FOR YOUR CHILD

It is impossible for us to create a perfectly safe environment, inside or outside, for our children. Try as we might, injuries and unanticipated situations will be a part of their little lives and ours. The best we can do is to try to anticipate dangers and safeguard against them. Here is our list of suggestions to help you create a safer environment for your child—and to allow you to breathe a little easier.

CAR SEAT INSPECTION

Thankfully, more and more parents restrain their children in child safety seats, but improper use is common. According to the US Department of Transportation's National Highway Traffic Safety Administration (NHTSA), nearly 80 percent of all child restraints are improperly used, needlessly exposing children to an increased risk of death or injury. That's why NHTSA is attempting to educate parents to correctly use child safety seats. The most common critical mistakes are loose harness straps, which secure the child, and a loose vehicle safety belt attachment to the child restraint. NHTSA also began rating infant and booster seats for safety and ease of use. Before you buy a car seat, you can now go to www.nhtsa.gov and click "child seat ratings" to see how the car seat you are considering is rated.

Texas law requires children who are under the age of four or are fewer than thirty-six inches in height to be secured in a child safety seat. Beginning September 1, 2002, all new vehicles and child safety seats are required to be equipped with the LATCH (Lower Anchors and Tethers for Children) system. It is a system authorized by the federal government in an effort to standardize and simplify the installation of child restraints. LATCH eliminates the use of a seat belt, which is a common source of user error.

ROAD RULES CAR SEAT SAFETY TIPS

- Infants must always be placed in rear-facing seats until they are at least one year old and twenty to twenty-two pounds.

- If a child is less than a year old and more than twenty to twenty-two pounds, be sure he rides in a seat approved for heavier babies and continues to ride rear-facing until at least one year old. Children may ride rear-facing in many seats until the child weighs thirty-five pounds.

- Never place a rear-facing infant seat in front of a passenger air bag.

- Once children are forward-facing, they should ride in a forward-facing toddler seat until they reach approximately forty pounds.

- All children who have outgrown child safety seats should be properly restrained in booster seats until at least eight years old, or are 4'9" tall and weigh eighty pounds.

- Always read the vehicle owner's manual and the instructions that come with the child safety seat, and keep them handy for future reference.

- Children of all ages are safest when properly restrained in the back seat.

- It's important to remember that the "best" child safety seat is the one that correctly fits the child, and the vehicle, and is used correctly every time.

- Children twelve years old and under should ride in the back seat, which is the safest part of the car in the event of a crash.

- Get your child safety seats checked by professionals!

We highly recommend that you have your car seat professionally installed. Car seat directions can be hard to follow, and why risk the safety of your child? The following have certified car technicians on staff and some may require a small fee, but it is worth it!

Carrollton Police Department
2025 East Jackson Road
Carrollton 75006
972-466-3530

Seats are checked by appointment only, for Carrollton residents only. Installation is free of charge.

Cook Children's Medical Center-Lewisville Specialty Clinic
401 North Valley Parkway, Suite 4000
Lewisville 75067
682-885-2634

Call and leave your name and phone number, and someone will call you between 2:30 p.m. and 5:30 p.m., Monday through Friday, to schedule an appointment. Appointments are thirty minutes per seat, and the child should be present unless the parent is expecting. Cook's asks that someone accompany you to watch your child during the appointment, and while you install the car seat. Installation is free of charge.

Dr. Babyproofer
972-380-1116

Thom Golden, a former RN and BSN, coupled his emergency room experience with his studies in child safety to start Dr. Babyproofer. You may remember the store locations on Garland Road and then on Preston Road. Those are gone, but Dr. Babyproofer still offers home and pool evaluations as well as car seat inspections.

Flower Mound Police Department
4150 Kirkpatrick Lane
Flower Mound 75028
972-874-3345

Residents of Denton County may call and leave a name and phone number and someone will call back to schedule an appointment. Inspections are free of charge.

City of Fort Worth Health Department Car Seat Safety Program
1800 University, Suite 220
Fort Worth 76107
817-871-7240

There are five technicians on staff and inspections can be done in English, Spanish, and Vietnamese. Car seat checks are done by appointment only on Monday through Thursday and are free of charge.

Harris Methodist Hospitals
888-4-HARRIS
www.texashealth.org

Harris Methodist Hospitals helps expectant, new, and experienced parents with car seat safety by offering free car seat safety checks. Certified safety technicians check to make sure there are no recalls on your car seat, and then the technician instructs you on how to install the seat. Bring your child, unless you are pregnant, so the car seat is accurately installed. Call or check the Web site for the days and times when this service is offered.

Presbyterian Hospital of Plano
6200 West Parker Road
Plano 75093
972-981-3948
www.phscare.org

Several times throughout the year, Presbyterian Hospital of Plano offers car seat safety checks. Dates and times can be found online under "Classes." The event is held in front of the Seay Child Care Center and provides Certified Child Passenger Safety technicians to assess your seat, the proper fit for the child and the car, and any seat recalls. Parents and caregivers will also learn how to properly install the seat and the child in the seat. If you have more than one car seat, they ask that you inform the registration center. Also, the children must be present unless you are pregnant.

Safe for Life
Owner: Craig Pfefferkorn
214-497-1650
www.safe-for-life.com

Safe for Life is a mobile child safety seat installation service. Craig has been a certified technician for the past three years, and he has two part-time technicians on staff. Appointments are approximately one hour. During that time, he checks for recalls, tells you about the seat itself, checks straps, adjusts the harness, and installs the child safety seat. After installation, it's your turn as he supervises you as you install the seat. Kim and Nevin, along with several of their friends, feel Craig's service is helpful and eye opening. You'll walk away knowing the look and feel of a correctly installed car seat. He prefers to have the child present in order to do the most correct installation. The cost is $45 for up to four seats, which don't have to belong to the same family. Safe for Life serves the Dallas area (excluding Fort Worth). Craig will also speak to groups and organizations on how to correctly install a car seat—a great idea for gathering your friends together.

Seat Check
866-SEAT-CHECK
www.seatcheck.org

Seat Check, sponsored by the National Highway Traffic Safety Administration (NHTSA) and Daimler-Chrysler, has a toll-free number and a Web site that offers a comprehensive listing of organizations and other entities that offer child safety seat inspection. They also provide information on the LATCH system and car seat recalls.

CPR EDUCATION

Knowing how and when to perform CPR can mean the difference between life and death in the case of an emergency. Anyone who takes care of a child should learn CPR and take refresher courses each year. There are online courses and books that claim to teach you how to perform

CPR, but most experts concur that there is no substitute for learning CPR in a classroom environment. Being educated in CPR should give you the confidence of knowing how to respond in an emergency. Some of the places listed offer individualized classes for children who are planning to babysit. Check other local area hospitals—many of them offer CPR certification.

American Heart Association
214-748-7212 or 877-242-4277
www.americanheart.org

The American Heart Association has an enormous compilation of places in the Dallas-Fort Worth area that offer CPR classes.

American Red Cross
214-678-4800
www.redcross.org

Arlington Memorial Hospital
817-548-6500 (Classes)
www.arlingtonmemorial.org

Baylor Healthcare System
800-4BAYLOR
www.bhcs.com

In addition to infant/child CPR classes, Baylor offers a Safe Sitter class in which children between eleven and thirteen years old learn basic lifesaving techniques and emergency response.

Dallas Association of Parent Education (DAPE)
972-699-0420
www.dallasparents.org

Frisco Fire Department
972-335-5525
www.friscofire.org

Harris Methodist Hospital
888-4-HARRIS
www.harrishospitals.org

They offer a Super Sitter First Aid and CPR class.

Medical Center of Lewisville
500 West Main Street
Lewisville 75057
972-420-1000
www.lewisvillemedical.com

Medical Center of Plano
3901 West 15th Street
Plano 75075
972-596-6800 (General)
www.medicalcenterofplano.com

The Nesting Place
Kay Willis, RN
877-625-6803
www.thenestingplace.net

The Nesting Place will teach you, family, and friends CPR in the privacy of your home for $50 an hour.

Presbyterian Healthcare System
800-4PRESBY
www.phscare.org

Besides infant and child CPR education, Presbyterian Hospital of Plano also offers a Safe Sitter course. Safe Sitters is open to eleven- to thirteen-year-olds, meets twice (each session is six and a half hours), and discusses topics such as babysitting as a business, safety for the sitter, care for a choking infant or child, and preventing and managing problem behavior. The course fee is $80 per adolescent, and registration is available online.

YMCA
www.ymcadallas.org

GUARDIANSHIP

Thinking about who would raise your child in the event that something should happen to you is the last thing anyone with children wants to imagine. Millions of parents don't have wills and have not designated who would be guardian for their child in the event that something was to happen. There are attorneys who specialize in helping parents set up these types of provisions. There is also an online service that is legal, quick, and inexpensive and allows you to designate who would take care of your child so that guardianship would not have to be decided by a court.

www.ChildGuardianship.com

www.childguardianship.com

Stork Avenue and the American Family Safety Network (AFSN) have partnered to develop a service that allows you to legally designate a guardian for you child. The documents they offer are valid in all fifty states and the cost is $10 for one parent and $15 for two parents.

HOME SAFETY

Safeguarding your children against potential dangers is a 24/7 job. Not only are you trying to protect them from the things around them, but also from themselves. If it can be climbed on, pulled or pushed over, or opened and closed, your child will try. Once little ones are on the crawl, the world rapidly grows and they come to know your home better than you do. Even with the best supervision, accidents can and will happen. Your job is to have the foresight to see what dangers are present and try to prevent them. If you decide to childproof your home yourself, get down at the same eye level as your child. This helps in detecting some of the temptations and dangers he might see. Some parents decide to hire an expert since they have no idea of all the dangers a baby can find. Professional "childproofers" know exactly what dangers to anticipate and will have access to products that the average consumer can't find.

HOME SAFE HOME

- Install smoke and carbon monoxide detectors throughout your home and make sure to change the batteries regularly.

- Check that your houseplants are not poisonous. The Poison Control Center will have a list of plants that pose a danger.

- Barefoot is best! If you have hardwood floors, don't allow your child to run around with her socks, as socks increase the likelihood that your child will slip and fall.

- Move dangerous items (such as glass, breakables, sharp or heavy utensils, cookware, and food wrap boxes with serrated edges) to an out-of-reach area.

- Set aside one drawer for your child that he is allowed to explore. Fill it with towels, wooden spoons, Tupperware, plastic measuring cups, and a colander. Try to have the drawer away from the stove and work areas.

- Never leave even an inch of water in the bathtub. A child can easily drown in that amount of water. Keep the toilets closed for the same reason.

- Think about using covered wastebaskets throughout your home to deter your child from taking out potentially dangerous contents.

- Make sure that bathroom door locks can be opened from the outside.

- Keep emergency numbers in a visible place and have a first aid kit handy in case of an emergency.

- Stay conscious of cords. Cords can easily be wrapped around a child's neck, causing strangulation. Once a child can climb up on her hands and knees, remove mobiles from the crib and use cord shorteners or wind-ups on window coverings.

Dr. Babyproofer
972-380-1116

Thom Golden, a former RN, BSN, coupled his experience in the emergency room and his studies in child safety to open Dr. Babyproofer. This is a business dedicated solely to protecting children. He will come to your home to evaluate your safety needs. Evaluations are $100 for a home 2,500 square feet or less, and anything over costs 4 percent of the square footage. Installation is $60 an hour at a two-hour minimum. You don't have to have an evaluation to take advantage of installation services, although it is recommended. Dr. Babyproofer encourages both parents to be involved in the process.

Little Bird Babyproofer
Owner: Brad Lemmon
972-712-3312
214-228-8518 (Cell)

In business since 1999, owner Brad Lemmon provides consultations and installation services for your home. Kim and Nevin found him to be thorough in his evaluation of their home and learned several potential hazards that are easy to overlook. Estimates are free in his service area, which consists of North Dallas, Plano, McKinney, and Allen. There is a $25 fee if you are outside this area, but if you employ his services, Brad will credit that charge to your bill. Installation is $40 an hour plus the cost of the products.

POISON CONTROL CENTER

The Texas Poison Control Network is a twenty-four hours a day, seven days a week, fully staffed hotline. Specially trained physicians, nurses, and pharmacists answer questions about the treatment of poisons or other toxic and harmful exposures. Make sure you have this number in a visible place in your home so you and your child's caregivers will know exactly whom to call. If you believe your child has swallowed a poisonous substance, try to obtain the following information before calling: the name of the poison your child has swallowed, the age and weight of the child, and the time the child took the poison. Call them immediately if you discover your child has been poisoned; they can tell you what to do.

Texas Poison Control Network
800-222-1222
www.poisoncontrol.org

POOL/SPA SAFETY

According to the National Safety Council, drowning is the second leading cause of unintentional injury-related death in children under fourteen years old. Since a child can drown in the time it takes to answer a phone, you cannot provide too many barriers in protecting your children from water accidents. Fences, gates, and other safety devices are not 100 percent childproof, but they do provide a layer of protection in case a child strays from an adult's watchful eye.

RULES FOR POOLS

- Instruct babysitters about potential pool hazards to young children and about the use of protective devices such as door latches and home security alarms.

- Never leave a child unsupervised near a pool. During social gatherings, designate a "watcher" to protect children from pool accidents.

- If a child is missing, check the pool first. Go to the edge of the pool and scan the entire pool, bottom and surface.

- Do not allow a young child in the pool without an adult.

- Do not consider children to be safe just because they have had swimming lessons.

- Learn CPR. Make sure that babysitters, caregivers, and members of the family also know CPR.

- Keep rescue equipment by the pool. Be sure a telephone with emergency numbers is poolside.

- Remove toys from around the pool when it is not in use. Toys can attract young children.

- Never prop open a gate to a pool.

Source: the US Consumer Product And Safety Commission, www.cpsc.gov, 800-638-2772.

Durafence
972-720-9977
www.guardianpoolfence.com

Guardian Pool Fence Systems has a patented self-closing gate specifically designed to operate with a removable mesh fencing system. The fence cannot be climbed and the gate can be locked with a key. Prices depend on pool size and the model of fencing you choose.

Katchakid
972-221-6605 or 888-552-8242
www.advanced-pool-covers.com

Our friends needed a safety net for a pond in their backyard after their son was born. They were most impressed with the service and quality of Katchakid. "Brad (a Katchakid sales representative) was efficient, the net is nonobtrusive, and the quality does not detract from our backyard but instead, blends right in." The company claims that they have never had a drowning with a properly installed Katchakid. These safety nets can be used on swimming pools, spas, split decks, and rockeries. Katchakid also offers custom-installed, removable safety fences. Prices depend on pool size, shape, and location.

Poolguard Pool Alarm
800-242-7163
www.poolguard.com

This pool alarm sounds as soon as anything weighing eighteen pounds or more touches the water. *Good Housekeeping* rated Poolguard pool alarms number one, and they come with a three-year warranty. The alarm costs around $200, and you can purchase one from One Step Ahead (800-274-8440) and from Leslie's Swimming Pool Supplies (800-537-5437 or www.lesliespool.com).

Protect-A-Child Pool Fence
972-681-7171 or 800-992-2206
www.protectachild.com

Nevin's parents used Protect-A-Child when it came time to safeguard their pool for their five grandchildren. This tightly woven mesh fence prevents toys from passing through but provides clear visibility to watch the pool. The fence can be installed to be removable, permanent, or semi-permanent, and it works with any pool shape. The lock on the fence is a patented, double-locking latch, and according to Nevin's mom, it takes some dexterity for the adults to unlatch it, let alone the children. Prices vary depending on the size of the pool and which grade of fence you select.

Protect 1 by Elite/SonarGuard
President: Michael Nantz
701 South Stemmons, Suite 210
Lewisville 76067
214-222-7233
www.sonarguard.com

Using advanced underwater technology called SonarGuard, this system creates an "invisible underwater sonar-net" so that when a child falls into the pool, a loud emergency signal is triggered in order to alert parents. Advantages of this type of device are that it is invisible, it works on any pool size and shape, and it is always "on." All the homeowner has to do is to put it into standby mode for a selected time period and SonarGuard will automatically rearm itself after the standby time is up. It is also able to differentiate between a child falling into the pool versus "surface disturbances," like a ball falling into the water. The average price is $5,000 but can vary according to special pool features such as spas, water features, irregular shape, and large pool sizes. For a small, simply shaped pool such as an oval or rectangular, the price can be as low as $4,000.

TOY AND PRODUCT SAFETY

TOY TIPS

- Choose age-appropriate toys. Follow the "recommended age" sticker when purchasing a toy.

- The bigger the better. For children under the age of three, make sure toy parts are bigger than their mouth to avoid choking hazards. A good rule of thumb is that if a part can fit through a toilet paper cylinder, it's too small for the child to play with.

- Beware of balloons. Children and balloons are not a safe combination. If a balloon pops, the pieces become a choking hazard. If you must have balloons around, use Mylar balloons.

- Secure stuffed animals. Before giving your child a stuffed animal, check that eyes, nose, and mouth are securely attached. Take off ribbons, buttons, or other choking hazards.

- Old is not new again. Be aware of older toys and products that are passed down or acquired at garage sales. Often, they don't meet current safety guidelines.

- Shhhhh! Don't allow children to play with noisy toys. They can damage a child's hearing.

The Juvenile Products Manufacturers Association (JPMA)
856-638-0420
www.jpma.org

JPMA is a national trade organization of more than four hundred companies that manufacture or import infant products. JPMA developed a certification program to assist parents in selecting products for their children that meet certain safety standards. You can find the JPMA Certification Seal on a product for added assurance the manufacturer designed and built the item with safety in mind.

US Consumer Product Safety Commission (CPSC)
800-638-2772
www.cpsc.gov

The CPSC is an independent federal agency whose job it is to protect the public from injury and death from over fifteen thousand types of consumer products. This is an extremely helpful Web site where you can sign up to be notified by e-mail of any recalls specifically involving infant and child products. You can also search the "child" and "toy" product categories to see which items have been recently recalled. The site displays a picture of the item and shows the press release that states the reason for the recall.

ORGANIC YARD AND HOME SOLUTIONS

Children are very vulnerable to environmental health threats. There can be many hidden dangers in your home and backyard, so it is important to be proactive in recognizing potential hazards. Many families such as ours are now using organic pesticides, pest control, and cleaning solutions. There are some companies that specialize in organic lawn and landscape maintenance, nonchemical and organic pest control, and chemical-free home cleaning services.

HOME AND YARD HEALTH HAZARDS

- Test for lead in existing paint.

- Make sure to change air filters every three months.

- Use nontoxic, all-natural household cleaning products.

- Store toxic products away from your house.

- Ask people not to smoke in your home.

- Frequently wash bedding in hot water, and choose hardwood floors over carpet to eliminate dust mites.

- Avoid using carpet in high humidity areas like the bathroom and kitchen.

- Check your yard for dangerous plants, and teach your child to never eat anything from a plant, no matter how tempting it may look.

Baker Environmental Services
469-443-0990
www.bakeresi.com

Baker Environmental Services, based out of Garland, has been serving the Dallas Metroplex since 1985. They are a quality company that offers many services, including mold remediation.

Blackmon Mooring Steamatic
877-730-1948
www.blackmonmooring.com

In business over fifty years, they offer chemical-free carpet cleaning, air duct cleaning, and twenty-four-hour emergency services for fire, water, and mold damage. They offer a two-hour window for appointments so you don't have to spend the entire day waiting at home.

Children's Health Environmental Coalition (CHEC)
609-252-1915
www.checnet.org

CHEC is a national nonprofit coalition dedicated to educating parents about environmental toxins that affect children's health. This is a wonderful online resource that offers suggestions for creating a safer environment for your children, and offers an online "Safer Products Store" that carries an enormous selection of products that are safe for use on or around children. They also offer a money-back guarantee if you are not satisfied with your purchase. We love getting our monthly e-mail newsletters to keep us in-the-know about the latest news and products for a safer environment.

Dirt Doctor
www.dirtdoctor.com

Howard Garrett, the Dirt Doctor, is a columnist for the *Dallas Morning News* and hosts "The Natural Way," a gardening show on WBAP. He specializes in organic landscaping and gardening. On his Web site, you can search for organic-friendly businesses in your area.

Earth Friendly Products
www.ecos.com

Whole Foods and Albertson's are two of our area's retailers who carry the Earth Friendly line of household cleaning products, which are nontoxic and consist of natural ingredients. They smell fresh and natural and work great.

Ecosafe Pest Control
3001 Wheelock Street
Dallas 75220
214-358-5201 or 800-710-4545
www.ecosafepest.com

Ecosafe specializes in nonchemical and organic pest control to eliminate insects, rodents, and other pests. Kim and Nevin have used Ecosafe for over four years and have the same serviceman who knows their needs and takes extra care due to the young children in their home. Ask about Mosquito Barrier, their garlic solution that helps control mosquitoes. Their quarterly calls remind you to schedule your next service—great for busy parents!

Green Living
Lakewood Shopping Center
1904 Abrams Parkway at Gaston Avenue
Dallas 75214
214-821-8444
www.green-living.com

This retail store sells products that are earth-friendly equivalents to everyday household items. If an item is recycled, organic, traded fairly, or sustainable, there is a good chance it's sold here. Green Living carries cleaning supplies, personal care products, apparel and linens, foods, and lawn and garden products and also offers recycling.

Jackson Mosquito Control

6950 Lemmon Avenue
Dallas 75209
214-350-9200 or 800-340-6747
www.jacksonmosquitocontrol.com

"It is expensive, but so worth it to us—and it works great," says Michelle Lockhart, a Dallas mother of two children. Their misting system uses a natural insecticide to eliminate mosquitoes and outdoor insects; nozzles are placed every eight to ten feet around the perimeter of your property. The system comes with a fifty-five-gallon reservoir, a fully automated timer, remote control operation, and battery back-up. They offer service contracts and a 100 percent refund the first year if you are not completely satisfied with the system. You can call for a free estimate.

Mosquito Nix

14288 Gillis Road
Dallas 75244
972-934-2000 or 866-934-2002
www.mosquitonix.com

Mosquito Nix uses natural insecticides to get rid of mosquitoes and other outdoor insects. The system is fully automated to mist three to four times per day at twenty- to sixty-second intervals. Unlike many other mosquito companies, Mosquito Nix is dedicated solely to installing these systems. They offer free estimates and provide a two-year warranty on parts and a one-year warranty on labor. The system can take anywhere from four hours to a few days to be installed based on the size of the area and the complexity of the installation. Becoming mosquito-free doesn't come cheap, but they do offer various financing options and a lifetime warranty.

Rhode's Nursery and Nature Store

1651 Wall Street
Garland 75041
972-864-1934 or 800-864-4445
www.beorganic.com

One of the first nurseries in the Dallas area to carry organic products, Rhode's sells only organic fertilizers and pest control products and their staff is extraordinarily helpful and knowledgeable. Don't be afraid to ask questions because they always seem to have the answers, and many times it doesn't involve trying to sell you anything. They provide mosquito treatment and many other organic products and services such as organic landscape maintenance service and landscape design and installation.

RID-All Pest Control
6812 Colfax Drive
Dallas 75231
214-340-6969
www.ridall.biz

Owned and operated by the Bosco family since 1955, RID-All specializes in using small amounts of organic products to eliminate indoor and outdoor insects and pests. They pride themselves on educating you so that you can make an informed decision on the specific treatment for your property. You can decide whether you prefer an organic approach, a more traditional approach, or a combination of both.

Soils Alive
972-272-9211
www.soilsalive.com

This lawn care company will send samples of your soil to be analyzed and will develop a prevention and maintenance program using nontoxic, chemical-free products. They also provide other organic services such as weed treatment and tree and shrub fertilization.

Walton's Lawn and Garden Center
8652 Garland Road
Dallas 75218
214-321-2387

Owned by Chuck and Ann Walton, this is a Dallas institution for organic lawn and garden solutions. They offer landscape design and installation, a full organic nursery, sprinkler installation and repair, and an enormous nursery. It is definitely worth a visit.

MISSING AND EXPLOITED CHILDREN

Unfortunately, we live in times where we can't be too careful or watchful when it comes to the safety of our children. Whether you are playing at the park or shopping for food at the grocery store, child abduction can happen within seconds. Did you know that every forty seconds, a child goes missing in the United States? We felt we would be remiss if we didn't include resources on missing and exploited children and measures that can be taken to protect our kids. The following Web sites provide information about safeguarding our children from abduction and exploitation:

The Federal Bureau of Investigation's Missing and Exploited Children's Program
800-843-5678
www.fbi.gov/kids/crimepre/abduct/abdmiss.htm

McGruff the Crime Dog

www.mcgruff-safe-kids.com

This program provides information for child safety, identification, abduction, fingerprinting, and crime prevention.

National Center for Missing and Exploited Children

800-843-5678

www.missingkids.com

National Child Identification Program

214-630-5895

www.childidprogram.com

The ID Kit allows parents to collect specific information by simply recording the physical character-istics and fingerprints of their children and placing the information on identification cards that are then kept at home. If ever needed, this ID Kit will give law enforcement authorities vital information to assist their efforts in locating a missing child.

THE NATIONAL CENTER FOR MISSING AND EXPLOITED CHILDREN (NCMEC) OFFERS THESE SUGGESTIONS AS PRECAUTIONARY MEASURES:

- Keep a complete description of your child.

- Take color photographs of your child every six months.

- Keep copies of your child's fingerprints.

- Know where your child's medical records are located.

- Have your dentist prepare and maintain dental charts for your child.

- Forgo storks or other forms of birth announcement signs in your yard.

- Choose a monogram rather than your child's name on clothing and bags to prevent strangers from knowing your child's name.

- Create a code word for you, your child, relatives, and caregivers and tell your child that he is never to go with anyone, even if it is a person he knows, unless the person knows the code word.

Follow these steps in case your child is missing:

- Immediately report your missing child to the local law enforcement agency.

- Ask the law enforcement agency to enter your child into the National Crime Information Center (NCIC) Missing Persons File.

- Limit access to your home until law enforcement arrives and has the opportunity to collect possible evidence.

SAFE KIDS COALITION

The Safe Kids Coalition is a national nonprofit organization that attempts to reduce preventable injuries to children who are under the age of fourteen. Injuries are the number one killer of children in this age bracket. Their Web site provides valuable and up-to-date safety suggestions, state child safety laws and regulations, BUCKLE UP events, and activities that can help you educate your children on how to be safe. There are local coalitions in Dallas and in Tarrant County if you are interested in more information.

Safe Kids Coalition
Dallas
214-456-8117

Tarrant County
682-885-1619
www.safekids.org

CHAPTER FOUR:
PARENT HELPERS

FINDING A CAREGIVER

Finding a caregiver for your child can be a stressful, complicated process to navigate and it may test your patience. You want someone who will be loving, honest, dependable, patient and smart . . . just for starters! While you probably won't find "you," it is possible to find someone who will meet most of your expectations. It is important to have a clearly defined view of what your family wants from the person you hire.

Salaries for nannies can range anywhere from $300 to $700 per week, depending on live-in/out status, age, experience, education, and the needs of your family. Beforehand, it is helpful to determine the duties and responsibilities you will expect from your caregiver. Will the nanny be exclusively responsible for child care, or will you expect her to perform household duties as well? All of these things will factor into the salary. There are live-in, live-out, and shared-care caregivers. Shared care is an economic alternative where two families share one nanny. If you decide to share a nanny with another family it's essential that the person you hire is able to please both families.

It's important to outline your expectations and what you consider to be acceptable up front. By establishing parameters before you hire someone, you are less likely to have conflicts down the road. For example, are there certain activities you would like your nanny to enjoy with your children? How many miles away from home do you think it is acceptable for your nanny to take your children? Do you expect the house to be relatively tidy and clean before she leaves for the day?

Also, consider the hiring of your nanny as a business relationship. Therefore, it is important to draw up an employment contract. You and your nanny should agree on how frequently the contract will be updated and clearly state that any necessary changes will be made based on your shifting needs. Some details to consider in the contract are the hours and days your nanny will work, vacation and sick days, how often a raise will be given, and what expenses you will expect to pay (such as a car seat for the nanny's car, car insurance, gas, trips to eat out, and visits to movies or the zoo). Not being up front from the beginning poses a bigger problem down the road. But realize that an employment contract is not legally binding. It may also help everyone if there is a written job description of duties, special needs of the children, the children's eating and sleeping schedules, and what the children are permitted and not permitted to do.

There are several ways to approach finding a suitable nanny.

AGENCIES

Many families in search of a nanny find it most efficient to enlist the aid of an agency. While most agencies do a background and criminal check, we cannot begin to stress how important it is to check references yourself. The Better Business Bureau can provide a "reliability report" on many agencies. The information in the report can help you determine if the company has had problems with other customers.

Agencies typically charge a fee: either a percentage of the nanny's annual salary (anywhere from 8 to 15 percent) or a contingency fee, which is paid only after you hire a nanny. All of the agencies listed here will provide a "replacement guarantee." This means that if you have to replace the nanny within a specified amount of time (typically three to twelve months) the agency will begin another search without charging you an additional fee. The entire placement process typically takes from two to six weeks if there are no extraordinary expectations or requests.

It's helpful to register with more than one agency in order to increase your applicant pool. Remember, many nannies will register with numerous agencies, so don't be shocked if two agencies send you the same applicant.

We would suggest visiting an agency's Web site if you want more information on a particular agency. Most Web sites can answer many of the questions you probably have. There are numerous agencies, but we have only included those which have come highly recommended to us.

Better Business Bureau
www.dallas.bbb.org
214-220-2000

Domestically Yours
President: Paula Schwartz
18352 Dallas Parkway, Suite 136-325
Dallas 75287
972-669-5059
www.domesticallyyours.com
Member of the Better Business Bureau

In business for fifteen years, Domestically Yours does not require an application fee. Upon placing a nanny in your home, Paula charges $1,895. They offer a six-month guarantee and employ an independent company to check nannies for felonies and misdemeanors. Additional services include maids, baby nurses, chauffeurs, senior citizen companions, cooks, butlers, and party servers. Nevin and Kim, as well as a few of our friends, have been very impressed with Paula's professional business manner and the quality of nanny candidates.

MBF Agency (Mom's Best Friend)
2121 North Josey Lane, Suite 202
Carrollton 75006
972-446-0500 or 866-26-NANNY
www.momsbestfriend.com
Member of the Better Business Bureau

MBF Agency was founded in 1994 and has offices throughout the state of Texas; its headquarters are in Austin. MBF has been used by quite a few of our friends, and the feedback we have gotten has all been positive. They require a $100 application fee and offer three different levels (bronze, silver, and gold) of permanent nannies based on the amount of experience the nanny has and your requirements. This agency charges 10 to 15 percent of your nanny's gross annual salary as a finder's fee. The guarantee is for ninety days, and they will offer a sliding scale discount after the guarantee period is over. They will extend the replacement period to 120 days if you attend an Employers of Nannies seminar before, or within a month of, your nanny's placement. The process takes approximately four to six weeks.

A criminal background check is performed in all counties in which your nanny has resided over the last seven years. MBF also arranges a state of Texas motor vehicle check going back three years, obtains a record of sex offenses, and verifies degrees in higher education. Other services include tutors, night nurses, doulas, lactation consultants, and in-home prenatal and postpartum consultants.

Park Cities Home Staffer
President: Adrienne Callaway
Two Galleria Tower
13455 Noel Road, Suite 1000
Dallas 75240
972-774-4550

In business for eleven years, PCHS works on contingency fees. Upon a client's approval and hiring of a nanny, there is a placement fee of $1,800 and a six-month guarantee. There is no application fee, and the hiring process typically takes two to four weeks. A Social Security trace, verification of work history, a county and state criminal background check, and a DMV search are performed on each candidate before she is hired. A friend of ours and mother of twins said, "I really think Park Cities Home Staffer is great. I know lots of other folks who have liked Adrienne, too. I have recommended her to others and will continue to do so."

REFERRALS

Kim and many of our friends have found a nanny through personal referrals. Ask child-care workers employed by friends whether they know of anyone who might be looking for work. Religious institutions and local ECPTAs are also valuable places to explore. Our local ECPTA chapter distributes a monthly newsletter which offers a no-cost ad service for families looking for child care or nanny-sharing. A visit to a local university, such as SMU, and approaching sorority houses might produce a student looking to work for a few hours a day. Even visiting a popular park and talking to nannies there can be a good source.

The downside of finding a nanny through word of mouth is that the priorities of the person recommending her may be different from yours. This is why it's important to understand what is expected from the nanny and how she performs the tasks at hand. It will also be your responsibility to perform a background check and reference check.

ADS

If you decide to place an ad yourself, beware that you will be doing most of the legwork. Carefully prescreen the candidates over the phone so that you don't spend a lot of time interviewing people who really aren't a good fit. Also, placing an ad may not produce the caliber of candidates that you would find through an agency or a referral. The following is a list of daily and weekly newspapers in the area:

The Dallas Morning News
214-977-8924 or 877-932-2390
www.dallasnews.com

Fort Worth Star-Telegram
817-332-3333 or 800-222-3978
www.dfw.com

People Newspapers
214-739-2244
www.peoplenewspapers.com

This pubication includes North Dallas People, Park Cities People, and Lakewood People.

Star Community Newspapers
972-422-7355
www.dfwcn.com

Star serves the following communities: Plano, Allen, Carrollton, Coppell, Flower Mound, Lewisville, McKinney, Mesquite, Rowlett, Southlake, and The Colony.

WHAT TO ASK A PROSPECTIVE NANNY

Before beginning the nanny search, decide what your expectations are. Give some thought to your family structure. Are you organized and do you like your child to follow a schedule, or are you more relaxed and spontaneous? These things will make a huge difference when choosing a nanny. Do you want someone who is a part of your family or strictly an employee? Either way, tension in a nanny relationship speaks volumes about how well your child is being taken care of.

As with any relationship, communication is key and the interview is the time to begin. The best interview questions are the ones that give you a sense of the day-to-day life and attitudes of the prospective caregiver. Here are some suggested interview questions:

- How long were you at your last job?
- Why did you leave your last job?
- Could you please expand on your previous child-care positions?
- Do you keep up to date with child development research and information?
- Are you certified in CPR?
- Have you ever taken care of sick children?
- Do you smoke?
- Do you have children of your own? If so, who watches them while you work? If your child were to become sick, do you have someone who watches him, or would you be unable to watch our children?
- How would you handle an emergency?
- Describe a typical day if you were taking care of my child.
- What are your hobbies and interests?
- Do you drive? Do you own a car? Do you expect us to provide car seats?
- If my child were doing something inappropriate, what words would you use to get him to stop?
- How many times in the past three years have you moved or changed your phone number?
- What do you expect from the family you work for?
- How would you discipline a child? Do you believe in spanking?
- What are your religious beliefs? (Are hers compatible with your family's beliefs?)
- What do you like to read?
- Are you currently or have you ever taken medication for depression?
- What is your favorite childhood memory?

CHECK, DOUBLE CHECK

Using an agency to hire a nanny should give your family peace of mind. It's assumed that the agency will have done the background checks and reference checks necessary to procure a reliable and trustworthy employee. Sadly, this is not always the case. A friend of ours used a supposedly reputable agency to find a nanny for her children. However, thirteen months after hiring the nanny, she discovered things that should have quickly taken the nanny out of the running for the job. If our friend had known the questions to ask and proper searches to conduct, she might have saved herself and her family a lot of heartache and tens of thousands of dollars in legal fees. She has graciously shared her painful lesson so that she can help prevent our readers from repeating the same mistakes.

1) **Get to the bottom of any and all inconsistencies in the employment background.** If there are gaps or overlaps in a candidate's employment history, get the full story in detail, and make it a point to verify it. If a nanny is unlikely to receive a positive reference from a previous employer, it is tempting for her to completely eliminate that family from her resume. You would not want to hire someone with something to hide. On the other side of the coin, when our friend looked over her nanny's résumé (after having a bad experience with the nanny), she was astounded at how many dates of employment overlapped. If she had questioned it further, she would have eliminated that candidate upon realizing that the nanny had deliberately falsified her employment record.

2) **Confirm the educational background.** Our friend's nanny lied about her degree, claiming a medical degree. She was compensated an additional $10,000 per year for this phantom degree. It was later discovered that she was not even certified in CPR, which the agency said she was. You are not being unreasonable when you ask to see the candidate's CPR card.

3) **Check and double check references.** Don't assume that just because a friend has recommended someone, the nanny has an impeccable background.

4) **Use a separate credit card with an intentionally low credit limit.** It is not unusual for families to allow nannies a credit card to pay for incidentals. However, do not allow her to have access to your main credit cards. The month before our friend's nanny was fired, she ran up $15,000 on one of the family's credit cards, insisting her fiancé was going to reimburse them. Unfortunately, the fiancé did not exist . . . and the reimbursement never materialized.

5) **Never sign an indemnity clause.** This clause states that if your nanny sues the agency, the agency is free of responsibility and you are responsible for the legal fees. If you ask the agency to eliminate this clause, most will do so without question.

6) **Perform a civil background check.** Agencies will do a criminal background check, but most don't do a civil check unless you specifically ask. If our friend had requested a civil check, she would have discovered this woman's history of suing prior employers. A civil background check also tells you if there are any restraining orders against the individual.

7) **Ask for a hard copy of the background check.** When our friend asked the agency for a copy she was told that everything came out okay and she was never sent a copy of the background check. However, when she finally pressed the issue and received a copy, employment at a strip club appeared at the same time she was supposed to be taking care of our friend's child full-time. When an agency tells you verbally that a candidate "checks out," be patient and cautious . . . and wait for the hard copy.

8) **Confirm your children's attendance at their scheduled activities.** The nanny changed the family's contact numbers to her own, so that when a teacher called the family to ask why their child had not made it to a number of classes, our friend had no way of knowing.

9) **Trust your intuition.** If you have a bad feeling, act on it. Social niceties should go out the window when it comes to protecting your children. Don't be afraid to ask questions of people who come in contact with your nanny on a regular basis to see if they have noticed anything unusual.

The Integrity Center
2828 Forest Lane
Dallas 75234
972-484-6140 or 800-456-1811
www.integctr.com/CheckNanny/

This is one of the most comprehensive Web sites we have seen to help you with the hiring process. They provide step-by-step instructions that help you to perform a thorough background check on your own. You mail them the required information, along with a fee, which is based on the number of checks you would like to have performed. For example, an ID and Social Security verification is $17.85. They will phone you with the results and prepare a written report. They also offer advice on the types of background and reference checks you should consider and why.

NANNY TAXES AND INSURANCE

To hire a nanny means that you become an employer. You are required to file payroll taxes with the Internal Revenue Service. The IRS requires a domestic employer who pays a domestic employee more than $1,400 in wages in a calendar year to pay Social Security, Medicare, and federal unemployment taxes. The IRS provides a guide, known as Publication 926, which helps determine your liability for these taxes. The guide also supplies a checklist of documents and the obligations you are responsible for as an employer.

In Texas, the Texas Workforce Commission (TWC) is the state government agency charged with overseeing employers and job seekers in Texas. TWC provides general information for employers, registration to obtain a TWC account number (which you need if you have to file state taxes), and forms. Worker's compensation insurance is optional in Texas and not a part of employment taxation. A worker's compensation insurance policy will cover you from lawsuits and liability in the event that your employee is injured on the job. If you choose to obtain this type of insurance, you can do so through an insurance company. Employers are required to pay state unemployment tax (also known as TUCA) if an employer pays "more than $1,000 in total cash wages during any calendar quarter." The following Web sites offer more information on federal and state taxes:

Internal Revenue Service
800-829-1040 (For tax-related questions)
800-829-3676 (To order forms)
www.irs.ustreas.gov

Texas Workforce Commission
800-832-9394
www.twc.state.tx.us

The following are online companies that specialize in filing taxes for household employees, and in providing useful tax information on their Web sites.

Breedlove & Associates
888-273-3356
www.breedlove-online.com

HomeWork Solutions
800-626-4829
www.4nannytaxes.com

Household Employment Tax Services
www.nannytaxusa.com

NannyTax, Inc.
888-626-6982
www.nannytax.com

NIGHT NANNIES

What a helpful person a night nanny or baby nurse can be! Usually a night nanny is hired to help take care of your newborn in the evenings and overnight at your home, while you are recovering from the birth. Night nannies can be helpful and instrumental with baby care tips, and they can offer a great emotional support system for the new parents. Now we must tell you that if you are given a recommendation for a "baby nurse," this is a term that is commonly used, but do not assume the nanny is a registered nurse. Please inquire further.

As with any outsider coming into your home environment, not only should you do an exhaustive amount of research before you hire her (please see the previous sections of this chapter), but she must also "check out" with you. From different personalities to styles and ways of thinking, another person in the home can be even more stressful even if she is a dear friend or family member. So know your methods, follow your "mother's instinct," and educate yourselves. This is the best recommendation we can offer.

We have found that good night nannies come word-of-mouth from friends and friends' networks who have used them and have had them living in their homes. Ask for references and a personal interview. Most are booked way in advance, and some ask for a deposit to secure your spot, which is understandable as they are a much-sought-after service. Make sure to get something in writing, or sign a mutually agreed upon "contract."

Confident Beginnings, LLC
Contact: Jill Walpole, RN, LCCE
972-390-0812 or 972-814-7556

Jill Walpole is a postpartum doula who describes herself as a "new mother's right hand." She is in your home not only to help you recover, but also to help teach you how to care for a newborn if needed. Jill will even run errands, help with laundry, do light housekeeping and light meal preparation, and offer breastfeeding assistance. She usually arrives about 8:30 p.m. or 9 p.m. and leaves at 7 a.m. However, she can tailor her hours to your needs. New parents usually hire Jill for up to eight weeks. Jill is a Texas state registered nurse and has two small children of her own, and she also does multiples. Call early, but if she is booked, she knows others who can possibly help you.

Kendell Dearing
214-346-9220

Kendell Dearing has fifteen years' experience as a nanny and five years as a night nanny and loves working with multiples. She is certified in CPR and first aid. Kendell has trained with NICU nurses at Presbyterian Hospital of Dallas and is extremely knowledgeable working with heart monitors and special medical requests. She works nights only from 10 p.m. to 6 a.m. When the baby is sleeping, she stays up washing clothes and bottles and organizing the nursery. Friends have told us that she keeps in touch and visits their children even after two years. She is typically hired on a minimum of two to three months, five days a week, at $20 an hour. You better call early, as she books far in advance.

She saved our lives, and if we hadn't had her, we wouldn't have gotten through the first three months at home with our twins. She monitored our children's heart monitors, gave them their medicines, and documented everything throughout the night so we could get the rest we needed. We wanted her to stay with us as our full-time nanny, but her love for helping new parents is her specialty. **—Melissa Brown, Richardson.**

Sharon and Cari Latham
903-473-2184

This mother and daughter team has been helping new parents take care of newborns at night for too many years to count. Found by word-of-mouth recommendation, Kim and Nevin used them when Sawyer was born and again with Ford. From bottles that produce less air when sucking to sleeping tricks of the trade, Sharon and Cari's helpful hints, coupled with their love of babies, is worth the $15 an hour charge. A typical night of their service is from 9 p.m. to 6 a.m., five nights a week. However, they are flexible with hours and prefer to stay twenty-four hours, with a few hours' break, during the first week to help create and maintain feeding and sleeping schedules. Several of our friends have used them and consider them the "baby whisperers," while others feel their strict timetables are more like the "baby police." With this said, it really depends on you and how you want to rear your child. Kim and Nevin's children were sleeping though the night by six to eight weeks and putting themselves to sleep without being dependent on rocking. Over time, the children Sharon and Cari have taken care of continue their great sleeping habits. They are very experienced with multiples and premature babies with heart monitors. Cari will tackle bottles, make formula, do wash, and organize drawers without asking. It is not unusual for them to travel out of state on the recommendation of previous employers, and they will do phone consultations for a minimal fee. Many call Sharon and Cari the minute they are pregnant to schedule them.

MBF Agency (Mom's Best Friend)

2121 North Josey Lane, Suite 202
Carrollton 75006
972-446-0500 or 866-26-NANNY
www.momsbestfriend.com

MBF offers trained and experienced care for mothers, families, and the newborn. You may choose a "post-partum caregiver," one who assists not only with advice and care of the baby, but with light housework, meals, errands, sibling help, and emotional support. The price is $17 an hour, including agency fees. The second choice you have is hiring a "night nanny/nurse," who helps new parents solely with newborn care during the night in ten- to twelve-hour shifts. She will feed the baby or bring him to mothers who are breastfeeding. An MBF nanny will diaper, rock, and do the baby's laundry and bottles. The fees range from $175 to $185 per night for single babies and $200 to $225 for multiples; both of these rates include agency fees. As you may have read earlier under Agencies in this chapter, MBF was founded in 1994 and is a member of the Better Business Bureau. We have had friends recommend MBF and a night nanny who has worked with them for over five years. The same friends say MBF is a "reliable, well-run company that treats you with respect."

The Nanny for Newborns, Lisa Stipe

214-734-0099
www.nannyfornewborns.com

For over eighteen years, Lisa Stipe has been "nurturing newborns and educating parents" as a nanny for newborns. She can help you around the clock for the first few days and then come just for the nighttime. You get rest while she monitors the baby, does laundry, and washes bottles. If you are nursing, Lisa will bring the baby to you to feed, and then she will change and put the baby back in bed. She will reinforce your particular parenting style, and if you don't have one, Lisa can help you synchronize wake time, feeding and sleeping cycles to achieve the routine of a baby calming herself and sleeping though the night. She is not rigid and has a very personable and loving demeanor. Lisa offers consultations; she will help with older siblings and is willing to travel on vacations with your family. We have been told that her service is "invaluable and trustworthy." Lisa has attended the National Academy of Nannies in Denver, Colorado, and is trained in infant CPR. Her fees are based on your needs and she books quickly!

AU PAIRS

The au pair program is a visitor exchange program that is closely monitored by the U.S Department of State. It is intended to be a cultural exchange program with an extensive child care component. Participants in the au pair program must be eighteen to twenty-six years of age and proficient in spoken English, and they are required to complete at least six hours of academic course work at an accredited educational institution. They choose either a year-long program or a ten- to fourteen-week summer program. Host families are required to pay up to $500 toward the cost of the au pair's required academic course work.

The au pair lives as an extended member of the host family and provides up to forty-five hours of child-care per week in exchange for room, board, and a weekly stipend (currently $139.05 based on minimum wage, less a credit for room and board). An au pair may not work more than ten hours at a time, is not allowed to stay with children overnight, and must be given a minimum of one and a half days off per week, one day which should be a weekend day, and one complete free weekend a month. Au pairs are not placed with families who have an infant under three months unless a responsible adult is at home. Families with a child under the age of two may only have an au pair placed in their home if the au pair has at least two hundred hours of documented infant child-care experience.

The au pair program also includes a component called EduCare, which is for families who have school-age children and require child care only before and after school hours. EduCare au pairs may not work more than ten hours a day, thirty hours a week, and they must complete twelve hours of academic credit. The host family is required to provide the first $1,000 toward the cost of the au pair's required course work, but the au pair only receives 75 percent of the normal weekly rate of compensation.

Something to keep in mind if you consider hiring an au pair is that she may not be planning a career as a nanny, so she may want to develop other interests while she is here. She may also experience culture shock or homesickness.

The following are organizations designated by the US Department of State to administer au pair visitor programs:

Au Pair in America
800-928-7247
www.aupairinamerica.com

AuPairCare Inc.
800-428-7247
www.aupaircare.com

Au Pair Foundation
866-428-7247
www.aupairfoundation.org

Cultural Care Au Pair
800-333-6056
www.culturalcare.com

EurAupair Intercultural Child Care Programs
800-713-2002
www.euraupair.com

Go Au Pair
888-287-2471
www.goaupair.com

BABYSITTING SERVICES

For many stay-at-home mothers a full-time nanny is not necessary, but an occasional reprieve from motherhood is needed (and well deserved!). The following is a listing of babysitting services that either provide help inside your home or are facilities where you can drop off your child. We also suggest that you ask your friends and church about mother's day out programs as well. Or, we have found it helpful and worthwhile to call sorority houses at a nearby university, such as SMU or TCU, because often, they can provide you with a list of girls who are ready and willing to babysit.

Babysitters of Dallas
214-692-1354
Twenty-four hour pager: 817-960-2174
www.babysittersofdallas.com

In business since 1955, Babysitters of Dallas is the oldest agency around, and it serves Dallas and Fort Worth. It provides both babysitters and nannies, but since we only know people who have used them for babysitting, we did not include them in our Agencies section of this chapter. Present day owner Sherry, who couldn't be sweeter, was a babysitter for hire with the agency for eighteen years before purchasing it. Babysitters of Dallas is state licensed and performs criminal and nationwide pedophile checks on its sitters. Sherry registers you over the phone, which only takes a few minutes, and then you are in the system; no registration fee required. A two- to three-day notice to hire a sitter is preferred, but she can sometimes place a babysitter in as few as two hours. There is a $10 agency fee per job. The fee is $10 an hour for one to two children, with a minimum of four hours. If both of your children are in diapers, the agency fee is $12, and the sitter is $12 per hour. A twenty-four-hour cancellation notice is a must.

Caring Hands
1824 Tracey Circle
Irving 75060
972-259-1184
www.caringhands.net
Office hours: Monday-Friday, 8:30 a.m. to 4:30 p.m.; Saturday, 8:30 a.m. to noon.

Caring Hands serves the Dallas-Fort Worth areas and has a staff of over 150 sitters. We have several friends who have used this babysitting service, and they have been very pleased with the quality of care. There is a $50 registration fee and a four-hour minimum. The rate for caregivers begins at $7 per hour with an additional $.50 per child/per hour. A $10 service fee per job will be billed on the tenth and twenty-fifth of each month.

Coughs & Cuddles at Presbyterian Hospital of Plano
6200 West Parker Road
Plano 75093
972-981-8585
www.texashealth.org

It's 7 a.m., your child is sick, forget mother's day out or daycare. You have an important meeting at 9 a.m. What will you do? Coughs & Cuddles is a temporary solution. This is a daycare facility for children with minor illnesses and injuries that prevent them from attending regular daycare or school. Nurses and child-care providers give children the extra love and attention needed when they are sick, giving you the peace of mind to go to work and know your child is in good hands.

Kiddin' Around Play Care
144 West Parkway
Coppell 75013
972-462-1300

9377 Lebanon Road
Frisco 75035
214-618-5433

www.kiddinaroundplaycare.com
Hours: Monday-Thursday, 8 am. to 10 p.m.; Friday and Saturday, 8 a.m. to midnight.

Kiddin' Around Play Care is an hourly drop-off sitting service for children six weeks to twelve years old. The brightly colored indoor playground with tunnels and slides, the movie theater, and the indoor basketball court might even make you want to stick around and play! The caregivers are first aid trained and certified in CPR. There is a $30 yearly membership fee per family, and sitting charges are $6.50 an hour. A Flower Mound location will open in 2005

The Little Gym

204 South Central Expressway, Suite 43
Allen 75013
972-396-7705
Every Saturday, 6 p.m. to 10 p.m.

740 South West Green Oaks Boulevard
Arlington 76017
817-465-9296
First and third Friday, 6 p.m. to 10 p.m.

2662 Josey Lane, Suite 229
Carrollton 75007
972-446-1122
Second and fourth Saturday, 6 p.m. to 10 p.m.

6465 East Mockingbird, Suite 410
Dallas 75214
214-515-0800
Every Saturday, 6 p.m. to 10 p.m.

11909 Preston Road at Forest
Dallas 75230
972-644-7333
Every Saturday, 6 p.m. to 10 p.m.

6295 Granbury
Fort Worth 76133
817-346-9655
First Saturday and third Friday, 6 p.m. to 10 p.m.

4017 Preston Road, Suite 522
Plano 75093
972-985-4545
Every Saturday, 6 p.m. to 10 p.m.

www.thelittlegym.com

Known for their motor skill developmental classes and camps, The Little Gym also offers a Parent's Survival Night. Children ages two to twelve enjoy games, music, and gymnastics while parents enjoy an evening out. Reservations are required. The cost is $35 for nonmembers and $25 for members; the fee for additional siblings is $12 per child.

PART TWO:

SHOP 'TIL YOU DROP

CHAPTER FIVE:
MOMMY STYLE

It is hip to be pregnant these days with all of the fun and chic wear for moms-to-be. From cashmere twin sets to summer halter tops, designers have worked hard to create fashionable, comfortable choices. When we were pregnant, we didn't buy very many maternity pieces because of the fear of "the tent look." Well, times have changed, and if you are brave like Kate Hudson, you too can show your belly during all nine months. However, if you are more modest like we are, you still can enjoy the tighter and sleeker designs offered today—without baring all!

To be honest, we, along with many of our friends, found nonmaternity clothes in larger sizes to be a great way to get by in the first and second trimesters. Check out Banana Republic, Anthropologie, The Gap, Old Navy, and even your favorite boutiques, but be sure to search out the low-riding hip cut of today or the generously cut waistlines and larger size T-shirts and tops. You can make these pieces work, and prices tend to be more affordable for something you won't wear for long. Now, just a word to those who think they will wear maternity clothes again during their next pregnancy . . . styles change, your body changes, and most likely, you will want a fresh look the second time around.

A. Hooper & Company
4601 West Freeway, Suite 216
Fort Worth 76107
817-348-9911
www.ahooperco.com
Hours: Monday–Saturday, 10 a.m. to 6 p.m.

This fashion-forward Fort Worth store carries some of the latest nonmaternity styles by designers such as Tracy Reese, Plenty, Trina Turk, and Nanette Lepore. It is not a full-scale maternity clothing store, but they just started carrying hip maternity styles by Michael Stars and Citizens of Humanity. Owner Amy Hooper Trott, a mother of one, also carries a small sampling of boys and girls toddler clothing (2T to 4T) by Rocket Dog, Cozy Toes, and Baby Talavera.

Babystyle
877-378-9537
www.babystyle.com

This California company, founded by a mother of two, carries the essentials, plus fun and dressy casual and athletic wear. Some designs and styles are exclusive to them (their label) and to lead designers such as Blue Dot, WhisperKnit, In-Transit, Earl Jean, and Michael Stars. It's a great place to get diaper bags, baby gear, and clothing, too!

Bella Band
415-642-2879
www.ingridandisabel.com and www.bellaband.com

The best-kept secret is a new product called the Bella Band. Created by a former Dallas mom, it is a seamless knit band that you wear around your waistline over unbuttoned, non-pregnant pants, to hide the open buttons, or over slightly big and yet-to-be-filled maternity bottoms. They are also great for skirts. "Instant hold, instant comfort, instant smooth." We only wish it was around when we were pregnant! It is the gift of choice for our friends, who are newly pregnant mommies.

BellaBlu Maternity
888-678-0034
www.bellablumaternity.com

BellaBlu Maternity is an online boutique with great designer maternity clothes. We love the bathing suits and so will you when you can see that even at nine months, there are tankinis and bikinis that are comfortable and forgiving—no grandma styles here. Just be sure to know your size and read about their return policy because swimwear is not returnable, but it may be exchanged with certain restrictions.

Belly Basics Pregnancy Survival Kit
www.babystyle.com or www.babycenter.com

Dressing yourself during pregnancy can be a no-brainer with the Belly Basics Pregnancy Survival Kit. The kit includes four basic pieces that are meant to mix-n-match, and are available in long, short, and 3/4 sleeve styles. The kit includes a dress; a short, slim skirt; a comfortable tunic; and a slim pant. The outfits can be dressed up for a night on the town or worn casually when you run around doing errands. The four-piece kit costs $152 and has been worn by stars such as Uma Thurman and Kelly Preston. We love how comfy they are and that they are machine washable.

BellyDance Maternity
888-802-1133
www.bellydancematernity.com

BellyDance Maternity, a full-scale boutique in Chicago, has a great Web site offering a wide variety of items that you can't always find here. They carry different styles, from jeans by Citizens of Humanity to Majamas nursing tops. You name it, this one-stop shop has it—including books and skin care products. Be sure to check out the hottest trend in baby bags by Skip Hop and Petunia Pickle Bottom. You can call the store, and the staff is very friendly and knowledgeable. Gift certificates are available.

Destination Maternity

5539 LBJ Freeway
Dallas 75240
972-788-4115
www.maternitymall.com
Hours: Monday-Saturday, 10 a.m. to 6 p.m.; Sunday, 11 a.m. to 6 p.m.

This is a great new addition to the Dallas area and a much-needed one-stop shopping adventure that includes parenting books, a refreshment bar, and a play area. Style is abound at Destination Maternity with hip, contemporary, and business wear by top designers—this is three stores in one: Mimi Maternity, a Pea in the Pod, and Motherhood Maternity. Shoppers can also find nursing clothes and bras, yoga mats, cards, "wonder" lotions for mom and baby, and gift items. They also offer free classes on exercise and education. Gift wrapping is complimentary.

Elements

4400 Lovers Lane
Dallas 75225
214-987-0837
www.elementsclothing.com
Hours: Monday-Saturday, 10 a.m. to 6 p.m.

Okay, this is not a maternity store, but it is so worth listing! Seriously, Elements has the hottest nonmaternity fashions that you can wear well up to the sixth month and after birth because there are several designer selections that are stretchy, low-waisted, or in the case of a dress, cut generously. Be sure to try out tops by Michael Stars, and look at James Perse's shirts and elastic waist skirts. We have gotten great use out of pieces by Susana Monaco and Ella Moss for during and after pregnancy. Be sure to look at their collection of beautiful jewelry and accessories. This boutique is husband-friendly, for the owner Connie Siegel and the gals who work there are knowledgeable and extremely patient—they will do the shopping for him! They offer refreshing beverages, a restroom, a dressing room filled with toys, and a small TV/VCR—complete with videos for the kids. For Children is just two doors down, and they have a wonderful selection of newborn to early teen clothing (See chapter 7, Kid Style).

Gap Maternity

Dallas Galleria
5220 Alpha Road
Dallas 75240
972-776-4750
www.gapmaternity.com
Hours: Monday-Saturday, 10 a.m. to 9 p.m.; Sunday, noon to 6 p.m.

Now that they carry their own line of maternity clothing, the fantastic, versatile styles you find at the Gap are now designed to get you through your pregnancy. Skirts, pants, and jeans are available with five different belly panels, and they come in sizes 0 to 20. They also have swimwear, active wear that is great for prenatal yoga, and nursing bras. Only a few select stores carry the maternity line, so you may have to order from their Web site. We are big fans of being able to return items you order by mail to the nearest Gap store.

Japanese Weekend

The Shops at Willow Bend
6121 West Park Boulevard
Plano 75093
469-366-4474
www.japaneseweekend.com
Hours: Monday-Saturday, 10 a.m. to 5 p.m.; Sunday, noon to 6 p.m.

This store was a much anticipated addition to our area, as for years you could only order their clothes online. Their contemporary maternity wear is designed by store owner Barbie White, a dancer, who designs the clothes based on a changing body. Japanese Weekend's "OK" patented waistbands "cradle the lower abdomen, support your lower back, and stretch as you grow," and were a world of comfort to us. Some have told us they "lived in them" before and even after giving birth. Prices are moderate for the trendy wear. The store has a restroom that is not outside in the mall, and the large changing rooms are great if you are toting other children with you. The staff is extremely helpful.

Liz Lange Maternity

888-616-5777
www.lizlange.com

This former fashion editor for *Vogue* created a name for herself and paved the way for better maternity fashions, thus creating the chic and fashionable mom-to-be look. You won't find maternity panels or tent shirts here. Clothing is trim and form fitting in casual, career, and Liz Lange's designs of Nike athletic wear. This is a great shop for a special occasion dress or a "night out" selection. A favorite find here is the bootleg stretch pants. Sizes do tend to run small. Prices are on the high end. Gift certificates and registry are available.

Mimi Maternity

Stonebriar Centre
2600 Preston Road
Frisco 75034
469-633-1465
Hours: Monday-Saturday, 10 a.m. to 9 p.m.; Sunday, noon to 6 p.m.

Northeast Mall
1101 Melbourne Road
Hurst 76053
817-284-0475
Hours: Monday-Saturday, 10 a.m. to 9 p.m.; Sunday, noon to 6 p.m.

University Park Village
1612 South University
Fort Worth 76107
817-332-7223
Hours: Monday-Thursday, 10 a.m. to 8 p.m.; Friday-Saturday, 10 a.m. to 9 p.m.; Sunday, noon to 5 p.m.

www.mimimaternity.com

Mimi Maternity offers contemporary, but affordable, maternity clothing in both trendy and basic styles. You can find almost everything here for fitness and yoga, plus career wear, special occasion dresses, nursing bras, sleepwear, and accessories. A variety of waists is available on their pants and skirts: mid belly, contour, under-belly, and classic belly. Their Web site is helpful and user-friendly—you can click on the waist you prefer, and it lists the available styles in pants and skirts. Most of the clothing is designed for Mimi Maternity.

Naissance Maternity

800-505-0517
www.naissancematernity.com

After former public relations executive Jennifer Noonan became frustrated at not being able to find stylish clothes during her pregnancy, she decided to do something about it and Naissance was born. They carry four different styles of maternity clothing: groovy mama, love goddess, hip chick, and funky diva. This unique clothing is a little pricey, but you probably won't find too many other people wearing your outfit!

A Pea in the Pod

7700 West Northwest Highway
Dallas 75225
214-346-9140
Hours: Monday-Saturday, 10 a.m. to 6 p.m.; Sunday, noon to 5 p.m.

The Shops at Willow Bend
6121 West Park Boulevard
Plano 75093
469-366-1018
Hours: Monday-Saturday, 10 a.m. to 9 p.m.; Sunday, noon to 6 p.m.

www.apeaninthepod.com

This nationwide store carries a large selection of casual, special occasion, and career clothing for the fashion conscious mother-to-be. There are hip fashions by big designers such as Bella Dahl, Diane von Furstenberg, Lilly Pulitzer, Anne Klein, and Three Dots. Hot denim jeans are hard to find, so be sure to stock up here for styles by 7 for All Mankind, Citizens of Humanity, and Chip and Pepper. The new NorthPark area location offers free exercise and education classes at their studio.

Pickles & Ice Cream

The Plaza at Preston Center
8300 Preston Road, Suite 700
Dallas 75225
214-361-1898
Hours: Monday-Saturday, 10 a.m. to 6 p.m.; Thursday, 10 a.m. to 7 p.m.

5813 Preston Road, Suite 564
Plano 75093
972-781-1898
Hours: Monday-Saturday, 10 a.m. to 6 p.m.

www.picklesmaternity.com

This store carries fashionable maternity clothes that make it hard to believe that they are for growing bellies. Brands offered are Ripe, Meet Me in Miami, Michael Stars, Japanese Weekend, and Pickles & Ice Cream's exclusive label. The store also carries a good selection of underwear, lingerie, and accessories such as a belly belt. A favorite find of ours here is the Mustela product line—great stretch mark cream!

Target and Super Target

Multiple locations
www.target.com
Hours: Monday-Saturday, 8 a.m. to 10 p.m.; Sunday, 8 a.m. to 9 p.m.

Target's maternity clothes are incredibly affordable and stylish—as are all of their clothes. They feature a line of maternity clothing designed by Liz Lange and their own line called In Due Time. Liz Lange is fun and trendy. In Due Time consists of more basic pieces. We highly suggest that you look in the women's section for nonmaternity wear. They have a great selection of loose-waisted styles, so you can get away with just a larger size.

CHAPTER SIX:

BABY FURNITURE AND GEAR

Hmm . . . Do you want a crib that can be made into a toddler bed later on? A rocker or a glider? . . . Nothing about the decision process is easy, but it is fun. We have made a list of items friends and we have found to be necessities. Researching products and seeing them at the store is helpful. We have borrowed a bassinet and baby swing from one another and encourage you to do the same and save hundreds of dollars. However, when it comes to car seats and mattresses, we must add that it is important to buy these items new. Now you don't have to rush out and buy everything, because you will get some necessities as gifts, but we do suggest furniture shopping during the fifth and sixth month of pregnancy, as an order can take four to ten weeks, depending on vendor and custom creations.

If you need help and ideas for decorating the nursery, we have found the furniture boutiques we have included to be extremely talented, as well as a valuable resource for muralists. Best of all, their "consulting" is free (when you order your furniture from them of course)! So let them come to your home with fabric swatches, lamps, pillows, and other accessories. Working within a budget is common practice for most, so don't be afraid to voice your limit.

THE ESSENTIALS

CRIBS

There are so many crib designs and makers to choose from today that it can be overwhelming, yet exciting too. Most importantly however, is that all cribs today should fit the strict codes and guidelines set by the Consumer Product Safety Commission (CPSC), 800-638-2772 or www.cpsc.gov, and certified by the Juvenile Products Manufactures Association (JPMA), www.jpma.org. You may also refer to our safety sections in chapter 3 for further information on these organizations and other nursery safety issues.

So what should you look for when buying a crib?

* A tight, firm mattress. A good test is to place your fingers between the mattress and the side of the crib, and if two or more fingers fit, then the mattress is too small.

* The slats of a crib. They should be no more than 2⅜ inches apart (about the width of a soda can).

* Crib hardware. Make sure the crib is stable and that wood joints are not splitting, and then check for rough edges. Does the crib have wheels? And can they be removed?

* Openings and decorative cutouts. The CPSC recommends passing on these, for the baby's head could get caught.

* A drop side. There is a benefit for access to your child, especially if you are recovering from a C-section. Make sure the side rail can be lowered easily with one hand by an adult, since one hand is usually holding your baby.

BABY SWINGS AND BOUNCY SEATS

From the beginning, we have found these to be lifesavers. From soothing a crying baby, feeding a child, and keeping her upright after eating, to letting you take a shower, a baby swing or bouncy seat is a portable, handy staple for all new parents. These are great items to borrow from your friends if their children have outgrown them, as new items can get quite expensive and infants are in them for a short period of time; usually the weight limit is up to about twenty pounds. A lot of these now have music, vibration, and toys in them. We have found that less is more. Brands such as Graco, Fisher Price, and Combi have proven to be reliable and durable for our friends and us.

BATHTUBS

Our most enjoyable part of the day has always been bathtime. For many this may not be the case, but bath time can be safe and fun if you know what features to look for. A sponge or mesh "cradle" is wonderful for tiny babies and it's a great device to keep them propped up. As they get older and are able to sit up on their own, you can remove the insert. Some tubs also come with temperature gauges, which change color to let you know if the water is too hot. We are fans of the Safety 1st inflatable duck tub—complete with a water temperature gauge, a nonslip bottom surface, and a quacking bill. Don't worry if you don't have a tub the day you get home from the hospital. The hospital and the pediatrician will tell you that your baby doesn't need a bath until her umbilical cord falls off—typically a week or so after delivery.

BEDDING

We could do almost an entire chapter on bedding locales alone because it seems that there are endless places and individuals that are in the custom-made baby bedding business. From fabric stores to small boutiques to super stores, you can find bedding in all price ranges and in various styles and quality. Picking the "theme" or "tone" of the room is the first step, and then shop from there. Touch the fabrics, rub them on your face, and ask if you can bring them home for a trial period.

In reality, all you need is a good bumper pad, a couple of basic sheets, and a bed skirt. Cute as they may be, you can save money and forget the blankets and comforters for now.

CAR SEATS

A car seat is one of the most significant items to purchase before the arrival of your child. While there are several brands on the market, we have found that asking friends and checking the consumer reports is the best way to choose a car seat. As mentioned in our safety sections, we can't suggest enough that you have your seat checked and installed by a professional. Kim and Nevin were shown by the nurses at the hospital before they left with Sawyer, as were Kelli and A.J. with Josh. And remember that all infants must be rear-facing until they are one year old and weigh over twenty pounds. The CPSC Web site, www.cpsc.gov, is a great place to check for product recalls.

We have found that infant carriers are great for taking your little one on the go, as they easily snap into a base attached to your car and can be unlatched for portability. A great bonus is that you can tote around the sleeping baby. There are stroller bases to hold the carrier, or there are also travel systems with more deluxe options, but all are very helpful. Be sure to watch your baby's growth, as Kim's kiddos were long, and by the age of six months, their feet and legs were hitting the backseat. So, she switched to a "convertible" seat that stays in the car at all times and converts from rear-facing to forward-facing. We have both found seats by Britax, which work for babies five to thirty-three pounds (rear-facing) and up to sixty-five pounds (forward-facing), to be of great quality with high ratings. And, this specific seat saved us from buying additional seats, including booster seats, as the children grew.

DRESSER AND CHANGING TABLES

We feel that one of smartest options today—and a cost-effective choice—is to choose a dresser for your changing table. We both did this after having trouble finding and affording both a dresser for the clothing and a separate changing table. Why did we need both when we could buy one functional piece of furniture that would take up less space and grow with the child? The drawers are great for diapers and diaper ointments and later can be used for underwear and other clothing. Options are limitless this way and "toppers" can be found at several area stores. You can use a foam changing pad and let it rest on the dresser, a custom wooden piece such as a "changing tray" exclusive to Stephanie Anne Room to Grow, or have a handy husband or grandpa-to-be who can make a pad for you (like A.J. made for Josh). Now, common sense does tell us that at all times you have to be aware of a rolling baby—even a newborn and especially a toddler!

HIGH CHAIRS

After early feedings in the bouncy seat or swing, transitioning to a high chair was a major photograph event in our homes. You better be aware: life and eating takes on a whole new meaning, as without a secure and stable chair, injuries can take place. Some features to take into consideration are a safety restraint, reclining and adjustable heights, a one-handed tray release, a comfortable and removable seat cover, and swivel wheels.

While feeding is the primary purpose of the high chair, we have found that a first-time experiment with coloring or having a snack while we unload the dishwasher makes this a beloved throne! We both, along with numerous friends and family, are extremely pleased with the Peg-Pérego Prima Pappa chair.

MONITORS

These smart devices allow you peace of mind when your baby is sleeping; you can hear him from another room or while outside. We have had to go through a couple of different brands to finally find one that works best with our homes and wireless phones. The 900 megahertz, two-receiver monitors allow you not only to have clearer sound with less interruptions and static, but also an extra receiver for downstairs or outdoors. We have friends who still watch their three-year-old on a video monitor allowing them to see even at night. These sound great, and are, but work better in certain homes due to the floor plan and multilevel designs. We have found Fisher Price, Safety 1st, and Graco to be reliable. There is also a new monitor, Angelcare by BébéSounds, that detects the slightest sounds and movements and if none are detected in twenty seconds, an alarm sounds. This award-winner further helps guard against SIDS. There are also television monitor systems, but while some pledge their handiness, we have had difficulty with excess static.

STROLLERS

Strollers are a necessity that you can use right away to save your back! There are several different kinds with various features, and the best way to choose is to go to the store and actually look at the different models. Some things to take into consideration are the details and extras that are important to you such as weight, reclining seats, a shade, storage, a tray and child cup holder, and so forth. We have owned several versions in our four years of parenthood and have found that a lightweight, collapsible stroller with a one-handed release is ideal. Also, the most expensive with the most bells and whistles is not necessarily the best buy. Our friends recommend Peg-Pérego, Graco, Kolcraft, and Maclaren. One of the latest and greatest (and very expensive) strollers to hit the market is the Bugaboo Frog stroller. Their award-winning design is smart, and has a reversible handlebar, seat/bassinet, the ability to go up and down curbs with simplicity ("frog-like suspension"), and so much more. Be prepared to hunt them down and pay about $729. We have found them at the Right Start and online at babystyle.com.

When looking for a stroller for twins, or an infant and an older sibling, Kim and her friends found the side-by-side model to be the most convenient, but the stroller with a landing for the toddler to stand on the back to be the easiest to control.

Baby joggers are a great addition to your baby gear, but we suggest that you wait until your baby's neck and head are strong enough before you hit the running or fast walking trails. We are fans of the joggers by Kelty and Baby Jogger for their five-point harness, light weight base, sunshade, and brake system.

ROCKER OR GLIDER

Whether you choose a rocker or a glider, you can't go wrong. Both will provide you and the baby a relaxing and rhythmic locale for either feeding or late-night soothing. There are various options and you can even choose your own fabric and details in design, so just have fun and be sure your husband likes it too! Oh, and be sure to invest in an ottoman to prop up your feet—some even glide as well! Many stores offer a small discount in price when you purchase both.

NURSERY TIPS

- Buy several sheets and waterproof mattress covers just in case there is middle-of-the-night leakage.

- Diaper disposal is a personal thing. Some swear by the Diaper Genie and others prefer using a regular kitchen bin with a deodorized bag.

- A sound machine or cool mist humidifier is great for soothing music, sounds of the ocean, or imitating the sounds from the womb while keeping out background noise. The humidifier also keeps rooms moist during the dry months.

- You can never have too much storage for future toys. From baskets to a toy chest, you can choose what best fits your needs and décor. Some like to have toys out of sight and use a chest. Just be sure that the storage device has a child-safe closure and round, smooth edges versus pointed ones.

- A nightlight is perfect for avoiding turning on the bright lights in the middle of the night and waking up the baby. Kelli found comfort in breastfeeding by the soft gentle light and could still see enough to read, if need be.

- A soft carpet or area rug is a must, especially for playtime on the floor and for when the baby gets moving.

- Wall hangings are great, but not in close proximity to the crib. Also, keep in mind the placement of the crib, keeping it away from heaters, air vents, windows, and window coverings with cords.

- Baby rolls or "positioners" are great to keep the baby in one position, such as side sleeping, or to keep her from rolling over onto her belly.

Babies "R" Us

420 East Round Grove
Lewisville 75067
972-459-9333

1501 West Arbrook Boulevard
Arlington 76015
817-784-2229

1701 Preston Road
Plano 75093
972-735-1229

3850 Beltline Road
Addison 75001
972-247-4229

1220 Town East Boulevard
Mesquite 75150
972-682-1450

5800 Overton Ridge Road
Hulen 76132
817-423-8829

www.babiesrus.com

Babies "R" Us is great and an inexpensive to moderately priced locale for a complete bedroom suite. Cribs start at around $150. The displays are helpful, but you might have to hunt down a salesperson. For an extra fee, they can assemble items for you, but you better bring an SUV because they don't deliver. Bedding selections are fun and bright and can usually include the whole ensemble including bed skirt, bumper pad, sheet, and comforter. This is a one-stop shop for everything from strollers and bottles to formula.

Be-dazzled!

The Shops at Legacy
5760 Legacy Drive
Plano 75024
972-378-3211
www.bedazzledplano.com
Hours: Monday-Wednesday, Friday and Saturday, 10 a.m. to 6 p.m.; Thursday, 10 a.m. to 8 p.m.

Be-dazzled! is a one-stop shop for creating your nursery or child's bedroom. From an on-staff muralist to a seamstress for custom bedding, let this friendly staff's creativity and knowledge work within your budget—and they will! "We can make a mansion out of a box," says owner Deb Hoffman, who has been in the children's bedding business for over twelve years. They carry "quality" brands, such as Morigeau-Lépine, Bonavita from Italy, and Bratt Decor. Be-dazzled!'s carpenter can make custom cribs and furniture.

Bellini

5600 Lovers Lane, Suite 142
Dallas 75209
214-352-2512
www.bellini.com
Hours: Monday-Saturday, 10 a.m. to 5:30 p.m.; Sundays by appointment

We like that Bellini's cribs all have a linen drawer for extra storage and that they can be made into a toddler bed. However, several of our friends have told us to order early because they are designed and manufactured in Italy and may take eight to ten weeks to be delivered. Prices start at $560, and there are five finishes to choose from. You can also find coordinating changing tables, dressers, juvenile coordinating furniture, desks, beds, and more. The friendly staff is willing to help you pick fabrics from their books to create customized bedding. For a fee, delivery and assembly of cribs are available (a great option because cribs can be tricky to put together). Bellini also carries great lightweight strollers by Maclaren, Britax car seats, and top-of-the-line B•O•B joggers. Gift certificates, complimentary gift wrap, and registry are available.

Cargo Kids

2787 Preston Road, Suite 1180
Frisco 75034
214-387-0109

812 Northeast Mall Boulevard
Hurst 75063
817-595-1225

www.cargokids.com
Hours: Monday-Saturday, 10 a.m. to 9 p.m.; Sunday, 11 a.m. to 7 p.m.

Cargo Kids has a variety of children's bed styles and companion pieces. They do not carry cribs but are great for basic nightstands, tables, and dressers. They will deliver for a fee and included in the fee is assembly. They will "take away the trash." Cargo Kids is a Pier One Imports company, and their furniture is sold under the Cargo Kids brand. Returns are accepted within thirty days with your receipt.

Designs for Children

4804 Camp Bowie Boulevard
Fort Worth 76107
817-732-6711
Hours: Monday-Friday, 10 a.m. to 6 p.m.; Saturday, 10 a.m. to 5 p.m.

This specialty market carries baby and children's furniture and a plethora of toys! There are several crib designs by Clark & Lee starting at $533 and going up to $1,600 for custom, hand-painted creations. Children's furniture is by PJ Kids and California Kids. Imagine fire truck bunk beds with a slide to twin and queen busy city headboards. Bedding, lamps, and toy chests are also available.

Haute Tot

818-448-8467
www.hautetot.com

After seeing a dear friend's baby carrier covered in adorable and hip fabric, Kim had to know where or who made it for her. Haute Tot, an online baby accessory boutique, has figured a way to make your standard infant and toddler car seats look dressed up—all are reversible and washable, and the infant cover is complete with a coordinating sunshade! Fabric selections for the car seats include leopard, cherry, fatigue, flower bouquet, and Zen prints—all of which can also be chosen for ready-made crib bedding. Prices for crib sets start at $500 and include a reversible blanket, bumper pad, bed skirt, and sheet.

The Land of Nod

800-933-9904
www.landofnod.com

Classic and fun furnishings by the Land of Nod (now partners with Crate & Barrel) are some of our favorites by far. Quality in design, customer service, and price—you really can't go wrong ordering from them. The Web site and catalog offer great design ideas, as well as humor and wit in their description of the items, such as "Curling Iron Bed," and "Honey, I Shrunk the Storage Bench." You can choose your crib, bedding, rocker, dresser, and wall art—it is a one-stop shop that delivers—for a fee of course. There are great rugs and accessories too.

One Step Ahead

800-274-8440
www.onestepahead.com

This online store carries innovative and quality products, and shopping online or through their catalogue makes life simpler. There are playpens, strollers, baby carriers, monitors, and infant tubs. We and our parent friends use One Step Ahead for numerous items and love their giant bath mats, safety products, toys, and clever items such as the TableToppers and Potty Toppers. They also have a Leaps and Bounds catalog for ages three and up—perfect for finding the newest in swim products to toddler bed rails. Visit www.leapsandboundscatalog.com or call 800-477-2189.

Posh Tots
866-767-4868
www.poshtots.com

Posh Tots, an online boutique, offers "the best of the best" for children of all ages. From nursery items to furniture and accessories for your child's playroom and "big kid" room, their items are expensive and unique. Just looking at their selections is inspiration for decorating any room. They also have an incredible new line of children's clothing and amazing gifts. One of our favorites is a great big cozy fleece blanket with your child's name on it.

Pottery Barn Kids
Knox Street
3228 Knox
Dallas 75205
214-522-4845
Hours: Monday-Saturday, 10 a.m. to 9 p.m.; Sunday, noon to 6 p.m.

Stonebriar Centre
2601 Preston Road
Frisco 75034
972-731-8912
800-993-4923
Hours: Monday-Saturday, 10 a.m. to 9 p.m.; Sunday, noon to 6 p.m.

www.potterybarnkids.com

If you like the catalog, you will love the store. PB Kids carries everything for a child's room from cribs to miniature versions of their popular adult-sized furniture. The colors and bedding themes are continually being updated but you can always find the basics. The staff is solicitous without being pushy, and they don't wince when your children try out the toys and furniture. They offer monogramming, gift wrapping, and gift certificates. Keep an eye out for terrific sale prices. Cribs range in price from $399 to $799, and they will assemble many items, excluding cribs, changing tables, and bunk beds.

The Right Start
Inwood Village
5550 West Lovers Lane
Dallas 75209
214-350-4070

Lakeside Market Shopping Center
5809 Preston Road
Plano 75093
972-781-0353

www.rightstart.com
Hours: Monday–Saturday, 10 a.m. to 6 p.m.; Sunday, noon to 5 p.m.

The "best of the best" is what you will find at the Right Start. Peg-Pérego, Maclaren, and Bugaboo strollers; Peg-Pérego high chairs; Britax car seats; and wonderful developmental toys and safety products are just a few of the superb items carried by the Right Start. The staff is extraordinarily knowledgeable and helpful, so don't be afraid to ask questions. On some items you will pay a little more than at a superstore, but the convenience and customer service outweighs the cost.

Shabby Palace
214-662-7477
www.shabbypalace.com

Shabby Palace is Valerie Masse Womack's baby. She has been sewing and designing since she was six years old and can create just about any bedding from her fabric or your own fabric choices. Shabby Palace also offers full service design services. For a custom made standard bedding set, which includes bumpers, crib skirt, and blanket, she charges $300 to $500. Prices vary as you add window treatments, diaper changing table covers, chair cushions, hampers, etc. to your order.

Shelbi's Stuff
8318 Preston Center Plaza
Dallas 75225
214-346-0404
www.luvstuffbaby.com
Hours: Monday–Friday, 10 a.m. to 5:30 p.m.

Shelbi's Stuff used to be one of the first boutiques to carry wonderful cribs and dressers. It now focuses on bedding by Luv Stuff for creating a "uniquely" designed nursery or child's room. You may choose from ready-made or custom bedding, and the fabric selections are endless. Shelbi's Stuff also carries a yummy selection of clothing and gifts. This is where Kim and several other local moms would practically line up to buy bottles of the Baby's Bliss GripeWater—a natural solution for babies and children for relief of gas, stomach discomfort, and hiccups. We swear it works like magic!

Small Fry World
7517 Campbell Road, Suite 500
Dallas 75248
972-380-2929

2985 South Highway 360, Suite 130
Grand Prairie 75052
972-522-0286

7200 Camp Bowie Boulevard
Fort Worth 76116
817-735-9936

www.babyexpressstores.com
Hours: Monday-Saturday, 10 a.m. to 6 p.m.

Small Fry World is an enormous warehouse of newborn to teen furniture, and baby gear such as strollers and high chairs. They carry the Ragazzi, Legacy, and Picci furniture brands and always have something for everyone. Cribs can take from eight to ten weeks and some up to twenty-four weeks for delivery. They also carry bassinets and a huge selection of gliders. Their prices are "less than retail," and they accept returns within ten days as long as the product is still in its box. Sale items are final and there are lots to choose from. Delivery is an additional fee and assembly is included. There is a large selection of strollers by Aprica, Pilko, and Graco.

Stephanie Anne Room to Grow
4346 Lovers Lane
Dallas 75225
214-368-3025
www.stephanieanne.com
Hours: Monday-Friday, 10 a.m. to 5:30 p.m.; Saturday 10 a.m. to 5 p.m.; Sunday, noon to 5 p.m.

Stephanie Anne's one-of-a-kind furniture is all designed and produced locally by Stephanie Anne. This furniture/interior designer has spent years, nights, and hours to create a comprehensive upscale line of cribs, children's furniture, and accessories to grow with your child. The heirloom quality cribs start at $700 and go up to $2,100. You may choose from a variety of Stephanie Anne exclusive colors and hand-painted embellishments for any piece. All furniture is "ergonomically" designed: corners are rounded for safety and the paint is child safe. The caring and very service-oriented staff will help you customize and create your own look for your nursery by sitting down and drawing out a floor plan if you desire. They will even travel to your home for no additional charge. This is a one-stop shop for items from custom bedding to a muralist, to a crib mattress, to unique gifts and art. There is a full baby and children's gift registry and a discount is offered when purchasing gifts off of the registry. Keep your eye out for their new private line of infant and children's clothing coming in winter 2004.

Target and Super Target
Multiple locations
www.target.com
Hours: Monday-Saturday, 8 a.m. to 10 p.m.; Sunday 8 a.m. to 9 p.m.

Target is a one-stop shop for strollers, diapers and formula, and toys and books. You can find your entire nursery here and more. We love that you can find great deals on quality products and brands such as Graco, Evenflo, Combi, Kolcraft, Safety 1st, and InStep. They have gift registry and gift cards available. Shopping online is easy and provides the resource of product information. Returns are now easier when shopping with your credit card. If you lose your receipt, bring the item back with your card, and all they do is scan both and you are done!

Toys "R" Us
9500 North Central Expressway at Walnut Hill
Dallas 75231
214-363-3192

2100 Town East Mall
Mesquite 75150
972-270-6164
3125 West Airport Freeway
Irving 75062
972-252-5959

3777 West Camp Wisdom Road
Dallas 75237
972-296-5936

300 Lexington Drive
Plano 75075
972-422-0408

2412 South Stemmons Freeway
Lewisville 75067
972-315-6210

2871 Preston Road
Frisco 75034
972-712-0054

4111 South Cooper Street
Arlington 76015
817-784-0843

1319 West Pipeline
Hurst 76053
817-589-7181

www.toysrus.com
Store hours: Monday-Saturday, 9:30 a.m. to 9:30 p.m.; Sunday, 11 a.m. to 7 p.m.

When you think of buying a Barbie, some Legos, a Matchbox car, or a bicycle, Toys "R" Us is probably one of the stores you might consider. But Toys "R" Us, which also owns Babies "R" Us, carries more that just toys. While they don't stock the extensive number of cribs, car seats, and high chairs that Babies "R" Us does, don't overlook them. You can choose from Graco, Cosco, and Evenflo car seats and strollers, Graco and Babytrend high chairs, and a large selection of swings and pack 'n plays. If you don't have a Babies "R" Us nearby, Toys "R" Us is a convenient place to pick up diapers and formula by the case and to buy bottles, clothing, and much more.

USA Baby
970 North Coit Road, Suite 3025
Richardson 75080
972-234-2552

2801 East Division Street, Suite 202
Arlington 76011
817-633-7040

9380 Prestmont Place
Frisco 75034
972-335-5222

Hours: Monday and Thursday, 10 a.m. to 8 p.m.; Tuesday, Wednesday, Friday, and Saturday, 10 a.m. to 6 p.m.; Sunday, noon to 5 p.m.
www.usababy.com

From bedding to car seats, strollers, and more—they have it all! Berg, Pali, Morigeau-Lépine, and Bonavita are among some of the furniture brands carried in this 10,000-square-foot store. They have some great prices and the staff is very helpful. For those moms carrying twins, they offer 10 percent off a second, duplicate item.

CHAPTER SEVEN:
KID STYLE

ittle clothes are such fun . . . and Dallas's children are as well-dressed as their parents, as the kids don both the latest trends and the classic styles. From cashmere to chenille to linen to a simple newborn sleeping gown, we have created a list of local finds that are friendly and customer oriented and have fashionable selections in all price ranges. Some of the stores' owners have shared in the emotions of watching our children grow, and other stores have been recommended to us by friends and those we have surveyed. So whether you are on the hunt for a special gift, in need of an array of staples, or want to resell your little fashion plate's outgrown clothes, this chapter will help you with your clothes adventure.

SHOPPING TIPS

Okay, you could spend a fortune on your little one's wardrobe—everything out there is precious! Just a hint that we try to remember each time we feel the urge—remember the sales! There are great sales in our city, and if you are patient, they are worth it. Ask the stores when their next sale is, or keep in mind that the end of one season means ushering out the old and bringing in the new. Buying for next season is tough, especially at the beginning, because you never know how much your child will grow. Use your best judgment, ask all the questions about returns, refunds, and store credit, keep the tags on until your child is ready to wear the item, and save your receipts. The Gap, Old Navy, and stores, such as Stein Mart, Marshall's, and TJ Maxx, are great places for stylish bargains. You may have to keep popping in periodically or ask them which days their shipments arrive, but the savings can be worth it.

Now choosing the right sizes can be daunting, but we have found that most salespeople are willing to help you slip an outfit on your child, or they urge you to take it home and try it on. It is also helpful to look at the tags for weight and height or length, or ask the salesperson what the size typically runs in terms of weight and length.

For those first few outfits, six to nine pounds or "newborn" is a safe bet, as are the sleeping gowns. These don't have all of the snaps and buttons, they are easy to put on, they have covers for baby's hands to keep him from scratching, and they are easy for diaper changes. Some of our favorite layette items that are useful essentials during the first few weeks and months are:

- Sleeping gowns—great for day and night and make diaper changing easy.

- Onesies—you can never have enough of these. They are perfect for the warm months and for layering during the cold ones.

- Socks

- Burp cloths—a package of Gerber cloth diapers found at the grocery store is inexpensive and the cloths can be used to wipe up anything!

- Washcloths—not only for baths, but for the first days (in place of baby wipes for those with sensitive bottoms)—a helpful hint from Kim's sister.

- SleepSack by Halo Innovations—this "wearable blanket," is relatively new on the market and the first product ever to be endorsed by the SIDS Alliance. It is sleeveless and collarless, and you put your baby in it, zip it up, and it keeps him warm without the worries of a loose blanket in the crib. They come in cotton or fleece and may be found at stores such as Babies "R" Us and on babycenter.com.

- Sleepers—as the baby gets bigger, cotton or terry sleepers are great for day and night—just watch out for all of those snaps!

- Cotton caps or hats—great at all ages for cool weather or air-conditioned locales.

- Hooded bath towels—these make great gifts and are easy to use when your hands are busy trying to hold on to a wet squirmy babe.

- Blankets—another great gift item that is not only useful for cool weather and air conditioning, but also for draping over the car seat when at the grocery store or in a crowded restaurant or for a last-minute changing pad.

STORES

Animal Crackers
120 State Street
Southlake 76092
817-416-6246
Hours: Monday-Saturday, 10 a.m. to 6 p.m.

This cute Southlake store, located on the square, carries infant, children's, and women's clothing. From Monkey Wear and Flowers by Zoe for girls, to Charlie Rocket and Johnny Boy for boys, you can find some adorable playwear and gifts. The bright and cheery gift wrapping is complimentary.

Babies on the Boulevard

6200 Camp Bowie Boulevard
Fort Worth 76116
817-737-7171
www.gordonboswell.com
Hours: Monday-Friday, 9 a.m. to 6 p.m.; Saturday, 9 a.m. to 5 p.m.

Dress your child from head to toe at this upscale Fort Worth clothing boutique. You will find House of Hatten, Piccino Piccina, Zackali 4 Kids hand-knit clothing, Susan Turner bags, Kecci Daddybag, and Little Bear Feet shoes made right here in Texas. They also have a large selection of party dresses and formal jon-jon outfits from sizes newborn to age four, along with many beautiful christening gowns to choose from. Babies on the Boulevard shares a space with Gordon Boswell flowers, which means it's simple to create a unique and beautiful gift basket. Their gift registry is unique and practical—the mother-to-be chooses items and then they are placed in a gift basket. People can browse through the basket to choose a gift—a convenient and time-saving way to shop. Delivery to both hospital rooms and the home is available.

Baby Bean, Vintage Daywear

www.babybeanwear.com
contact: christine@babybeanwear.com

This is a new and well-welcomed addition to children's wear that we just think is unique and elegant, yet practical and functional for every day. If you are looking to dress your child in something that others don't have, Baby Bean is it—well, for girls thus far, that is! Christine Visneau, owner and creator, designs are made from 100 percent vintage fabrics and are comfortable and handmade. New to the market, Christine, a former New Yorker who moved to Dallas with her photographer husband and her "baby bean," offers a jacket and pant set ($58), a tunic ($48), and others. She welcomes custom orders and also offers adorable ponchos and matching berets ($60). We embrace Baby Bean because what is a dress one year can be a tunic over jeans or a skirt the next.

Baby Gap

Multiple locations throughout Dallas-Fort Worth
800-GAP-STYLE
www.gap.com

This is a great place to buy staples for the different stages in your child's life. You can find amazing bargains, and if you fall in love with something, wait . . . it is sure to go on sale. Layette and receiving blankets are soft and run pretty true to size, even for those early outfits. They have shoes and hats, and their socks are the best—they have treads on the bottom for beginning walkers.

Babystyle
877-378-9537
www.babystyle.com

Babystyle offers soft, fun-loving clothes for newborns to 5T. Whether it is a baby basic romper, a toddler's retro-printed dress, or genuine Levi's for the little one, they offer mostly the exclusive Babystyle brand. We have found their boys' clothing to be a savior because they seem to fit a tad more generously for a tall and bigger babe. For us and our friends, ordering by phone or via their Web site has always been quick and easy. Shipments have always been sent on time.

Bamboo & Bananas
The Shops at Willow Bend
6121 West Park Boulevard
Plano 75093
469-366-2084
Hours: Monday-Saturday, 10 a.m. to 9 p.m.; Sunday, noon to 6 p.m.

When owner Karen Gonzalez had to return to the United States after living in Singapore for almost two years, she decided to bring something back: a unique line of clothes called "bumwear." Her 100 percent Javanese (from the island of Java) cotton clothing is designed using the traditional method of printing called batiking. The prices are very reasonable; most outfits seemed to be around $25. Since garment workers are paid on a piece-by-piece basis, Gonzalez tries to keep the prices affordable to keep people coming back. There are shirts and shorts for boys. Girls' sizes go from infant to 14, and boys' sizes are newborn to size 10. The store also carries Kaboo and Michael Simon.

Bebe Grand
2013 Abrams Road
Dallas 75214
214-887-9224
www.bebegrand.com
Hours: Monday-Saturday, 10 a.m. to 6 p.m.

This is a one-of-a-kind boutique nestled in Lakewood. Owner and grandmother Susan O'Neill is an endless talent. From creating a nursery, to choosing from her extensive book collection, to sizes, be sure to ask her for help with anything. Beyond the sweet, hip, and classic array of clothing, there is a phenomenal selection of toys, unique gifts, talking backpacks, hand-painted high chairs, furnishings, and so much more . . . a true treasure! Bebe Grand offers free gift wrapping, complete with a baby-inspired fortune cookie.

The Children's Place

Multiple locations
877-PLACE-USA
www.childrensplace.com

Sold under the Children's Place brand, these clothes are fun, colorful, and durable basics at affordable prices. Sizes run from newborn to 14 for both boys and girls. Boys do not get shortchanged here. The Children's Place carries an equally large selection of boys' and girls' apparel, which dads and moms of boys appreciate.

Chocolate Soup

10720 Preston Road, Suite 1015
Dallas 75230
214-363-6981
Hours: Tuesday, Wednesday, and Saturday, 10 a.m. to 6 p.m.; Monday, Thursday, and Friday, 10 a.m. to 8 p.m.; Sunday, 1 p.m. to 5 p.m.

The store's motto is "great taste in kid's clothes," and it is a store filled with a lot of variety. The clothes are arranged by size on numerous racks everywhere, and the aisles are narrow, but it is worth it to thumb through for great prices. There is even a small play area. Be sure to get on their mailing list because it seems like they are always having sales. Sizes range from newborn to preteen.

Dillard's

13343 Preston Road
Dallas 75240
972-386-4595

100 NorthPark Center
Dallas 75225
214-373-7000

1101 Melbourne Road
Hurst 76053
817-284-4566

3901 Irving Mall
Irving 75062
972-258-4968

2501 Dallas Parkway
Plano 75093
972-202-4730

581 South Plano Road
Richardson 75081
972-783-2598

www.dillards.com
Hours: Monday-Saturday, 10 a.m. to 9 p.m.; Sunday, noon to 6 p.m.

Fashion-forward adults can clothe children in their likeness at this well-known retailer. Polo by Ralph Lauren, Le Top, and Tommy Hilfiger are some of the labels you can choose. They have a large selection of layette for newborns, and clothes run up to girls' size 16 and boys' size 20. Dillard's always seems to have items on sale, so keep your shopping radar tuned to get some great deals.

Flora and Henri
888-749-9698
www.florahenri.com

Flora and Henri is a high-quality line of children's clothing created out of fine European fabrics. The designs are similar to vintage styles, but with updated flair. The Seattle flagship store and the New York City stores are fun to visit, and they carry the soft colors and traditional lines as well. They stock minimal accessories, but we love the Italian wingtip boots in pink or navy and the softness of the Dore-Dore French socks and tights. You can order online or by phone.

For Children
4408 Lovers Lane
Dallas 75225
214-363-1651
Hours: Monday-Saturday, 10 a.m. to 5:30 p.m.

This store grows with you—literally. The minute you walk in, there are newborn items in the front, and it casually graduates to young boys' clothes up to size 7 and girls to size 14 as you walk toward the back of the shop. From smocked dresses to fun print cotton pajamas to party wear, be sure to take some extra time to look at the wide selection of bows and accessories. Monogramming is a special feature on towels and little girl panties. There is a great, clean play area.

Good Night Moon
5934 Royal
Dallas 75230
214-691-9393
www.gnmdallas.com
Hours: Monday-Saturday, 10 a.m. to 5:30 p.m.

The "Premier Signature Store" of Lilly Pulitzer for moms and children has great children's clothing and accessories. Here you can find wonderful and pricey European fashions. Some of the precious brands include Bonpoint, Lili Gaufrette, Cacharel, and Grain de Lune. Their gift selection is unique and worth the visit, and their staff is very friendly. They carry boys' sizes 2 months to 2T, and girls' sizes 2 months up to 12 years.

Gymboree
Multiple locations
877-4GYMWEB
www.gymboree.com

These are fun, bright clothes and accessories for newborns to eight years. The prices are fair and the sales are better. The clothes are the Gymboree brand (yes, this is owned by the same company as the classes) and are "active wear." They make it easy too—they have several options that coordinate, from socks to hair bows to hats to shoes to dresses, shirts, and pants. There is a TV with a video usually playing in the small area where children can sit down.

Hanna Andersson
800-222-0544
www.hannaandersson.com

Hanna Andersson's clothes are bright, fun, and oh-so-soft. A friend gave a gift to Kim for her daughter and son, and after several washings, the clothing has yet to shrink or fade in color. We are very pleased with their customer service, the premium quality fabrics they use, and their selections for infants to adults. Hanna Andersson also offers underwear, shoes, hats, and pajamas. Gift certificates are available.

Haute Baby
5350 West Lovers Lane, Suite 128
Dallas 75209
214-357-3068
www.hautebaby.com
Hours: Monday-Saturday, 10 a.m. to 6 p.m.

Fun and fashionable finds by Houston mom and designer Linda Jeffcott are found at this great store. She "sweetens" adult fashions for little ones, evident in her signature Haute Baby private label animal print shirts for toddler boys, the rose silk pants for infant girls, and even in the layette gowns. You will be entranced once you walk in and may think you have come to buy one perfect gift, but trust us, you will leave with several "gifts" for your little one. They also carry bedding, christening gowns, wonderful blankets, and Moses baskets. We love the mini suede pink cowgirl boots!

Hip Hip Hooray!
6805 Snider Plaza
Dallas 75225
214-369-2788
Hours: Monday-Friday, 10 a.m. to 5:30 p.m., Saturday, 10 a.m to 5 p.m.

Hip Hip Hooray!, in its new location in Snider Plaza, continues to be a favorite of ours. You can find soft baby blankets, newborn sleepers, smocked outfits, and bathing suits for boys (newborn to 4T) and girls (newborn to 14). Little ones are easily entertained at a small play table. Monogramming is available, which makes this a great place to find a special gift. There is also a selection of shoes, toys, bows, and books at this small, friendly, neighborhood boutique.

Janie & Jack

Stonebriar Centre
2601 Preston Road
Frisco 75034
214-618-6430

The Shops at Willow Bend
6121 West Park Boulevard
Plano 75093
469-366-0707

www.janieandjack.com
Hours: Monday-Saturday, 10 a.m. to 9 p.m.; Sunday, noon to 6 p.m.

This national chain store carries clothes that are stylish compared to their more fun and "themed" playwear sister store, Gymboree. All clothes are Janie & Jack private label and are for preemie to 3T. Visit the Web for nursery bedding by Peacock Alley and for their adorable accessories and silver gift items.

Keedo

3921 West Park Boulevard, Suite 120
Plano 75075
972-867-6100
Hours: Open on Tuesdays and Fridays only, 10 a.m. to 1 p.m. Call for times as they can change.

Soft and yummy, "fun-to-wear," cotton clothing from Cape Town, South Africa. Styles range from breezy and light linen for girls with hip bell-bottom-shaped pants, complete with ruffles, to adorable animal print T's and shorts for infants. Call to get on their e-mail list because they have great sales!

Kid Biz

8408 Preston Center Plaza
Dallas 75225
214-692-5437
Hours: Monday-Friday, 10 a.m. to 5:30 p.m.; Saturday, 10 a.m. to 5 p.m.

A treasure beyond clothing. You can't miss a gift from Kid Biz due to their cow-print tissue paper. From newborn to teens, the clothes are fun, traditional, and hip. Infant wear is practical and cute with several European selections. There are too many gift items to name, but a favorite is the Prudence Knox photo necklaces. There are great private dressing rooms, and there is a play area for the children. There is an ice cream store just a few steps away. This store is extremely dad friendly!

Kidcrazy.biz
214-696-6287
www.kidcrazy.biz

This new Web site is an online replacement for the former local favorite children's store, Kids Next Door (closed October 2004). Customers will still find that it is "the place" for pajamas by At Home, PJ Salvage, Sara's Prints, and Skivvydoodles. They also carry a small selection of bright and fun clothing, as well as this family biz's (three local sisters, a brother-in-law, and a friend) soon-to-be-patented product—a decorative cover for the Diaper Genie. Many might know one of the sisters, Jessica Kramer, of the coveted Swimmers by Jessica summer program (See chapter 16, Tired Child, Happy Parent).

Korshak Kids at Stanley Korshak
500 Crescent Court, Suite 100
Dallas 75201
214-871-3668
Hours: Monday-Saturday, 10 a.m. to 6 p.m.

Korshak Kids, located on the second floor of Stanley Korshak, is as close to a couture store for children as you can get. It's a great place to find something different and special. Be prepared to spend a lot on brands such as Cavalli, Miss Blu Marine, Tse Cashmere, Simonetta, and Moschino. Ask for Jessica Melton, and she will assist you with size or finding that special gift. She can even help find something for Mom! Dads, shopping can't get any easier for you—the ladies love children, they serve a cool beverage for all, and crayons are an added perk.

Life Size at Fred Segal
500 Broadway
Santa Monica, California 90401
310-458-1160
www.lifesizekids.com

If you are looking to dress your babe in something a little more hip, fun, and different, this is a must and a favorite of Kim's. Totally L.A. baby! Some of the brands include Paper Denim & Cloth, Juicy Couture Kids, One Tomato, Madonna, James Perse, Adidas, and Fred Segal's own Life Size line. Gift registry is now available.

Little Bo-tique Children's Apparel

310 Parker Square
Flower Mound 75028
972-899-8787
www.littlebotiquewest.com
Hours: Monday-Saturday, 10 a.m. to 6 p.m.

This store is a quaint, upscale children's boutique with party dresses by Sarah Louise from England and fun playwear by vendors such as Chicken Noodle and Lipstik. Their prices are reasonable for higher-end items, and they carry a good selection of Petit Bateau. Sizes are for infants to 16 for girls and go to size 7 for boys.

Marshalls

888-MARSHALLS
www.marshallsonline.com

You can outfit your child from head to toe (and then some) here—at great prices. From designer wear to Carter's sleepwear, you can't go wrong as long as you are willing to look through the racks. It can be hit or miss, but you will also find great educational toys and books. Most stores carry newborn to size 16.

Mini Boden

866-206-9508
www.miniboden.com

This London mail-order company has fun children's and infant clothes, shoes, and accessories with a style that is comfortable and fresh. We love that they are practical clothes with great quality and reasonable prices. They also have a great adult selection. Orders are filled within two weeks. Returns are easy and sent to a return center in Florida.

Neiman Marcus

The Shops at Willow Bend
2201 Dallas Parkway
Plano 75093
972-629-1700
Hours: Monday-Friday, 10 a.m. to 9 p.m.; Saturday, 10 a.m. to 8 p.m.; Sunday, noon to 6 p.m.

NorthPark Center
400 NorthPark Center
Dallas 75225
214-363-8311
Hours: Monday-Friday, 10 a.m. to 9 p.m.; Saturday, 10 a.m. to 8 p.m.; Sunday, noon to 6 p.m.

One Marcus Square
Dallas 75201
214-741-6911
Hours: Monday-Saturday, 10 a.m. to 6 p.m.; Thursday, 10 a.m. to 8 p.m.

www.neimanmarcus.com

Neiman Marcus has a beautiful selection of clothing for children of all ages. From timeless designs to some trendy wear, shopping here is always a special treat. You'll find miniature Burberry treasures, Helena, Petit Bateau, and Heartstrings. Neiman's is THE place for christening gowns and special occasion dresses. We love that they have swimsuits out for midwinter retreats before anyone else. Returning or exchanging a gift from Neiman's is one of the easiest procedures in town, and leaves you with enough time to have lunch at the infamous Zodiac Restaurant.

Nordstrom
Dallas Galleria
5220 Alpha Road
Dallas 75240
972-702-0055

Stonebriar Centre
2613 Preston Road
Frisco 75034
972-712-3794

www.nordstrom.com
Hours: Monday-Saturday, 10 a.m. to 9 p.m.; Sunday, noon to 6 p.m.

This upscale retail store is known for its outstanding customer service. Nordstrom carries the well known brands of Baby Lulu, Ralph Lauren, Tommy Hilfiger, Oink Baby, and clothing sold under the Nordstrom brand. They have one of the nicest, most comfortable women's lounges we have found—it's great for nursing. They also boast a terrific shoe department for children (See Happy Feet, Children's Shoes).

Oilily Dallas
NorthPark Center, Suite 216
Dallas 75225
214-692-5173
www.oilily-world.com
Hours: Monday-Saturday, 10 a.m. to 9 p.m.; Sunday, noon to 6 p.m.

Oilily's clothes are fun, bright, and creative. They carry sizes newborn to 12 for both boys and girls, and women's clothing as well. We have found that sizes do run small. Each season expect to find a theme, which is exhibited through the various patterns on the clothes and accessories. We are fans of their shoes.

Old Navy

Multiple locations through out the Dallas-Fort Worth area
800-653-6289
www.oldnavy.com

The less expensive sister store of The Gap, Old Navy offers a combination of high quality, wide variety, and affordable prices. Clothes are sold under the Old Navy label and range in size from newborn to girls' size 16 and boys' 18. Look out for sales where excellent bargains can be found. They have great pajamas, a good selection of shoes, and the clothes are adorable and fashionable.

Orient Expressed

888-856-3948
www.orientexpressed.com

This Web site offers adorable sister and brother matching outfits, mostly hand smocked bubbles, rompers, and dresses. They offer monogramming and fun swimwear. From infants to toddlers, you can see the clothes in person at local in-home trunk shows. Visit their Web site or call their toll-free number for contacts.

Papo d'Anjo

888-660-6111
www.papodanjo.com

This store has wonderful-feeling clothes from Lisbon, Portugal, with classic and unique lines. It is a must to find out who is having in-home trunk shows near you. You will not find their clothes in very many stores, which is nice. And for the money, we don't think you will find even a near match in quality, design, and fabric. The clothes do run small, so you might want to order a size or even two larger. All fabrics are 100 percent cotton or wool and are from some of the best fabric mills in Europe. The blouses for both boys and girls are timeless. The summer collection is our favorite. Go to their Web site and e-mail them for a contact near you.

St. Michael's Woman's Exchange

5 Highland Park Village
Dallas 75205
214-521-3862
Hours: Monday-Saturday, 10 a.m. to 5:30 p.m.

From House of Hatten smocked dresses and bubbles for both boys and girls to the finest christening gowns in Duponi silk, you will find some of the dreamiest dressy wear for your little one. Be sure to walk over to Celebrity Café for a quick snack or iced cookie for the little one.

Safari Kids

5960 West Parker Road at the Tollway
Plano 75093
972-473-3336
www.safarikidsplano.com
Hours: Monday-Saturday, 9:30 a.m. to 6 p.m.; Sunday, 1 p.m. to 4 p.m.

What a fun shop for kids! Sizes range from infant to early teens. There are gorgeous christening gowns and fun soft cotton pajamas. Brands range from Baby Lulu for girls and Pepper Toe for boys, to Zutano, Sweet Jane, Heartstrings, and Monkey Wear. They even have a birthday party event for girls starting at age four—complete with a fashion show!

Stein Mart

Multiple locations throughout the Dallas-Fort Worth area
www.steinmart.com
Hours: Monday-Saturday, 10 a.m. to 9 p.m.; Sunday, noon to 6 p.m.

This national chain has several designer brands to choose from at fantastic prices. From Ralph Lauren layette to Carter's pajamas, you can't go wrong here except to shop on the day before they restock. There is also a great selection of toys, wooden Melissa & Doug puzzles, and Baby Einstein products.

Strasburg Children

The Shops at Willow Bend
6121 West Park Boulevard
Plano 75093
469-366-0099

Dallas Galleria
13350 Dallas Parkway
Dallas 75240
972-934-2074

www.strasburgchildren.com
Hours: Monday-Saturday, 10 a.m. to 9 p.m.; Sunday, noon to 6 p.m.

Seventy-five percent of this store's collection is for formal events and special occasions. They carry christening gowns and flower girl dresses. The hand embroidery, feather stitching, and smocked clothing is primarily for little girls, but there is a distinct small collection of adorable cotton and silk JonJons for boys.

Target and Super Target

Multiple locations
www.target.com
Hours: Monday-Saturday, 8 a.m. to 10 p.m.; Sunday, 8 a.m. to 9 p.m.

We can't say enough good things about this national mega store. They carry baby basics, playwear, swimwear, pajamas, shoes, nursery décor, baby gear, toys, books, and they have a great selection of maternity clothes. You can shop for all of your nursery needs and join the registry. Don't worry if you lose your receipt. If you make a purchase on a credit card and return the item, they simply swipe your card.

Ten Monkeys

5600 West Lovers Lane, Suite 143
Dallas 75209
214-350-2888
www.ten-monkeys.com
Hours: Monday-Saturday, 10 a.m. to 6 p.m.

Ten Monkeys is one of the latest and greatest stores to arrive in Dallas. Owners Shahla Southerst and Maryam Mortazavi, both moms and former children's retail professionals, opened Ten Monkeys because they always wanted to dress their children in something different that is not "mass produced." The majority of the clothing is for girls ages newborn to 14, but they are expanding their boys' line this year. Our favorites here are the soft fabrics used by Luna Luna from Denmark and the Biscotti line. Other brands include Little Mass, Flowers by Zoe, Sister Sam, Tina Newman, Rosetta Millington, and Submarine. Their gift wrapping is adorable!

TJ Maxx

Multiple locations
800-2TJMAXX
www.tjmaxx.com
Hours: Monday-Saturday, 9:30 a.m. to 9:30 p.m.; Sunday, noon to 6 p.m.

This store is all about "quality brand name designer merchandise at affordable prices." It can be hit or miss, but worth the search, for European designer clothing and an extensive Ralph Lauren layette and toddler collection. You can also find an enormous selection of toys, videos, socks, and other accessories, and then shop for mom, dad, and home.

You and Me Babe

870 North Coit, Suite 2651
Richardson 75080
972-669-2110
www.youandmebabe.com
Hours: Monday, Friday, and Saturday, 10 a.m. to 5 p.m.; and Tuesday-Thursday, 10 a.m. to 6 p.m.

This small store makes the most of their space by carrying everything from cribs and breast pumps to maternity and children's clothing. The owner, Debi McGaffey, strives to supply a combination of casual and special occasion clothing for preemie to size 16 by Le Top, Feltman, Carriage Boutiques, Little Me, and Alexis. They have one of the largest assortments of christening clothing we have found and carry quite a few items by House of Hatten.

RESALE SHOPS

Kids Kloset
6138 Luther Lane
Dallas 75225
214-369-2243
www.kidskloset.com
Hours: Monday-Saturday, 10 a.m. to 5 p.m.

Close to the Park Cities, this shop has great finds daily and an area for the kiddos to play. From "smocked dresses to sport coats," you will find yourself stopping in often. It is also great for gently used maternity brands such as a Pea in the Pod to the Gap, and also for strollers and more. We have even seen Peg-Pérego high chairs.

Kidswap
6829 Snider Plaza
Dallas 75205
214-890-7927
Hours: Monday-Friday, 10:30 a.m. to 6:30 p.m.; Saturday, 10 a.m. to 5 p.m.

If you hunt and dig though this jam-packed store with no aisle space to spare, you can find silk dupioni shortalls for boys and Mally & Co. dresses for girls. Keep checking for wonderful, gently used designer styles. It is a perfect place to take your little one's clothing. They do not take clothing items from Old Navy or Target.

Kid to Kid
2035 West McDermott
Allen 75013
972-390-1117
Hours: Monday, Wednesday, Friday and Saturday, 10 a.m. to 6 p.m.; Tuesday and Thursday, 10 a.m. to 7 p.m.; Sunday, 1 p.m. to 5 p.m.

6405 West Parker at Midway
Plano 75093
972-781-2543
Hours: Monday-Saturday, 10 a.m. to 6 p.m.; Sunday, 1 p.m. to 5 p.m.

At this small store, you will find used clothing for newborns up to teen size 14. The brands run the gamut from Ralph Lauren to Old Navy. There is a limited selection of gently used cribs, car seats, strollers, toys, and maternity wear. Returns are taken within seven days as long as the tag is still attached to the item and you have a receipt.

Mudpuppy . . . Gently Housebroken Kidswear
5714 Locke Avenue
Fort Worth 76107
817-731-2581
Hours: Monday–Saturday, 10 a.m. to 6 p.m.

Save yourself the trouble of having a garage sale and take your items to Mudpuppy. They carry gently used clothing for boys and girls, sizes newborn to 14, maternity clothing, shoes, bedding, strollers, and toys. Make an appointment and bring your clothes in. Clothes are taken on a seasonal basis. Items are priced for about a third of what they cost new, and when one of your things sells, they pay you 40 percent of the sale price. Checks are mailed every other month.

Once Upon A Child
2311 Cross Timbers Road
Flower Mound 75028
972-874-0779

7200 Independence Parkway
Plano 75025
972-618-5800

www.ouac.com
Hours: Monday–Friday, 10 a.m. to 7 p.m.; Saturday, 10 a.m. to 6 p.m.; Sunday, noon to 5 p.m.

This massive national chain store has everything from new and used children's clothing to maternity wear, toys, and strollers. On-the-spot payment for your items and a small play area with a television make this store worth the trip.

HAPPY FEET: CHILDREN'S SHOES

The day when babies stop putting their toes in their mouth and begin their wobbly first steps comes quickly! Barefoot is best, especially for beginner walkers, but at some point they need shoes for the new territory they're navigating. Remember that it is important to find the proper fit for their tiny feet. Fashion forward may be your first priority, but don't compromise fit for design. Imagine how miserable you are in a pair of shoes that don't fit properly. Our list includes stores that have knowledgeable salespeople. If you don't get one who takes the time to ask about your child's needs, how long he has been walking, or to measure each foot individually, ask for a manager. When you step up to the cash register, remember that shoes are one of the most important and worthwhile apparel investments you will make for your child. The right shoe fit will promote healthy steps—get ready to run!

Dillard's

13343 Preston Road
Dallas 75240
972-386-4595

100 NorthPark Center
Dallas 75225
214-373-7000

1101 Melbourne Road
Hurst 76053
817-284-4566

3901 Irving Mall
Irving 75062
972-258-4968

2501 Dallas Parkway
Plano 75093
972-202-4730

www.dillards.com
Hours: Monday-Saturday, 10 a.m. to 9 p.m.; Sunday, noon to 6 p.m.

Little shoppers can choose from Stride Rite, Kenneth Cole, Keds, Polo, Nina, and Tommy Hilfiger, to name a few. Kelli can't tell you the number of times she has witnessed "shoe negotiations" between parent and child at Dillard's. They always seem to have a "compromise shoe" that satisfies all parties. Sizes range from newborns to size 12.

Kid's Shoe Cottage

2021 Justin Road
Flower Mound 75028
972-691-8474
www.kidsshoecottage.com
Hours: Monday-Saturday, 10 a.m. to 6 p.m.; Thursday, 10 a.m. to 7 p.m.; Sunday, noon to 5 p.m.

We feel you can never have too many pairs of shoes and Kid's Shoe Cottage supports our belief. They carry Hush Puppies, Primigi, Nina, Jumping Jacks, New Balance, and Dr. Martens. Newborn to girls' and boys' size 12½ are stocked and they carry hard-to-find widths (narrow to EEE).

Kidzfeet
5960 West Parker Road at the Tollway
Plano 75093
972-398-0860
Hours: Monday-Saturday, 10 a.m. to 6 p.m.; Sunday, noon to 4 p.m.

Kidzfeet is jam-packed with a variety of brands, including Robeez, Naturino, Timberland, Elefanten, Teva, Stride Rite, Jumping Jacks, and Nina. Girls who like to accessorize will love the large selection of hair accessories. Sizes range from newborn to girls' and boys' size 12.

Naturino
108 Preston Royal Village
Dallas 75230
214-363-7757
www.naturino.com
Hours: Monday-Saturday, 10 a.m. to 6 p.m.; Sunday, noon to 4 p.m.

It's never too soon to introduce your kids to the luxury of Italian shoes. For thirty years, Naturino has concentrated on making the most comfortable and "developmentally correct" shoes for children. Infants can begin wearing the "Falcotto" line, which has a flexible bottom and soft upper, and progress to "Naturino" when they become walkers. Sawyer lives in the N Sport collection, which is great for more athletic days. The sales staff and owner Patti are beyond helpful . . . they are forthright in selecting the perfect and appropriate fit for your child. These shoes are pricey, but they last. You can bet that not all the kids on your block will be wearing them.

Nordstrom
Dallas Galleria
5220 Alpha Road
Dallas 75240-4316
972-702-0055

Stonebriar Centre
2613 Preston Road
Frisco 75034
972-712-3794

North East Mall
1101 Melbourne Road
Hurst 76053
817-590-2599

www.nordstrom.com
Hours: Monday-Saturday, 10 a.m. to 9 p.m.; Sunday, noon to 6 p.m.

Nordstrom is known for their phenomenal women's shoe department, and their kid's department is equally impressive. Elefanten, Merrell, Ugg, Nike, Jumping Jacks, Kenneth Cole, and the Nordstrom brand are just a few of the well-known kids' brands they carry. Salespeople go above and beyond and are knowledgeable when it comes to fitting shoes. They offer sizes for newborns all the way to "big kids" (eight to twelve years old).

Stride Rite
Also carried at Dillard's, Nordstrom, and select JC Penney's and Foley's.
Preston Center
6129 Luther Lane
Dallas 75225
214-373-1182
Hours: Monday-Saturday, 10 a.m. to 6 p.m.; Sunday, noon to 4 p.m.

Town East Mall
2063 Town East Boulevard
Mesquite 75150
972-270-6487
Hours: Monday-Friday, 10 a.m. to 9 p.m.; Sunday, noon to 6 p.m.

Valley View Center
1074 Valley View Center
Dallas 75240
972-661-8948
Hours: Monday-Friday, 10 a.m. to 9 p.m.; Sunday, noon to 6 p.m.

The Shops at Willow Bend
1621 West Park Boulevard
Plano 75093
972-202-8453
Hours: Monday-Friday, 10 a.m. to 9 p.m.; Sunday, noon to 6 p.m.

Southlake Town Center
1240 Prospect Street
Southlake 76092
817-481-9992
Hours: Monday-Friday, 10:30 a.m. to 6:30 p.m.; Saturday, 10 a.m. to 7 p.m.; Sunday, noon to 6 p.m.

420 East FM 3040, Suite 113
Lewisville 75067
972-459-9163
Hours: Monday–Saturday, 10 a.m. to 6 p.m.; Sunday, noon to 5 p.m.

2601 Preston Road, Suite 1032
Frisco 75034
469-633-1282
Hours: Monday–Saturday, 10 a.m. to 9 p.m.; Sunday, noon to 6 p.m.

www.striderite.com

We remember our mothers and grandparents taking us to Stride Rite when we were young. Today, Stride Rite continues to be one of the most popular brands of shoes for tiny feet. "Certified Fit Specialists" participate in an extensive training program to learn how to properly fit shoes for children. Sizes range from prewalkers to boys' and girls' size 12. They continually update their selection of shoes whether it's sandals for the beach, special occasion dress shoes, or sneakers for play. Stride Rite shoes are not inexpensive, but they are a value for their durability and style. They also carry Capezio ballet shoes, socks, and hair accessories.

Target and Super Target
Multiple locations
www.target.com
Hours: Monday–Saturday, 8 a.m. to 10 p.m.; Sunday, 8 a.m. to 9 p.m.

Kids love shoe shopping at Target. Choose from a variety of seasonal styles and "character" designs such as Hello Kitty sandals and Dora the Explorer sneakers. They also carry a less expensive brand by Stride Rite. Don't worry if you get home and the shoes are the wrong size or if you lose your receipt. If you made your purchase on a credit card, it takes a simple swipe through their computer to locate and then refund your purchase price.

CHAPTER EIGHT:
STORY TIME AND PLAYTIME

BOOKS AND TOYS

A happy, healthy childhood is one of the greatest gifts we can give. What parent doesn't want to re-create his or her own happy memories—only bigger and even better for their own little ones? Books and toys are often an integral backdrop to many educational and emotional moments in a child's life.

When you introduce your child to the joy of reading, you get to share the books you loved as a child and also discover new literary treasures. We have some marvelous bookstores in our area, and while shopping the hours magically tick away. Some of them even offer story time for youngsters—a fantastic way to introduce your child to literature. Look for a book symbol next to the stores that offer story times. Don't forget to check out your local library, too. It is a convenient (and best of all, free) way to try out new authors without worrying that your child might not like the book. There's no point in wasting money on a book that will sit unread on a shelf.

Undoubtedly, the word "toy" will become one of your child's favorites. Educational, whimsical, or just plain noisy, toys can be a source of amusement and wonder, and a medium for creativity. We have listed several local stores that carry some of our favorites. One thing to keep in mind: it is easy to feel your house has become overrun with toys. Consider swapping with a friend or shop at stores like Tuesday Morning, TJ Maxx, and Marshalls, where prices are substantially lower, which makes your investment less.

Babies "R" Us
420 East Round Grove
Lewisville 75067
972-459-9333

1501 West Arbrook Boulevard
Arlington 76015
817-784-2229

1701 Preston Road
Plano 75093
972-735-1229

3850 Beltline Road
Addison 75001
972-247-4229

5800 Overton Ridge
Fort Worth 76132
817-423-8829

www.babiesrus.com

While they don't have as extensive a selection as their parent company, Toys "R" Us, they do have tons of toys and videos to choose from. Lamaze, LeapFrog and VTech are just a few of the best-selling brands they stock. They carry a variety of play mats, walkers, and bouncy seats as well. A do-it-yourself gift wrapping station with complimentary wrapping paper is handy for oversized and odd-shaped gifts.

Barnes & Noble
362 East FM 1382
Cedar Hill 75104
972-293-7397

7700 West Northwest Highway
Dallas 75225
214-739-1124

14999 Preston Road at Beltline
Dallas 75254
972-661-8068

2601 Preston Road
Frisco 75034
972-668-2820

1612 South University
Fort Worth 76107
817-335-2791

1217 West Highway 114
Grapevine 76051
817-251-1997

7615 North MacArthur
Irving 75063
972-501-0430

3634 Irving Mall
Irving 75062
972-594-8187

2325 South Stemmons
Lewisville 75067
972-315-7966

801 West 15th
Plano 75075
972-422-3372

2201 Preston Road at Park
Plano 75093
972-612-0999

501 South Plano Road
Richardson 75081
972-699-7844

www.bn.com

Barnes & Noble has a wide selection of books with topics ranging from parenting to children's story books as well as videos and music. Most locations have story time and other events for kids and families. The staff is friendly and willing to help. Most have a café—a great spot for a quick snack.

Bebe Grand
2013 Abrams Road
Dallas 75214
214-887-9224
www.bebegrand.com

Back in the corner of this Lakewood neighborhood store, you can find what may look like a small selection of books, but truth be told, there is a treasure trove of unique, award-winning, and all-time favorites here in gift condition. Owner Susan O'Neill is great at helping you find an age-appropriate book and combining it with a toy or trinket for a memorable gift. Bebe Grand has a wide selection of fun, educational toys for kids of all ages—you won't find these goodies at other stores (See chapter 7, Kid Style).

Bookstop
5550 West Lovers Lane, Suite 47
Dallas 75209
214-357-2697
www.bn.com

Bookstop is owned by Barnes & Noble and has a large selection of parenting and children's books.

Borders
5500 Greenville Avenue at Lovers Lane
Dallas 75206
214-739-1166

3600 McKinney Avenue-Uptown
Dallas 75204
214-219-0512

10720 Preston Road at Royal
Dallas 75230
214-363-1977

4613 South Hulen
Fort Worth 76132
817-370-9473

4601 West Freeway
Fort Worth 76107
817-737-0444

2403 South Stemmons Freeway, Suite 100
Lewisville 75067
972-459-2321

1601 Preston Road
Plano 75093
972-713-9857

Multiple locations
www.borders.com

We have so enjoyed hearing tales with our children at the Greenville Avenue Borders. There is a small stage and a large area for spreading out, which the kids just love. They often feature music and special events like face painting or sidewalk chalk drawing. Call the store nearest you to find out times and special family events. The children's section has a vast selection of board books and soft books, as well as audiocassettes, videos, and big kid books. We love to grab a snack and beverage at the café and always visit the grown-up book and music sections for the latest releases or sales. Gift wrapping is available and we have found the staff to be very friendly.

Collectible Trains & Toys
10051 Whitehurst, Suite 200
Dallas 75243
214-373-9469 or 800-462-4902
www.trainsandtoys.com

All aboard! Collectible Trains & Toys is one of the biggest specialty toy stores around, and it's family owned. Some of the toys to choose from are Schleich hand-painted animals, the Radio Flyer classic red wagon, K-Line electric trains, Steiff teddy bears, Thomas the Tank Engine, and Scalextric slot cars and sets. Located inside Collectible Trains & Toys is Lone Star Toys, which is dedicated to toys of the past, such as Lionel, American Flyer, and Matchbox. They also have a library with the most up-to-date titles about toy trains, train collecting, layout building, and railroading in America. When you visit, plan on staying awhile—the store is located in an old movie theatre, so there is plenty to see.

Designs for Children
4804 Camp Bowie
Fort Worth 76107
817-732-6711

For over twenty years, Designs for Children has been making kids and parents happy with their tremendous range of toys. Choose from Lamaze, Shelcore, Alex, Felt Kids, Madeline, Franklin, Thomas the Tank Engine, Corolle dolls, and much more. Creative gift baskets are perfect for baby and birthday gifts, and gift wrapping is available. They have just added furniture, bedding, and lamps to make this a one-stop shop for children's rooms and play areas (See chapter 9, Unique Gifts).

Discovery Toys
Local consultant: Allyson Toler
214-821-7688
www.tolertoys.com

800-341-TOYS
www.discoverytoys.com

Discovery Toys was founded by a mother over twenty-six years ago and, ever since, they have been making innovative educational toys, books, and software. They have bright colors, involve the senses, and are for various developmental stages. Many of their toys win product excellence awards, and new items are added to their "classic" line each season. Kelli held a Discovery Toys "party" at her house where grandmothers, mothers, and moms-to-be were highly impressed with the quality of the toys, but, more importantly, the children were completely absorbed in playing with them. You may order online or if you are interested in hosting a party (you get a discount on purchases) it's possible to have a consultant meet with you and a couple of friends or speak at a PTA meeting. A great selling point with their toys—if you lose a piece, you can replace it without having to buy the entire toy again.

Doubleday Bookshop
18 Highland Park Village
Dallas 75205
214-528-6756

Doubleday Bookshop in Highland Park Village is a great place to shop for a wide selection of children's books and parenting ones as well. While the store's selection is not on as grand a scale as a Barnes & Noble (its sister store), the books are not picked over or worn by playful hands. There is not a story hour, but there are child-friendly eateries within walking distance.

Lakeshore Learning Center
13846 North Dallas Parkway
Dallas 75240
972-934-8866
www.lakeshorelearning.com

Lakeshore Learning Center is a not-to-be-missed store for fabulous educational toys and more. You can find cushiony climbing centers, washable dolls, wooden toddler kitchens, dress-up trunks, arts and crafts, giant fruit, and book display shelves. We suggest that you make plans for a craft hour on a Saturday, typically held from 11 a.m. to 3 p.m.

Learning Express
6818 Snider Plaza
Dallas 75205
214-696-4876

4760 Preston Road
Frisco 75034
214-387-8697

Willow Bend Market
5964 West Parker Road, Suite 120

Plano 75093
972-473-8697

4900 El Dorado Parkway
McKinney 75070
972-542-8697

www.learningexpress.com

When visiting Learning Express for the first time, you'll find it difficult to hold back, especially with the kids in tow—there are so many irresistible toys for all ages. Brands include Lamaze, Brio, Small World, Melissa and Doug, Kettler, Peg-Pérego ride-on toys, Thomas the Tank Engine, and Madeline. There is also a good selection of books and videos. This is a sure winner for birthdays and holidays and a fun place to visit anytime! Fun, bright gift wrapping is free. Be sure to get your frequent buyer card stamped to earn a discount down the road.

Logos Book Store
6620 Snider Plaza
Dallas 75205
214-369-3245

6115 Camp Bowie Boulevard, Suite 130
Fort Worth 76116
817-732-5070

www.logosbookstore.net

While primarily known as one of the best "Christian" bookstores around, Logos has a wide variety of book titles to choose from in their snug space. Owners Rick and Susan Lewis really try to cater to their loyal clientele. Popular titles like Goodnight Moon, as well as religious-themed books and Bibles are available. They carry the Veggie Tales videos and have some adorable baby gifts. The staff is incredibly helpful and knowledgeable.

Sensational Beginnings
800-444-2147
www.sb-kids.com

Sensational Beginnings, an online shopping catalog, celebrates childhood with an extensive selection of indoor and outdoor toys and swim gear. If your household is as busy as ours, you'll find their twenty-four-hour phone ordering service helpful, especially during the holidays. There really is too much to mention, but some of our favorite finds are the top-of-the-line Kettler tricycles, a Safety tub with a temperature gauge, a Baby Bjorn potty trainer, a Bilby shopping cart liner, LeapFrog and LeapPad learning toys, SunSafe suits, the Driveway Barrier sign ("Caution Kids at Play"), and the weatherproof

New England pine table and chair set that comes with a canvas umbrella. They donate 50 cents, for every catalog order, to a different children's charity each season. We have been very satisfied with their customer service and shipping. They have gift certificates, and gift wrapping is free.

Southern Methodist University Bookstore, Barnes & Noble College
3060 Mockingbird Lane
Dallas 75205
214-768-2435

Saturdays at 11 a.m. you will find parents, grandparents, and kiddos gathered in the children's area for story time at SMU's bookstore. The bright and cheerful miniature stage decorated with trees and a backdrop makes stories come to life. This is easily one of Sawyer and Ford's favorite pastimes. For crawlers and walkers, there is plenty of space to roam, and for little readers, there are small tables for paging through books from their impressive collection. A wide variety of magazines and newspapers, coupled with their full-service book store/café, makes this is a great spot for a family outing. Hey, you may even run into an SMU student who "just loves to babysit."

Target and Super Target
Multiple locations
www.target.com

Target has just about every toy, infant play station, and walker at some of the greatest prices in town. They carry Playskool, Hasbro, Little Tikes, Step 2, Tiny Love, Fisher-Price, Safety 1st, Edushape, LeapFrog, Baby Einstein, and toys by *Parents Magazine*. We frequent their book and video aisles for popular titles and books on tape (several titles are available in Spanish). For summertime fun, they have temporary pools, safety vests, goggles, and more. For bigger kids, they have bikes, scooters, games, Barbie dolls, video games, and so much more. There is a baby registry, and ordering online is great for finding the hard-to-locate items. Their hours make it convenient to make those early morning or late evening runs for potty training rewards and last-minute birthday gifts. Stock up on diapers, formula, and adorable clothing.

Toys "R" Us
9500 North Central Expressway & Walnut Hill
Dallas 75231
214-363-3192

2100 Town East Mall
Mesquite 75150
972-270-6164

3125 West Airport Freeway
Irving 75062
972-252-5959

3777 West Camp Wisdom Road
Dallas 75237
972-296-5936

300 Lexington Drive
Plano 75075
972-422-0408

2412 South Stemmons Freeway
Lewisville 75067
972-315-6210

2871 Preston Road
Frisco 75034
972-712-0054

4111 South Cooper Street
Arlington 76015
817-784-0843

1319 West Pipeline
Hurst 76053
817-589-7181

www.toysrus.com

Toys "R" Us is such an obvious listing, but seriously folks, we are truly impressed with the selection at this, the supermarket of toy stores. They carry all of the most popular brands and have equal space for both boys' and girls' toys. Fisher-Price, Playskool, Little Tikes, and Mattel are just the tip of the iceberg. They also have an impressive selection of videos and DVDs, and a section devoted to hosting birthday parties with decorations and goody-bag gifts. The prices are hard to beat, but be aware—around holiday time the most requested toys can sometimes be hard to find. They also carry baby necessities.

Toys Unique!
5600 West Lovers Lane
Dallas 75209
214-956-8697

The type of toys you will find at Toys Unique! isn't unusual, but the selection they carry is. These are things you don't find just anywhere. While they do carry a huge selection of Melissa & Doug, Kid Craft wooden toys, and Thomas the Tank Engine toys, they also offer unusual games, arts, crafts, puzzles, and dress-up costumes. Don't hesitate to ask the staff for suggestions because they are incredibly helpful and in the know.

Whole Earth Provision Co.
5400 East Mockingbird Lane
Dallas 75206
214-824-7444

Well known for their outdoor clothing and accessories (backpacks, compasses and walking shoes), Whole Earth Provisions is a fun place for the entire family to hunt and capture nature books and bestsellers. For a great learning experience, Kim and Sawyer love their butterfly and frog habitats in which you can watch them grow and blossom. They also carry Alex art and crafts, kites, cute frog umbrellas and rainboots and mosquito be-gone T-shirts by Buzzoff.com. There is a great section and the staff is incredibly friendly—even if your little one is crawling all over the displays.

Wooden Toys and More
888-213-8278
www.woodentoys-and-more.com

This online store sells the highest quality unique wooden toys, puppets and puppet theaters, puzzles, educational games, and pedal cars. If you like handcrafted toys that will last a lifetime and are up for a change from all-things-plastic, this is a sight for your eyes.

Zebra Hall
www.zebrahall.com
800-834-9165

This online catalog has unique toys for all ages, toys from around the world. Just viewing the online store or the catalog is fun. Some of their items will remind parents and grandparents of younger days while other viewers will simply wish to be a kid again. We fell for Zebra Hall's colorful Zamiloo House, the Shopping List Memory game, the Ultra Soft Night Light Bunny, and the mini Miele Action Washing Machine for washing doll clothes—gotta love that! Shop here and you will be sure to put Santa to shame! Gift wrapping is extra, as is shipping.

CHAPTER NINE:

UNIQUE GIFTS

Remember that a gift doesn't have to cost a bundle. Creating a basket of your favorite items, complete with a personal "helpful hints and use" note, can easily win the unique gift award. One mom told us that she gives out mini food grinders along with recipes for homemade baby food, while another prefers giving a "new mommy" care package of a massage and facial. Bottom line . . . whether it is a basket of Kiehl's yummy baby products or an embroidered keepsake, gift giving is fun and a joyful time to celebrate a new baby, an older sibling, a new grandparent, or a godparent.

American Forests
202-737-1944
www.americanforests.org

Having a tree planted in honor of a loved one is a special and perfect gift, not only for a new baby, but also for any significant occasion for which you want to celebrate life. Starting at $15, American Forests plants a tree in a rural or urban area across the United States and the world. They send you or the recipient a gift certificate and the rest is up to Mother Nature. American Forests plants trees for environmental restoration and is the nation's oldest nonprofit citizens' conservation organization. Another great option for gifting a tree is to send a four-bag case of Mother Nature Diapers to new parents, and they in turn will plant a tree for your baby though American Forests. If you want to send some environmentally friendly and great absorbent diapers to help stock a friend's nursery, go to www.mothernaturediapers.com.

Arm Hole
1910 Abrams Parkway
Dallas 75214
214-824-9544

Arm Hole carries a great selection of cool decals for baby and adult T's, or you can make up your own! We love this place for sassy shower gifts and have had shirts made for our little ones—from a glittery "Rockstar," a colorful The Who, to a pink Hello Kitty. Service is fast and friendly. Arm Hole also has fun shoes and clothing for women and men.

Art by Anne Hines
214-207-1106

Anne Hines creates some of the most breathtaking and spiritual artwork that we have encountered! Kim was given one of Anne's Noah's ark creations with an intricate, hand-painted scene of Noah, his wife, animals, and nature. This may sound basic, but each time Kim or a guest views this piece, a new detail is revealed. (The artwork is painted on a piece of wood cut to the shape of an arc). Anne calls these "Personal Devotionals." They are illustrations of Bible scriptures for an individual or family to have and be inspired by. This former interior designer, who began painting and drawing at the age of six, now devotes her time entirely to her artwork. Prices vary, but typically start at $200, depending on the detail, and take two to four weeks. Anne also does art for interiors, whether creating a piece for your child's room, a wall mural, or a ceiling mural.

Baby Rags Company
214-868-3452
www.babyragscompany.com

After not having what her husband labeled "spit rags" around, local mom Ashley Blomberg decided to create simple, yet "funky" rags to clean up all of the drool and dribbles. Cute and simple bundles of "absorbent rags" in an array of designs, from western to polka dots, are all tied up in clever packaging of white crates. A great gift idea for new parents or grandparents—a friend of Gwyneth Paltrow thinks so and sent baby Apple some! Available online or at select stores.

Belly Casts by Mara Black
214-327-8863

Mara Black has been a midwife, doula, and teacher of infant massage for over fourteen years. Her love for mothering is obvious from the minute you hear her soothing voice describe her experiences. A favorite activity of Mara's for her clients is to create a plaster casting of their expectant belly. In the comfort of your home, and with your husband's help if desired, she will have you stand over a drop cloth at your bathroom sink, have you oiled, and then carefully place individual plaster strips from your breastline to your pelvic area. Within thirty minutes you will be done and have a keepsake belly cast that you can hang on your nursery wall. Mara suggests having the footprints of your child on the cast.

Bunnies and Bows
972-317-2962
www.bunniesandbows.com

Bunnies and Bows has items that make a great sibling gift! Kim was introduced to Bunnies and Bows when she met the owners at a local market. They love what they do, have fun doing it, and create adorable personalized pillowcases, tote bags, nightshirts, laundry bags, tooth fairy bags, and much more. The whimsical designs are drawn in water-based inks and are soft, bright, and ecologically friendly. No need to worry about sleeping on stiff paint! Prices for pillowcases start at $17.95, and turnaround time is fast.

Burdick Baby

7151 Preston Road, Suite 181
Frisco 75034
972-712-1377

1679 West Northwest Highway
Grapevine 76051
817-310-3358

www.burdickbaby.com

Owner Rene Burdick began Burdick Baby as a Web site for unique and innovative children's products and only recently decided to open a store. She carries Buggy Baggs, which cover 100 percent of a shopping cart's seat surface, providing a barrier for your child against germs and bacteria. This particular one has more padding than the others we have seen on the market. Sleep Sack can also be found at Burdick Baby and is the only sleeper sack endorsed by the SIDS alliance. She also carries Svan of Sweden high chairs, which have been sold out in the United States and are the only adjustable wooden high chair certified by the JPMA. Definitely worth a visit if you are trying to find a unique, but practical gift item.

Calyx and Corolla

800-800-7788
www.calyxandcorolla.com

Sending a wreath from Calyx and Corolla is one of Kim's favorites for a new baby, a grandmother, or a thank-you gift. Their service has been dependable, and the flowers fresh and charming. We suggest the Enchanted Heart Wreath for $69, or a New Baby Wreath for $44. There are also traditional and elegant fresh flower baskets and herb garden variations to choose from.

Cheekie Designs

214-691-5328

These adorable, hand-embellished note cards, calling cards, announcements, and invitations are a fabulous and unexpected gift. Cheekie Designs are created by two local moms, Melanie Cheek and Sara Brown, who work word-of-mouth and in between taking care of their families. We are big fans and love the simplicity, yet detail in each design. You may choose from a frog, a train, a spaceship, flowers, holiday motifs, or custom creations. Orders are filled as quickly as possible with full attention to every detail. You can visit with Melanie and Sara and view their samples. A gift pack of ten fold-over notes and five calling cards is $30.

Chiffoniers

3905 West Vickery
Fort Worth 76107
817-731-8545

Owner Susan Jose has a created a refreshing and bright California-chic store that carries an array of gift items and House Inc. baby bedding (think Rachel Ashwell's Shabby Chic, but more affordable). Some of our favorite finds are vintage pillowcase skirts with elastic waist bands for the mom-to-be's expanding belly, silver crosses, Corkey's Kids dresses for toddlers, and French milled soaps by Pre de Provence. The vintage-inspired, fabric laminated bags by Farmhouse Productions (Susan's private label) make great bags for carrying kid stuff! This super friendly store can create gift baskets and ship anywhere.

The China Belle
972-231-0335

For over thirty years, Mary Ann Reese has been creating keepsake porcelain baby shoes which she hand-paints with flowers; the baby's name, date, time of birth, and weight; and gift giver's name on the bottom. She promises that even after twenty years, they can be washed in the dishwasher! These are sweet and perfect to remember a baptism or christening.

The Copper Lamp
208 Preston Royal Shopping Center
Dallas 75230
214-369-5166 or 800-765-6519
www.copperlamp.com

The Copper Lamp has some of the most exquisite fine silver and china we have seen. We love their rare antique silver baby cups, spoons, and brushes. Their active collections are more affordable and can be engraved in your presence on Tuesdays and Thursdays from 10 a.m. to 2:30 p.m. Be sure to look at their silver and silver-plated rattles and china figurines. Herrand animals make quite a gift and start a special collection for little girls. Gift wrapping is free.

EmbroidMe
3411 Preston Road, Suite 6
Frisco 75034
972-668-8530
www.embroidme-frisco.com

At EmbroidMe, it's just as easy to monogram one bib as it is to embroider shirts for your daughter's entire ballet class. It's one-stop shopping because they offer an enormous selection of clothing, bags, towels, and hats, along with bibs and onesies. Bring your own monogramming idea or choose one of their designs. Prices are reasonable.

Exposures
800-222-4947
www.exposuresonline.com

Exposures offers an extensive selection of great photo albums, frames, and personalized products that make great gifts for any occasion, especially Father's Day! We love their custom collage canvas where you send in five photos and they design a collage for you on canvas stretched over a wood frame. The custom photo cards are perfect for holiday cards and are made with your favorite snapshot. A true treasure is the custom canvas album, a great gift with a cover made of a reproduced photo of your little one or one of her drawings—our favorite for a sibling gift. Exposures now carries several jewelry options such as bracelets and charms for your children's pictures—think grandmother gift!

For Goodness Sake!
437 NorthPark Center
Dallas 75225
214-691-9411
www.forgoodnesssake.net

This is a haven for the gift giver for all occasions. Whether you choose a frame, blanket or book, it is a guaranteed hit! All funds from each purchase go directly to over fifteen area agencies such as Equest, Buckner Children and Family Services, Wednesday's Child Benefit Corporation, and the Wilkinson Center.

GoToBaby
866-510-baby
www.gotobaby.com

This New York CIty store has great gift baskets and new-parent gifts that can be shipped just about anywhere. Nevin loves the limited edition chrome racer, which is fashioned after the 1952-1957 Ferrari F2—just something for daddy to dream about and son to ride! Their gifts are cute and different. Their exclusive T-shirts for the new family (mom, dad, and baby) are a best seller (Happy, Sleepy, and Grumpy). Gift wrapping is available.

Keep U-N Stitches
1152 North Buckner, Suite 110
Dallas 75218
214-321-0505

"If we can hoop it, you can have it" is owner Gina Volpe's motto behind her successful Lakewood embroidery business. She specializes in embroidery and monogramming of christening gowns, blankets, burp cloths, pillowcases, sheets, and anything else you can imagine. Monogramming is anywhere between $8.50 and $20. Gina makes you feel like you have known her forever and is tremendously helpful. If you are picking up an item and have the kids in the car, call ahead because she will meet you curbside.

Kelco Designs, Inc.
405-341-9425
www.Kelcodesignsokc.com

Kelly LeShelle Cotts has been creating wonderful charcoal, pencil, ink, or watercolor renderings of families, children, and homes for over ten years. From your photos, she will take the best expressions and the background you choose for your one-of-a-kind portrait. Prices vary per portrait, and a deposit is required before she starts the project. These make a super keepsake gift and can take over one month for completion.

Kidoodle
972-596-5456

Let artist Mindy Carter turn your child's art into a keepsake. Give her five to seven pieces of her work and a photograph. You will be blown away, not only by the collage Mindy creates, but by the specialty of having an assembly of your child's art and photo on canvas—a one-of-a-kind masterpiece to treasure!

Korshak Kids at Stanley Korshak
500 Crescent Court, Suite 100
Dallas 75201
214-871-3668
www.stanleykorshak.com

Korshak Kids is a knockout for children's couture clothing, but it is the work of Fran Chibib of Austin that has left us with our mouths wide open. Her Prayers for Children books are hand-embossed with 23K gold-gilded pages of splendor; books start at $350. Another keepsake is her hand-embellished, framed spiritual sayings and verses starting at $40—perfect for a baby gift, a baptism, or for grandparents and godparents. Personalization is available and requires several weeks. So worth the wait!

Lavish
415-565-0540
www.shoplavish.com

Lavish is a fantastic San Francisco boutique that thankfully offers their adorable gifts online. Our favorites are the "snapsuits" or onesies with "I might barf" or "I eat dirt" and the Pee-pee Teepees—a washable fabric cone to keep your little guy from squirting you in the face during diaper changes! A classic addition tied to the top of any baby gift or included in a basket, are the small crochet elephants or rattles.

Judith Leiber
866-542-7167
www.judithleiber.com

Judith Leiber's signature Austrian crystal evening bags may be the ultimate collectible for the woman who has the money to spend. When we heard about her new "Kids Artwork" bags, we thought the $3,000 and up price tag may be over the top, but the rare opportunity and idea alone are worth mentioning. Your one-of-a-kind bag would feature a color reproduction of your child's artwork hand-set in crystals and engraved with the child's name and date. Both sides of the handbag can hold designs and the price is determined by detail and difficulty of the artwork. "Only in Dallas," we may say, but a portion of the proceeds will benefit Cancer Care for Kids.

Little Words, one-of-a-kind stories for children
214-208-4052
www.littlewordscreations.com

Parents, grandparents, siblings, or friends relay life moments and generational anecdotes, which are compiled into an original, personal story—written for your family! The rhyming story, handwritten and illustrated, is destined to become a family treasure. Author and illustrator Kim Radtke Bannister (yes, she is one of the authors of this book!) has been creating little words books for over three years. Each one-of-a-kind "creation" takes six to ten hours (from interview to drawing the final book), and Kim only makes sixty little words books each year. It is the perfect personalized gift for a new baby, a child's birthday, or to celebrate friendship, say thank you, or to give at a graduation. Prices vary per book. The Web site depicts the process of the book, explains your choices, and provides samples to view.

The Monogram Shops
East Hampton, NY
631-329-3379

Locust Valley, NY
516-676-5411

www.themonogramshops.com

The Monogram Shops, located in East Hampton and Locust Valley, New York, offer some classic treasures online. After seeing a friend's children in matching his-and-her monogrammed swimwear, we had to know where to find the pale pink gingham ensembles. Now we are hooked on the cotton roll neck sweaters, canvas baby bags, and cotton pajamas—all can be monogrammed. A favorite is having a poem stitched on a baby blanket. Kim loves getting calls updating her on the latest arrivals, and the shop employees couldn't be friendlier or more helpful with gift selections. Be sure to check out their gifts for men and the home—one-stop shopping for busy families!

Paper Doll
4812 B Camp Bowie
Fort Worth 76107
817-738-8500

Paper Doll, located in Fort Worth, has fantastic gifts. Good luck choosing from their array of items such as personalized ceramic plates, silver baby cups and frames or monogrammed items such as baby-soft terrycloth bath robes, Nantucket Chicks bags, canvas laundry bags, bright fleece blankets, and more. Standard monogramming is $8. Paper Doll wraps for a colorful presentation and can ship anywhere. They also carry baby announcements and invitations.

Personalized Railcars for the Trains at NorthPark

214-631-7354

www.rmhdallas.com

For a unique or different gift to honor a new baby, big sibling, birthday, or holiday, a personalized railcar for the Trains at NorthPark would make anyone smile—especially those kids and families at the Ronald McDonald House of Dallas who benefit from your purchase. An artist will paint the railcar, which starts at $150 for a standard car, $200 for a caboose, and $250 for an engine. This is a tax-deductible donation.

Red Llama Studio

214-215-3049

www.redllamastudio.com

Shari Ledji, a local mom of two daughters, has turned her beloved hobby of quilt making into a business of cherished and one-of-a-kind handmade quilts, pillows, and receiving blankets. These phenomenal, whimsical, hand-embroidered creations can include a child's name. Red Llama Studios has in-stock items, but their custom designs are worth the wait and can include swatches of sentimental clothing, old pajamas, and memorabilia. We love the quilts that include a replica of your child's self-portrait or hand prints—a perfect gift from the big sister or brother; the gift will become an heirloom. Prices for in-stock receiving blankets start at $40 and quilts start at $100. Custom orders vary in price.

Rue 1

6701 Snider Plaza

Dallas 75205

214-265-0900

Rue 1 is a gorgeous store that sells French furniture and goodies, plus all kinds of gifts, and it smells fabulous. We love the yummy soaps and lotions for expecting and new moms as well as a little grandma gift. In the back of the store, you will find an adorable selection of baby items such as clothes, bibs, blankets, plates, and cups. Our favorites are the picture frames embellished with antique children's book pages and the fabric teepee tents.

St. Michael's Woman's Exchange

5 Highland Park Village

Dallas, Texas 75205

214-521-3862

St. Michael's Woman's Exchange is a favorite shop of many, and the shop carries fabulous finds for every occasion. Gorgeous silver picture frames, children's books, spiritual gifts, smocked children's clothing, children's pearl bracelets and necklaces, along with christening gowns, are just the beginning. Kim makes this her one-stop gift store because she can find cards; hostess, graduation, and baby gifts; as well as holiday décor—all at once. You may choose from several gift wrapping selections, but be prepared to wait—sometimes two days—as they are always swamped. The Woman's Group of St.

Michael's and All Angels Episcopal Church opened the store in 1958. All proceeds go to grant funding decided upon by the Woman's Group gift committee.

Sew Write Embroidery
2311 Cross Timbers Road, Suite 303
Flower Mound 75028
972-874-1150

Have you ever wanted to create and place a family crest or logo? This large store can help you. Known for creating custom designs and monogramming, Sew Write Embroidery can do just about anything. Bathrobes and towels make great gifts. Prices start at $8 for small embroidery. The staff is extremely helpful and efficient.

Spilled Milk Kid Couture
214-566-2610
www.spilledmilk.biz

Spilled Milk is a unique collection of children's clothing made from vintage fabrics, trims, and embellishments. Each custom-made, one-of-a-kind piece is designed and created by local mom of three, Stephanie Bernal. A hobby of cutting up old linens and making dresses for her daughter turned into a business for Stephanie about four years ago, and her distinctive and fun "Kid Couture" clothing has become some of her most sought-after items. Kim loves the free-flowing dresses with a T-shirt top, the baby cashmere sweaters, and the soft European cotton boy bubbles. Just meeting with Stephanie is worth the visit. You may call for an appointment. Prices range from $50 to $165 and more, depending on the style and fabrics.

Spiritual Garden
120 West Virginia Street
McKinney 75069
972-548-9229
www.myspiritualgarden.com

Spiritual Garden, housed in a fabulous old McKinney building near the square, has some special gifts and room accessories that you won't see everywhere. The fabric umbrellas, vintage fabric banners, and vintage chandeliers are dreamy. They also have a small selection of vintage-inspired cribs and soft bed linens by Little House, Inc.

Sweet Classic Baking Co.
Sue Whiteside
214-349-9780

Ann West
214-342-2526

These two moms and longtime friends who love to bake started catering for friends and neighbors just two years ago. It didn't take long for the word to spread about their decadent baked goods. Sue and Ann will cater a shower, "sip and see," or deliver treats to a friend in the hospital. Some of their items include scones, sour cream coffee cake, muffins, dipped macaroons, banana cake with whipped butter-cream frosting, and the Italian panna cotta custard. Gifts may be boxed or delivered on a bamboo tray, tied with a ribbon, and accented with a fresh flower.

TuTu Cute Creations, Inspiration for Everyday Play
214-707-6123
tutucutecreations@sbcglobal.net

These are the cutest and fullest tutu's we have seen and we love the fact that they are all handmade by a local mom—who has been known to get up before the sunrise just to complete orders! When she's not running after her two young daughters, Tracy Cutrona finds time to create precious tutus in a variety of themes. Whether it's her clown tutu (a white tulle tutu with pastel ribbons and a white satin birthday hat with pastel pom-poms), or the cowgirl ensemble (a bright turquoise tutu with a hot pink cowgal hat and a pink bandana), each tutu (handmade out of sixty-six yards of tulle) is adorned with theme embellishments and accompanied with a headpiece, cheerleader pom-poms, or a wand. Sizes start at 6 months and go up to 6T, and prices range from $40 to $50. Custom orders are welcome and a Web site is her next creation!

Unmistakably Molly
6619 Snider Plaza
Dallas 75205
214-696-8686

Unmistakably Molly is a University Park treasure box. There are special little finds for a new baby, a teacher, a grandparent, and a friend. The Annibanani buddie blankets, leather Robeez shoes and Little Giraffe pillows and blankets are hard to find, but Unmistakably Molly has a great supply, as well as sweet cards for all occasions. The friendly staff is very helpful, and they will wrap your gifts in a bag with tissue and ribbons for free.

The Well Appointed House
888-WELL-APP
www.wellappointedhouse.com

Dubbed "the place for luxuries for the home," the Well Appointed House has an amazing selection of children's collections. They are classic, unique, one-of-a-kind, and truly keepsakes—especially at those prices. From prams to hand-painted high chairs to silver cups, you can't go wrong. For the golf-loving daddy-to-be, grandpa, and future pro, the Child's PGA Tour golf cart rocker is sure to be a hit. If you don't mind spending a lot for a crib, armoire, light fixture, rug, or chest, their hand-painted selections are gorgeous and come in a variety of themes such as An Enchanted Forest French design and On the Beach. Gift certificates and registry are available.

The Write Invite
4415 Lively Lane
Dallas 75220
214-956-9966

In her private and relaxed home, which she shares with her husband and two sons, local business-savvy mom Jaime Gerard can help you find the perfect gift. Choose unique baby and mommy gifts, from private label "Baby G Wear," to custom onesies and matching burp cloths, or all-natural baby products by Erbaviva and California Baby. There are also custom hand-painted frames for your child's birth announcement and items by Little Giraffe, Cherry Pie, and Icky Baby. You will not leave empty handed and will most likely ponder whether to tell your friends of your new find! One of our favorites is the personalized footprint plates and bowls by Lori Dodson. Jamie is great to work with and is by appointment only. Be sure to get on her mailing list for seasonal trunk shows. The Write Invite started primarily as a provider of invitations, birth announcements, calling cards, and holiday cards and has some of the latest and greatest (See chapter 10, Announcements, Stationery, and More).

Yo My Booties
310-717-4912
www.Yomybooties.com

We like to think of designer Kris Pettit's angora baby booties as the Jimmy Choo for babes. These adorably soft creations come in an array of colors such as cotton candy pink, electric blue, and pumpkin, and in two sizes (0 to 6 months and 6 to 10 months). Kris Pettit, who began sewing at the age of five, started making the booties when she was pregnant. She once gave them away to moms in her yoga class, and now they are sold around the world. Her sweaters are yummy, too, and are available in sizes 6 months to 5T.

PART THREE:

SPECIAL MOMENTS
AND CELEBRATIONS

CHAPTER TEN:

ANNOUNCEMENTS,
STATIONERY,
AND MORE

Selecting baby announcements is perhaps one of the most fun items on the to-do list prior to having your little bundle. We have included a list of popular area stores, individual artists, and online services that provide unique and one-of-a-kind selections for baby announcements, shower and birthday invites, and personalized stationery. We also highly suggest that you refer to chapter 13, Photographers, as most of them offer wonderful announcements that feature your baby's picture.

There are endless choices, and many are economical. You can even make your own stationery by pasting a photograph on simple cardstock. The owners of the stores listed below are helpful and creative. Ask their opinions about what is being used too much because you want something unique. Bring a snack and a drink because it can take some time. We highly suggest that you make your selection at least five weeks prior to your delivery date (order time varies per line and can take up to eight weeks). Even if you don't know the sex of your child, make two selections, or settle for a unisex announcement. Most stores will help you with wording, take your information and payment method, and provide you with envelopes to get a head start on all of that addressing and stamping. All you need to do next is call in the baby's name, date of birth, weight, and length. Coordinating personalized stationery is a great idea for thank-you notes—be sure to order those at the same time.

Our list is also a resource for birthdays, baptisms and christenings, holiday cards, enclosure cards, and personalized stationery for you!

Bow Tied, Too!
6323 Camp Bowie
Fort Worth 76116
817-732-4595

We are big fans of this Fort Worth find and can't get enough of their in-house "hot stamping," which has a raised, almost engraved look. In three to five days you can have note cards, cocktail napkins, fold-over notes, and hand towels for the perfect personalized gift. They have a good selection of baby announcements and shower invites. Brands include Paper So Pretty, Spare Bedroom Designs,

Inviting Company, and Putnam House. Sherry and Kim (the mother-daughter dynamic duo and partial owners) can help you with wording while the kids find toys in the small play area. Printing (outsourced) has a setup fee and can take up to one week.

Carté

6719 Snider Plaza
Dallas 75205
214-559-6168

Located in Snider Plaza in University Park, Carté (French pronunciation) carries a wide range of announcements, invitations, stationery, and gifts. You can select from the albums of Crane's, William Arthur, Bambino, Elite, Sweet Pea Designs, and Regency, or the "imprintables" displayed along the walls. Carté offers in-house printing or engraving on selected lines and calligraphy. Service is friendly and they are always willing to spend time helping you with the wording and getting envelopes to address before your baby is here. There are choices in all price ranges.

Cheekie Designs

214-691-5328

Cheekie Designs was created by two local moms, Melanie Cheek and Sara Brown, who work word-of-mouth and out of their homes. They do adorable hand-embellished announcements, invitations, note cards, and calling cards. We adore their simplicity, yet detail in each design. You may choose from a frog, a train, a spaceship, flowers, holiday motifs, or custom creations. Orders are filled as quickly as possible with individual attention to every design. You can visit with Melanie and Sara, view their samples, or create your custom design. For a one-of-a-kind creation, prices vary depending on details. In-stock designs are approximately $115 for fifty invites, not including the $30 setup charge.

Extravaganza

640 Parker Square
Flower Mound 75028
972-899-3550

Extravaganza's name is quite fitting. They have an array or "extravaganza" of stationery, invitations, announcements, and gifts. Selections include Meri Meri, Cross-My-Heart, Penny Laine Papers, Itty Bitty Baby, Inc., Inviting Company, and Crane's. They also carry boxed note cards and announcements if you don't have time to wait for printing!

Finestationery.com

888-808-FINE
www.finestationery.com

This is a fantastic online store for all your stationery needs! Ordering is simple, and there are countless choices for showers, baptisms, and correspondence. Some of the lines available are Sarah LeClere, Odd Balls, Style Press, Checkerboard, Tree House, Anna Griffin, and Inviting Company. They also carry choices for you to print at home, fill-ins, boxed selections, and calling cards. This is a great way to order some of the best selections and in the comfort of your home. Shipping is dependable.

French Blue
888-474-5585
www.frenchblueonline.com

This Austin retailer, which started in Dallas, carries a large selection of announcements (Paper Prince, Max and Lucy, Cross-My-Heart) and invitations, but it is their custom creations that are just fabulous. Engraved baby announcements from Crane's and Pepperite are also available, as are enclosure cards and selections printable on the computer. Orders are usually shipped five days after you approve the proof. An order of one hundred announcements or invitations will cost about $90 and up.

JLD Greetings (Junior League of Dallas)
214-357-8822

The Junior League of Dallas carries lines such as Stacy Claire Boyd, Crane's, Sweet Pea Designs, and Masterpiece Studios. The friendly staff will help you with shower invitations, birth announcements, and holiday cards. One hundred percent of the profits aid the JLD community service fund, which goes to over forty-seven area nonprofit agencies. Prices vary.

Needle in a Haystack
6911 Preston Road
Dallas 75205
214-528-2850

The minute you walk into Needle in a Haystack, you will see just about every design for any occasion. The baby announcements and children's invitations cover the walls of the small back room. There is a table to accommodate a variety of albums such as Crane's, William Arthur, Cross-My-Heart, and Sur Tout Pour Vous. The majority of the printing is done in-house and takes about four to five business days, which includes proof time. Engraved selections depend on the company. All price ranges are available, and the staff is eager to help. With a credit card on file, they will take an order and wait for you to call with your baby's name, etc.

The Paper Lion
2310 West Virginia Parkway, Suite 160
McKinney 75071
972-540-5966

This store in McKinney seems continually busy. Why wouldn't it be with all of the products and services they offer? From custom printing for invitations, announcements, and stationery, to business cards, cups, and napkins, some of the lines they carry are Crane's, Studio Chevalier, and Caspari. They also have a grand selection of greeting cards, photo albums, candles, and gift wrapping essentials.

Polka Dots

8306 Kate Street, Suite 3
Dallas 75225
214-739-2107

Polly Campbell and her friendly staff make choosing from hundreds of designs and fonts a fun and smooth experience. Polka Dots stocks hip and traditional lines of invitations, announcements, enclosure cards, holiday cards, and stationery. Lines include Fitzgraphic, Julia D. Azar, Rockabye Baby, Sweet Pea Designs, Stacy Claire Boyd, and C'est la Fete. They do printing in house and offer engraved items by William Arthur and others. The turnaround time is fast and the work, top quality. If you are looking for special gifts, you can find custom hand-painted crosses by Mollie Owens, plus burp cloths, bibs, and other items by Swankie Blankie. A fun alternative to the traditional announcement is offered here—personalized chocolate candy bars. Don't miss this petite shop hidden inside a small office center in Preston Center.

Pretty Girl Events

214-929-5510

These handcrafted invitations and announcements are creative, fun, and of the highest quality. Attention to detail by artist/designer Lauri McKay's Pretty Girl Events doesn't go unnoticed and neither will the price, which can be $9 to $12 each. She uses only the highest quality papers and double-sided ribbons, and hand creates and embellishes each card. Lauri, a junior high teacher in Frisco, meets with each client to show her samples and to discuss creating an individualized design for a baby announcement, shower, or birthday invitation. These are original designs that you will not see anywhere and are truly a keepsake.

The Social Bee

5960 West Parker Road, Suite 256
Plano 75093
972-781-0151

The Social Bee is a one-stop shop for invitations and party needs. From paper goods to gift bag goodies and decorations, owner Kristina Selakovich has assembled quite a collection. Stocked invitations and announcements include Posie by Paper Prince, Cross-My-Heart, Mara-Mi, and Paper Girls. They also carry baby announcements, children's fill-in thank you notes, and calling cards.

Socially Write

The Shops at Legacy
5760 Legacy Drive
Plano 75024
469-241-0059

This "noteworthy" store, owned by two sisters, carries the latest and greatest designs such as Posie, Caspari, Inviting Company, and Sweet Cheeks. An extra special touch is their by-hand application of glitter to just about any announcement and invitation. They have an assortment of gift items, such as candles, frames, and albums, as well. Prices vary, starting at about $1.75 per announcement.

The Write Invite
4415 Lively Lane
Dallas 75220
214-956-9966

Jamie Gerard's The Write Invite truly is a gem and a one-stop shop for announcements, invitations, stationery, holiday cards, enclosures, and gifts. She has one of the best selections including Checkerboard, Inkwell, Martin and Frank, Little Knot, Madame T Productions, 2 Skirts, Mara Mi, Julia D. Azar, Unique Artistry, and too many more to name. While The Write Invite is by appointment only (Jamie works out of her home), your scheduled time is personal and all about you. We like this because you can bring your newborn, it is quiet, and a new mom needs to feel "pampered." Jamie's service is all about these luxuries, but her prices really aren't any higher. Get on her mailing list for seasonal shows (See chapter 9, Unique Gifts).

Write Selection
314 Preston Royal Village
Dallas 75230
214-750-0531
www.writeselectiononline.com

This Preston and Royal area store carries every kind of invitation, announcement, and stationery imaginable. From the traditional William Arthur and Crane's, to two of Kim's favorites—the unique Sur Tout Pour Vous and Julia D. Azar—the helpful staff will even assist you with wording. They carry boxed selections and various gift items. Owners Betsy Swango and Susan Foxworth are always "in-the-know," so be sure to ask for their guidance.

CHAPTER ELEVEN:
BIRTHDAY CHEER

Birthdays mark the crossing into a new year of life—and should not go unnoticed. It's a time to have a memorable party that will mean a lot to the little guest of honor. However, before you go all-out and book a marching band, dancing elephants, or a circus tent, think about what is appropriate for your child's age. You can really tailor the theme to his or her interests and make it truly a personal celebration without going overboard (or over budget).

So whether it is a small family affair or one that includes lots of friends, adding a personal touch or family tradition will make it even more special. For her daughter's first birthday, Kim hung a ribbon garland with a picture of Sawyer from each month of her first year. It made for a perfect keepsake, and guests could see how she had changed and grown. For her second birthday, the invitations were actual party hats made from a pictorial collage of Sawyer . . . a special touch that's easy and fun.

Just remember, it doesn't take much to overwhelm little ones, so be conscious of nap time, the number of guests, and the length of the party. For toddlers, we favor interactive entertainment and playtime environments, and we always include parents. Generally, it is not until the third birthday that organized games and special locales are big hits. Themes at home add fun and imagination that lend to a variety of activities, food, and decorations. Naturally, children of all ages can have party meltdowns. The icing on the cake is to keep it relaxed and not to expect perfect behavior.

There are countless entertainers in our city in the birthday party gig business. We have listed a variety of talents, all of whom have proven to us and to our friends that they're ready to go the extra mile to make your child's day special. Many of these are also great for school and church festivals. Their professionalism is fueled by the ethic: "it is all about the kids."

BIRTHDAY ENTERTAINMENT

Adventure Railroad
972-293-0634

Adventure Railroad will bring their trackless train to your house and take kids and parents up and down the street or around the neighborhood for $250 an hour. One hour is the minimum and an additional one-half hour is $75. There is a $50 deposit to hold your day and time. The train has music and double latches on doors, and some cars have seatbelts for smaller children. From our experience, we recommend parents ride with the little passengers.

Mr. Barnaby
972-266-5747
www.mrbarnaby.com

Mr. Barnaby's cast of characters is sure to please little ones at your home. Dora, the CareBears, Big Bird, a princess, or a superhero can make an appearance and entertain. Prices start at $145, which includes music, games, balloons, and bubbles for forty-five minutes. Mr. Barnaby serves Dallas and Fort Worth, and costumes are available for the daring parent who doesn't mind dressing up and putting on his own show!

Melody "Afi" Bell, Griot/Storyteller
214-374-1192

Do you want a one-of-a-kind celebration? Melody "Afi" Bell will engage, enlighten, and captivate children and adults with her African storytelling, music, and poetry. In traditional African dress, this mother of two and former Dallas public school teacher is working to keep the oral tradition alive and has received numerous community awards. Kim and Sawyer have seen her perform and were quite impressed. Afi is a rare find and puts on a quality program for the little ones. A friend of ours used Afi for her child's second birthday party, and the guests left in awe!

Bonkers the Clown
Poppy Productions, Jon Rainone
214-221-9779

Bonkers is perhaps the sweetest and friendliest clown in town. For $125 a half hour or $175 an hour, Bonkers entertains party goers with live juggling, balloon art, and a mini magic show during which he produces a live rabbit. Kids love this show and it is appropriate for ages three and up. We have even seen him at charity events, donating a portion of his appearance fees.

Broadway Babies
972-672-2308

The hills are alive with the sounds of Broadway Babies and their musical show tunes! This is one of the most fun types of party you could give a child of any age. Talk about interactive . . . each tune has a different instrument for children and parents. There is dancing, bubbles, hats, lights, and much more. Owner Ivy Lester is a dynamo who gets the kids moving and singing at the top of their lungs, all while introducing classics from musical Broadway hits such as *The Music Man, The Sound of Music,* and *Hair.* This one-hour show is a hit for boys and girls and parents. It is only $150! There is a $50 deposit to secure your event date. Ivy's Broadway Babies also offers private group classes.

Capers for Kids
972-661-2787
www.capersforkids.com

You will see drama at its best from the birthday child and her guests at a Capers for Kids party performance. For $175, a teacher will come to your home for one and a half hours, with a box of costumes, face paints, and small props, then read the children a "story drama." They will then warm up and go straight to rehearsal—all before parents return to see a princess story or a tale of pirates. This is too cute, and absolutely loved by the three-and-up set. Parties may also be held at Capers for Kids in Plano for $350, with the final production on the grand stage. Either way, a $75 deposit is required when you book, and the final payment is due one week prior to the party.

Country Carnival
817-477-5556
www.countrycarnival.com

Jalapeño Pepper the Clown will entertain little ones with her cheery demeanor. She does an age-appropriate comedy routine and either balloon animals or face painting for $135 an hour. A fun addition to her show is Miki the monkey, who can sit on kids' laps and do tricks. Booking Miki requires an extra $200! You can also rent popcorn, hotdog, and cotton candy machines, and even a trackless train that runs on the street and seats both adults and children for $225 an hour. While Kim's daughter, Sawyer, and some of her little friends were afraid of the clown's big red shoes and wig, other kiddies lined up to meet her.

Critterman & Safari Sue
940-365-9741
www.critterman.com

This friendly duo rivals any TV animal guides. Critterman and Safari Sue can surprise, educate, and engage age groups from toddlers to adults. Their "Original" Safari Guide party is forty to forty-five minutes, $225, and features eight animals: a hedgehog, a hissing cockroach, land tortoise, a legless lizard, a native king snake, a rose hair tarantula, a red Tegu lizard, and a ten-foot Burmese python. With all of that said, they do have other options for the three-and-under set.

David Chicken
214-929-4376
www.davidchicken.com

For an entertaining party that has people in a buzz, call David Chicken and his SCAKLE TIME! Call him crazy (he dresses in an Elvis-like suit, red cape, and a chicken hat) or call him a marketing genius . . . his one-hour, high-energy musical show is a hit with parents and kids alike. For $300, tots are the stars. You get dancing, singing, large pretend instruments, contests, and prizes (his CD and video). Be sure to ask for a guest appearance by Super Joanie, David's entertaining Chihuahua. You can buy a chicken hat on his Web site in advance—his mom hand-makes each one.

Emergency Ice
214-747-6746
www.emergencyice.com

Whoever knew that countless bags of sno-cone ice could imitate snow and entertain children for hours? Since Sawyer's birthday falls during the winter when there is not much to do outside, Kim and Nevin thought it would be fun and different to have her friends show up with mittens and hats for the chilly surprise. And that it was! Emergency Ice is a professional ice supply company that loves the opportunity to supply "snow," especially during the holiday season. They have worked through the night on Christmas Eve to cover a customer's roof and yard in "snow" as a surprise for the grandchildren! Of course this comes at a cost. The ice is $8 a bag and there is a minimum order of ten bags. For approximately four hundred square feet, you will need about one hundred bags. Good thing they deliver for free, right before the party. You just supply the plastic tarps, which help the ice last longer. Ours lasted for almost two days! Be sure to ask for Earl.

Face Painting by Germaine
214-826-5009

Germaine does some of the prettiest and most realistic face painting we have seen anywhere. She is great with kids and truly can do any bug, princess, dinosaur, or seasonal figure imaginable, either as a full-face design or on the cheek. One hour is $75. There is an additional travel charge if she has to go outside of the Dallas Metroplex.

Fun on the Farm
2300 West McGarity Lane
Lucas 75002
972-390-1933
www.funonthefarm.net

For a petting zoo and pony rides, Fun on the Farm will come to your home or host your party at their spread. Children can sit on the ponies for rides while parents snap photos. The Farm gang can bring everything from ducks to donkeys for your little crew to feed. Friends say their service is "organized, reliable, friendly, and clean."

Jessica's Princess Parties
214-686-1056
www.jessicasprincessparties.com

Mirror, mirror on the wall, which princess can entertain all? Jessica of Jessica's Princess Parties is the queen of characters and can portray Snow White, Cinderella, Belle, or Jasmine, with an enchanting fairy princess as well. For $130 to $165, there will be an interactive story, a treasure hunt, face painting, games, balloon swords/wands, and crowns. The birthday girl will get a tiara, a wand, and a gift. Boys will be transformed into princes. Moms say Jessica is "sweet, one-of-a-kind, and has made their daughters' days." The show, available throughout the Dallas and Fort Worth areas, is typically one hour for fifteen children, but it can be longer depending on the number of guests.

MiMi's Pony-Go-Round
214-460-0245

When all a little girl wants is a pony for her birthday, appease her with two! For $125, Mimi's Pony-Go-Round will bring one pony, or for just $150, they'll bring a second one! Their fee is $200 for a five-horse carousel. We have used them, and they are friendly and the horses are calm and well groomed. Plus, they won't leave your yard a mess!

Zooniversity
972-979-9847
www.zooniversity.net

Whether your little one likes bugs, rabbits, snakes, or safari animals, Zooniversity's owner and zookeeper Allison Blankenship can make even the squeamish beam. Her knowledge and talent coupled with innovative programs offer forty-five minutes of a fantastic adventure and learning experience. Appropriate for ages three to thirteen, the parties should have no more than twenty-five children. Your child is featured as a junior zookeeper. All the kids are awarded a diploma as a favor, and there are animals for kids to pet and touch. There are several themes to choose from, since there are over twenty-five tame and touchable animals. Allergy-free animals are available. The standard forty-five-minute party with six animals is $190. The additional feature of balloon animals is a fun touch and worth an additional $25—it was a highlight at a friend's party. Allison, a mother of two, is a member of the American Association of Zookeepers and has over twenty years' experience as an award-winning educational designer and trainer.

RENTALS

All-4-Fun
972-234-1700
www.all-4-fun.com

For inflatable fun, balloon art, and face painting, All-4-Fun can help you create a festive event. For the child who loves cars, All-4-Fun will bring to your home a mini inflatable NASCAR track with five remote control cars and a staff member—all for $175 an hour (two-hour minimum). Some favorites include a princess bounce house and an inflatable Twister game for twenty. Most inflatables can fit in your garage in case of rain.

Bill Reed Decorations

717 South Good Latimer
Dallas 75226
214-823-3154
www.billreed.com

Would you like to transform your party space into a "Big Top Circus" or "Alice in Wonderland" tea party? Bill Reed Decorations can do and create just about anything. From tents to pretend character picture stands to life-size wooden carriage props, his team can set up and even custom make quite a set for you. For over thirty-eight years, Bill has been designing and making props for social events. His services are great for school carnivals. There is a minimum $200 rental fee. Delivery, set up, and take down are free. Currently, Bill Reed serves North Texas and surrounding areas.

Ducky Bobs

3200 Belmeade Drive
Carrollton 75006
972-381-8000

4987 South Hulen
Fort Worth 75132
817-370-8400

www.duckybobs.com

We love that you can rent toddler-sized tables and chairs that are a perfect fit for the kids. They also rent standard-height tables and chairs, cloths, high chairs, tents, and concession stands. Tables start at $8 a table, and chairs can be $2 a chair. A sno-cone machine, a hot dog vendor, or a popcorn popper cart is $113. Fixings are available for an extra fee. While prices can be high, they are reliable. If you aren't home when they deliver, tell them ahead of time where to place your items. We suggest that you try to be there and ask them to help set up your tables and chairs. You can pick up items at their warehouse if you want to save on cost. Delivery and return is an extra $50 (throughout the Metroplex). Rentals are picked up the next day.

Just Jump'n

2021 Copper Street
Garland 75042
214-634-5867
www.justjumpn.com

You can rent a bounce house for almost any theme at Just Jump'n inflatables. Whether you want a princess castle, a dinosaur, water slides, or climbing walls, they are friendly and dependable. They even have some toddler-sized bounce houses. We love that they also rent sno-cone, cotton candy, and popcorn machines. Just this year, they have started table and chair rental—and all can be delivered! No hassles here, friends have told us, and their products are clean and in good condition. You can pick up your rental to save on cost. Rental for basic bouncers starts at about $90 for eight hours. Delivery is extra and varies per order and distance.

M & M Rental Center
2525 West Mockingbird Lane
Dallas 75235
214-350-5373
www.mmspecialevents.com

Formerly Abbey Party Rentals of Dallas, M & M is a reliable source for child-size tables ($9.70 each) and chairs ($1.30 per chair), tents, and glassware. Located near Love Field, their friendly staff can help load your car to save on the $50 delivery fee, with a minimum order of $50. We like that rentals can be picked up on Friday and don't have to be returned until Monday, at no extra charge!

Simply Pretend
972-396-1486
www.simplypretend.com

Playing dress-up is just not for girls! Simply Pretend has trunks of fun for all children. For $85 (for fifteen children) you can rent a dress-up trunk, choosing from heroes, pirates, princesses, or a tea time social bee. They will preselect costumes according to the number of children and gender. All trunks come with a dance party CD, age-appropriate games, coloring sheets, props, and accessories. Invitations and thank-you notes are cute and only 60 cents each! Favor bag goodies are also available. A $50 deposit will reserve your trunk and is refunded upon return. A party hostess is available if needed.

The Social Bee
5960 West Parker Road, Suite 256
Plano 75093
972-782-0151

The Social Bee is a one-stop shop for parties. From concession rentals, children's chairs and tables, and party planning, to invites, paper goods, and favors, owner and mom Kristina Selakovich and her staff can help you with it all!

PARTY LOCATIONS

Having a party at your home can be quite personal and a great venue for the wee one's birthday celebration. Once your child reaches age three, we have experienced a location party to be a trend and favorite for the kiddies because it ties into a cherished pastime. Location parties are also a favored choice for parents, due to less mess, fuss, and clean-up at home.

As for the grand finale of food and party cakes, some locations do provide the fare, paper goods, and decorations. We prefer (as do several moms we know) to bring the cake and goodies. We have listed some fun, interesting, educational, and interactive places that will be sure to entertain with games, food, and silliness galore!

Age of Steam Railroad Museum
Fair Park
Dallas 75315
214-428-0101
www.dallasrailwaymuseum.com

With paper conductor hats and plastic whistles, partygoers can learn about trains and have a tour of the Age of Steam Railroad Museum. For $100, twenty guests get free admission, a short presentation, and the outdoor picnic area is reserved for cake time. A guided tour is extra. You bring the cake and refreshments. Candles are not allowed. The museum is open on Wednesday through Saturday, 10 a.m. to 5 p.m.

Artzy Smartzy
8400 Abrams Road at Royal
Dallas 75243
214-341-0053

For $150, the birthday child and ten guests can have a ball while creating a masterpiece and their own party favor. The birthday child gets a special T-shirt. You bring the snacks and cake. Choose a tea, mask, bug, or a bedazzled theme for four-year-olds and up. Additional guests are $10.

Barnyard Buddies
3316 North Central Expressway, Building C
Plano 75074
972-633-9779
www.fairview-farms.com/barnyard.htm

This popular petting zoo is nestled in the middle of the hustle and bustle of city life (Joe's Crab Shack and more), but the kids don't even notice as they are busy feeding a pig, horses, and goats—just watch out for the sneezing goat (hint: he is a big guy!) Birthday parties are a hit, as long as you don't schedule one during the summer heat. Beyond feeding the animals, party-goers will also enjoy a trail ride, a hayride, a goat chase, sack races, and even a piñata. Parents bring the cake and refreshments and let Barnyard Buddies supply the paper goods and favors or loot bags. Prices start at $300 for fifteen children for two hours (adults are free). If you want a pony in your backyard, no problem—it is $150 for two hours.

Birthday Avenue
972-333-4150
www.birthdayavenue.com

Birthday Avenue, in Lewisville, is a great place for a party (ages three to ten) and for those who like to have fun. Parents will like it because the party planning and details are all taken care of at this one-stop party locale, and the staff is friendly. For a toddler's party, you can choose a Big Top Circus, Tea Cup Café, or a superhero theme. The cost is $150 for eight to twelve children, for one and a half hours. For an additional $75, you can include invitations, cake, decorations, party favors, and balloons. Face painting, pizza, and character appearances from Cinderella, Strawberry Shortcake, Ariel, Tinkerbell, Batman, or others are great "add-ons."

Central Market

5750 East Lovers Lane
Dallas 75206
214-234-7000
214-361-5754 (Cooking School)

320 Coit Road
Plano 75075
469-241-9336

www.centralmarket.com

Great feasts with good friends are an invaluable treasure—even at four! Central Market's cooking school can customize and create a cooking birthday celebration that is sure to make happy tummies and smiling faces all around. So parents, let your imagination run. From individual pizzas to hamburgers to cookie or gingerbread house decorating to healthy eating discussions coupled with sandwich making, be sure to reserve the cooking school in advance because this is one popular venue for people of all ages. Kim's good friend had a party for her daughter, and the kids loved decorating aprons she brought in while their food creations baked. Fees are structured to your event.

The Dallas Arboretum and Botanical Garden

8617 Garland Road
Dallas 75218
214-515-6500
www.dallasarboretum.org

Do you care for a garden party, picnic, or perhaps an enchanted fairy dessert event? We suggest this locale as a gathering spot for moms and babes, and it is suitable for a first birthday through toddler age. If all you want to bring is food, blankets, treats, and a camera, then no reservations or fees beyond admissions are required. A great shady spot is near the frog fountains—very sprinkler-like. This is one of our best-kept secrets. Now, if you want something grander or more planned, contact the arboretum directly. Hours are 10 a.m. to 5 p.m. daily (all year).

Dallas Zoo
650 South R.L. Thornton Freeway
Dallas 75203
214-943-2771
www.dallas-zoo.org

For $450, you can rent the Party Place at the Lacerte Family Children's Zoo for your little animal lover's party. A crowd pleaser for people of all ages, the Dallas Zoo supplies everything from hot dogs to pizza, with lemonade, cake, ice cream, and even party favor bags. Admission and parking for thirty guests is included. Parties can be scheduled seven days a week at 10 a.m., noon, 2 p.m., and 4 p.m. Winter hours are 11 a.m., 1 p.m., and 3 p.m. This is a favorite locale of ours for combining celebration, family, and fun.

Emler Swim School
4621 West Park Road
Plano 75093
972-599-SWIM
www.iswimemler.com

For $210, and under the watchful eye of a lifeguard, you can have a parent and tot swim party in their small pool. Afterwards, you can order pizza to be delivered and enjoy cake (brought in by you) in the private party area. Owner and founder Jan Emler has worked to train her instructors and lifeguards for over fifty hours each and puts her heart into her business. There is a larger indoor pool with two slides for the big kid celebrations. Parties are on the weekends only and a $50 deposit is required to hold your date and time.

Fort Worth Museum of Science and History
1501 Montgomery Street
Fort Worth 76107
817-255-9300
www.fortworthmuseum.org

The Dino-Mite Birthday Party at the Fort Worth Museum of Science and History is sure to capture the heart of the birthday child and guests. The party is perfect for ages three to twelve and gives kids a chance to explore and experience first hand many engaging, science-based activities in the party area. The Dino-Mite package, for fifteen children and four adults, includes a reserved table in the play area, invitations, paper, tableware, a Dino-Mite hot dog, chips, a small drink, party favors, and a $5 museum gift coin for the birthday child—all for $225. Each additional child is $10, and there must be two adults for every ten children. A hit for the older kids is the smoking Mad Scientist liquid nitrogen ice cream demonstration for an extra $50.

Fort Worth Zoo
1989 Colonial Parkway
Fort Worth 76107
817-759-7200
www.fortworthzoo.org

The Fort Worth Zoo is a "wild" place to have a party for animal lovers and their friends—and so worth the drive (ages four to twelve). For $205 (nonmembers), thirty individuals (parent or child) can celebrate with a Wild Wonders presentation and all-day passes. The party also includes the Education Center room for two hours and games. Reservations are required, and parties are typically held on Saturdays at 1 p.m. and 2 p.m.

Frisco Fire Station

8860 Tomlin Drive
Frisco 75034
972-335-5525
www.friscofire.org

A special party with Frisco firefighters is fun for all, we hear. How could it not be with a chance to climb on a fire truck; learn to stop, drop, and roll; dial 911; and eat cake in the firehouse kitchen? Parties are usually booked one year in advance and are open to Frisco residents and employees or grandchildren of residents. This educational and enjoyable party is free. (Some party givers have chosen to make small donations.)

Life Time Fitness

7100 Preston Road
Plano 75024
972-202-8100
www.lifetimefitness.com

"Wow!" is all a group of moms could say after attending a toddler party at Life Time's wading pool area. Picture a beach-like entrance for the wading pool, with fountains, an indoor tunnel slide for older kids, and of course a life guard—what more could a beach babe or winter birthday child want? For $20 a child, you get one hour in the party room with pizza and drinks, and then an hour in the pool. If swimming is not for you, they also offer a gym event with games, parachute play, and rock climbing for those over six years old. To hold your date and time, you must pay a deposit for the first ten children ($200). Prices are less for Life Time Fitness members.

The Little Gym

6441 East Mockingbird Lane, #410
Dallas 75214
214-515-0800

11919 Preston Road at Forest
Dallas 75230
972-644-7333

Multiple locations
www.thelittlegym.com

Much like their classes, this popular "gym" offers parties for children age one and up. You get the entire gym, with age-appropriate fun, and the party room. You bring the food and cake. Be sure to reserve it early as the schedule fills up fast. We have seen many families have great fun at The Little Gym, not only because some of the children were already familiar with "Mommy and Me" classes, but also because the wonderfully outgoing staff puts newcomers at ease. The bubbles are a great way to end playtime and introduce cake!

My Gym

4654 South Cooper Street, Suite 322
Arlington 76017
817-937-5552

2021 Justin Road, Suite B-197
Flower Mound 75028
972-874-5700

3241 Preston Road, Suite 1
Frisco 75034
972-378-9000

910 West Parker Road
Plano 75075
972-578-6630

www.my-gym.com

These action-packed parties book up fast, so call now to reserve your date with a $50 deposit, which is applied to the cost of the party. The "basic" party ($250) for twenty children is a fun-filled hour and a half. It includes teachers leading a creatively planned celebration with hip music, games, full use of the play area, all paper goods, decorations, invitations, and thank-you notes. The staff is incredibly friendly and energetic. The birthday child (typically two and up) gets to ride on a mini Harley-Davidson while guests sing . . . all before cake! There are variations at the assorted locations.

Playtime

5964 West Parker Road, Suite 100
Plano 75093
972-781-2244
www.mytimeplaytime.com

Playtime partygoers can have use of the entire space for an hour and a half. For $300, they supply the fun, games, balloons, table, chairs, and cleanup! All you have to do is supply the food, cake, drinks, and favors. It will be hard to choose from their themes. A favorite is the Princess Tea, which includes a dress up and fashion show in custom princess dresses and royal knight costumes. The Pirate Treasure Hunt includes dress up in pirate costumes and maps to hunt for hidden treasure. For the athletes or climbers, the Sports Time party includes scaling a "volcano" climbing wall, sliding down a beach lighthouse, and tumbling on gym equipment. If a puppet show is more your style, the Create and Play Puppet Show gives kids a chance to make their own puppets and create a story. Now, for the older child who wants to be a star, Star Time Karaoke has everyone singing and entertaining one another to their hearts' content. We have been very impressed by Playtime's creative and well-planned activities and their kindhearted staff. For those who don't live near Plano, it is well worth the drive just to see this fantastic kid's fitness/learning center attached to the MyTime Gym (for women only). It is a great concept and will be expanding in the near future. Parties are available on Saturdays and Sundays only.

Premier Club

Contact: Terri Arends
5910 North Central Expressway
Dallas 75206
214-891-6641

Kids can be kids at a Premier Club party. They can run, play games, swim, and do yoga—all under one roof and all without your worrying about your house being torn apart. You can create your own theme or select from one of theirs, such as Fun & Fit, with classic games like tug-of-war, scooter, and relay races, or Swim & Gym, a combination of free swim and gym time with games. All parties are ninety minutes of fun for $225 with an additional fee for the instructor (about $75). The staff is friendly and works with you as a team. All you have to do is bring the decorations, paper goods, and utensils for the cake. We recommend the club for ages three and over.

Pump It Up

7164 Technology Drive
Frisco 75034
Reservations: 214-387-9663

9201 Forest Lane
Dallas 75243
Reservations: 972-792-9663

Multiple locations
www.pumpitupparty.com

Pump It Up is an indoor "inflatable party zone" that is fun for the older toddler. Up to twenty-five friends can join your child for a one-and-a-half-hour party in the private play area and then enjoy cake and presents in the decorated party room. Cake, chips, drinks, and candy are the only outside foods allowed. For an extra fee, they can provide pizza, drinks, party favors, and balloons. Friends say they have enjoyed having parties here because it is entertaining for all, with a no-hassle clean up. All you really have to do is send out the free invitations from Pump It Up, and order a cake of course. Parties cost more on the weekends, so check weekday availability.

The Purple Cow
4601 West Freeway
Fort Worth 76107
817-737-7177

Trains, a jukebox, and great food make the Purple Cow a favorite party locale for many. This Fort Worth eatery has a side room that seats eighteen to twenty and does take reservations. We only wish that the other locations in Dallas and Plano would reserve space for partygoers. The Purple Cow milkshake makes a great addition to cake after a burger or grilled cheese and fries. (See chapter 18, Child-Friendly Eateries).

Scottish Rite Hospital for Children's Playground
2222 Welborn Street
Dallas 75219
214-559-5000
Jeannie.Munoz@tsrh.org

A fabulous playground, a playhouse, and a covered pavilion complete with a bathroom—the Scottish Rite Hospital's shaded park is one of the best kept secrets in town for a child's birthday party. There is lower-to-the-ground equipment, which makes this a perfect venue for both tots and older children. While there is no fee, we highly suggest that you make a donation to the hospital, for this venue can fill up three months in advance. When asked what the fee is, Jeannie Munoz said, "There isn't one." They just want the public to enjoy the park—could they be any nicer? Well, yes they can . . . they set up tables, chairs, and tablecloths.

Sunshine Glaze Creative Studio
405 North Carroll Avenue
Southlake 76092
817-424-1417
www.sunshineglaze.com

Sunshine Glaze promotes the creativity of all ages. Let the birthday child and his guests choose from a large selection of ready-to-paint ceramic objects (piggy banks to animal figurines) to decorate and paint during the one-and-a-half-hour party. For $18 a child, the staff decorates the room and cleans up, and you bring the cake, favors, and paper goods. This is also a fun place for baby showers, and they have special fee days such as "Mommy-N-Me" Thursdays and "Family Day."

Sweet & Sassy

Southlake Town Square
1246 Main Street
Southlake 76092
817-251-6353
www.sweetandsassy.com

Calling all princesses in training! Sweet & Sassy is the perfect party place for young girls ages four and up to be pampered. All party packages include makeovers, nail polish, group photo favor and choice of dress-up attire—there is also a special area to enjoy cake and unwrap presents. Packages include the "Jammin' Jewelry" party, where each girl designs her own bead accessory and gets a hair up-do, makeover, nail polish, and runway show ($29.95 per girl with a six-girl minimum). Or maybe the "Sassy Spa Girl" party where everyone puts on a spa robe and pair of fluffy slippers is more to your diva-in-training's liking. This party includes a manicure, pedicure, facial, makeover, and a hair up-do ($49.95 per girl with a five girl minimum). Call or visit the Web site for more information and to see all of the party packages offered.

University Park Fire Station

3800 University
Dallas 75205
214-987-5383

For the little future firefighter, this is a special moment for all to meet the friendly neighborhood firemen and to try on boots, hats, and coats and climb on the big red trucks. The meet, greet, and educational event is typically thirty to forty minutes, depending on the age (two and up). Be prepared for the crew to get called out if there is an emergency—the party could be delayed or cut short. The adjacent Gore Park gazebo is a great place for cake and ice cream. There is no fee and this is available to University Park residents only (grandchildren of residents are included).

Van Grow: Studio for the Arts

3434 West 7th Street
Fort Worth 76107
817-348-0505
www.vangrowstudio.com

Budding Picassos will love to have a birthday party at Van Grow. Parties are hassle free because Van Grow provides the tablecloths, napkins, forks, crafts and supplies, party favor bags, staff, and best of all, clean up! There are a variety of themes to choose from depending on your child's age. Two- to five-year-olds can choose between the princess, dinosaur, pirate, ballerina, tropical luau, western cowboy, jungle or zoo animal, pink poodle, or fairy theme party. Five to six different activity tables are set up, and kids can decide between creating a collage, painting, working with beads or stamps, or designing something out of clay. Older children, between the ages of five and eight, can select a princess party and can decorate a tiara or jewelry box. There is also a paint-a-canvas party and a clay party. Van Grow has invitations available for $1 each and they can be customized. Directions to Van Grow are printed on the back. Parties take place on Saturdays and can accommodate up to twenty-five guests ($15 per child).

Whole Foods Market
Contact: Suzan Mackay
11661 Preston Road at Forest Lane
Dallas 75230
214-361-8887

Okay, call us crazy, but a Whole Foods Market tour with Suzan Mackay (only available at the Preston/Forest location) is a fun-filled adventure that is perfect for a birthday party. It may sound different and it is, but who better than the experts to give an educational, yet funny, marching and singing tour. Kids will march through the aisles tasting and learning that blueberries are "brain food" and that meat and eggs from free-range animals, which feed on grass and natural grains, will help give them muscles (without the chemicals, that is). This is a great class trip or playgroup adventure as well. Suzan and her staff not only make this a unique birthday idea, complete with gift bags filled with stickers, a nutritional fun book and a pencil case (you may add your own goodies too), but they make sure you leave with full tummies and kids begging parents to buy a new food they just tried! Customized tours are available by contacting Suzan.

DECORATIONS, GOODIES, AND FAVORS

Theme or no theme, every party needs some celebratory decorations. Themes allow for a full range of parent imagination! While the older kids can have fun making homemade decorations, you can opt for keeping things simple by simply purchasing them. Most locales, such as grocery stores, Target, and Dollar Tree, also sell decorations, paper goods, invitations, thank-you notes, and favors—making them a one-stop shop.

For favors, we have found that the options are endless and that you can go overboard. The party alone is a big event, so we suggest following the theme and going low key. We have been to parties where the children make a craft, which is their favor, and to others where gift bags with stickers and Play-Doh suffice. For the wee ones, useful and playful items such as a rubber duck or soft bath toy are cherished. Favors should not be expected, but are a nice touch to thank guests for coming. Remember to give age-appropriate gifts. Parents will be thankful if you steer clear of potential choking hazards. Stay away from junky items that you wouldn't want around the home. Our favorite and unexpected favor thus far was a CD Kim's friend burned with her daughter's lullabies and sing-a-longs.

Birthday Express
800-424-7843
www.birthdayexpress.com

You name the theme, and they supply the plates, napkins, and favors. Piñatas galore! Mail delivery is dependable.

Card and Party Factory

6441 East Mockingbird Lane, Suite 354
Dallas 75214
214-824-6223

Multiple locations

We will simply say that if you can't find it at Card and Party Factory, good luck finding it. With aisles conveniently divided into categories such as Bulk Party Favors, Home Entertaining, Preschool Party, Baby's 1st Birthday, Girl's Party, Boy's Party, Cake Decorating, Luau, and Halloween, shopping is a breeze at this massive store. There is a large room solely dedicated to costumes and other Halloween or costume party necessities. Card and Party Factory also carries the basics like balloons, cards, wrapping paper, and invitations, and the not so basic items, like life-size cardboard cutouts of Elvis or Bart Simpson. You can't go wrong by stopping in.

Oriental Trading Company, Inc.

800-875-8480
www.orientaltrading.com

The Oriental Trading Company can send you a catalog that offers theme items for parties and school events. From party favors to decorations, they have it all! The Bannisters love the bubble machine they purchased three years ago. Talk about a bubble show! The glow-in-the-dark necklaces make great Halloween treats.

Party City

305 Medallion Shopping Center
Northwest Highway between Skillman and Abrams Road
Dallas 75214
214-891-0200

1701 Preston Road, Suite D2
Plano 75093
972-380-0844

Multiple locations
800-477-4841
www.partycity.com

Party City has balloons, table roll paper, invites, and total theme collections for birthdays, showers, and more. Discount prices.

CHAPTER TWELVE:
CAKES AND TREATS

Vanilla, chocolate, carrot, strawberry, Italian crème, oh my . . . who would have thought that the options were so endless for a child's birthday cake? It seems like yesterday when we were grinning ear to ear over our first "shaped" cakes. We can even remember the white fluffy icings, sugar crunching against our teeth, and its thick residue on the roofs of our mouths. Watching your child experience this for the first time is special, not to mention his curious touch and sly grin as he relishes the unknown taste of sugar!

Whether you choose to make a homemade cake with butter cream icing or begin with a bakery-bought creation, we think decorating has never been so fun. Themes lend us this creative freedom to dream and to embellish. We have listed some fabulous and fun options, but the best tip we have is to either make your own cake or buy a simple round or sheet cake and decorate it yourself with decorated sugar cookies or toy trinkets. Cupcakes are also great for decorating and are an easy choice. Just be sure to take off any decorations before serving to the little ones.

If you want easy, most of the local grocery stores have great options: such as Tom Thumb, Kroger, Minyard's, and Albertson's. Sam's and Super Target are good options too. They are a great alternative to the local bakeries, and can usually inscribe the cake while you wait. Some of these stores also offer kosher and sugar-free cakes. They do take special orders and most have a book of theme designs to choose from. Often, Kim will pick up cupcakes just for fun, or to have Sawyer and her friends decorate them on a rainy day.

BAKERIES

A and J Bakery
3535 Oak Lawn Avenue
Dallas 75219
214-526-0077

1910 Pacific Avenue, Suite 210
Dallas 75201
214-880-0850

17509 Coit Road, Suite 2
Dallas 75252
972-72-7724

www.aandjbakery.com

One of our favorites is A and J Bakery for their willingness to create any design imaginable. And their cakes are quite tasty, too! From baby showers and birthdays to christenings, designer cakes vary in price. A basic nine-inch round, two-layer cake starts at $22 and feeds fifteen to twenty people. The banana-chocolate chip cake can't be beat!

Amazing Cakes by Tom Lawson

214-521-3456
www.amazingcake.com

In his twenty-sixth year of baking, Tom Lawson's love for decorating and handcrafting chocolates is a true Dallas treasure. His cakes are some of the most decadent in taste and design. Give him at least four days and he will custom-create a cake for your little one, as well as make party favors, including homemade chocolate lollipops, individual take-home cakes, and iced cookies. Delivery is included if you live within a fifteen-mile radius of Park Cities. Prices start at $85 for about twenty-five servings. Tom Lawson will also teach cake baking and decoration at your home for children, or you might want to try his beloved "girls' night out parties." Beyond his gorgeous and yummy creations, his fun-loving personality alone will make you a repeat customer.

Aston's English Bakery & Catering

4342 Lovers Lane
Dallas 75225
214-368-6425

Just ask for the owner Mary Aston Rains when ordering a cake for your special occasion here. She will be sure to make your sheet cake or round cake fit any affair. Cakes can be custom decorated to match your theme or invitation and are moderately priced, starting at $28 to $38 for an eight-inch round that will feed eight to ten people.

Cakes to Go & More

2623 Manor Way
Dallas 75230
214-357-2488
www.cakestogo.com

Cakes to Go & More can't make it any easier than this—delivery throughout the Dallas area for cakes, cupcakes, party trays, balloons, Blue Bell ice cream, and ordering online! We have friends who use them year after year because of their customer service and adorable character cake designs. Cakes with a character design are $49 and serve fifteen to twenty people. They also offer cupcake cakes starting at $30.

Central Market

5750 East Lovers Lane
Dallas 75206
214-234-7000

320 Coit Road
Plano 75075
469-241-9336

www.centralmarket.com

Central Market's cakes are gourmet tasting, and it is so easy to run in and pick up a gorgeous round cake, elegantly decorated with flowers, in the bakery section. Baked that morning, the cakes are typically vanilla or chocolate with white or chocolate butter cream icing and serve fifteen to twenty people for about $27. Just ask the bakery to write your message while you shop. Layer cakes can be requested in sheets with forty-eight-hours notice. The vanilla cake is one of the moistest we've ever tasted. Cupcakes are also available.

Dallas Affaires Cake Company

2307 Abrams Road
Dallas 75214
214-826-9409

Dallas Affaires Cake Company has some of the prettiest and best tasting cakes in Dallas. Decorated with fresh flowers and ribbons or chocolate dipped strawberries, these "basic" eight-inch, double layer cakes are $45 and feed about twenty people. Known for their wedding cakes, they elegantly embellish a round, square, oval, or rectangle cake for your little one's celebration. Let them know your theme and together you can create a cake of your dreams. Kelli and Kim have used Dallas Affaires numerous times and have always been happy, as have their guests, with the quality and designs. Call for an appointment, or stop by to view their creations. Just remember that Saturdays are busy wedding days, and they are closed on Monday.

La Duni Latin Kitchen & Baking Studio

4264 Oak Lawn Avenue
Dallas 75219
214-520-6888
www.laduni.com

This is one of Kim's favorite for cakes and special treats for adults. These are the most delicious sweets! Known for their cuatro leches cake (perfect for a shower) and wedding cakes, it is La Duni's fondant-covered cookies, carmelized Swiss meringue-filled ice cream cones, and gorgeous cupcakes that will win your heart and your tummy. Just imagine a dozen cupcakes adorned with a delicate, handmade, white chocolate butterfly! If you are looking for an elegant presentation, European flair, and award-winning taste, call at least twenty-four hours in advance for a hand-decorated birthday cake that will be sure to make your party one to remember! Prices are high and vary per creation.

Magnolia Café & Bakery

2601 South Stemmons Freeway, Suite 190
Vista Ridge Market Place
Lewisville 75067
972-459-3100

Magnolia Café & Bakery does amazing old-fashioned homemade cakes. Their handsome custom decoration is not extra—yes, you read that right! Owners Susan and Mike Matta are all about customer service and quality. Some popular flavors to choose from are strawberry, chocolate, or carrot cake, and all of their icing is butter cream. Prices start at $27.50 for an eight inch, two layer cake, which serves twelve to fifteen people. Adorable iced sugar cookies in practically any shape and theme can be made to order, and they are big! Cupcakes are available too. If you need other food or bakery items for your event, make it a one-stop shop because their food is great, easy, and fun.

Moonlighting Cakeworks

972-418-7663

Owner and sole baker/decorator Vicki Prusaitis has been creating custom cakes since her son's first birthday, over thirty-five years ago! Moonlighting Cakeworks, which has only been in business for ten years, can create just about anything from pictures or your invitation, and at the last minute. Prices vary per design and size and start at $35 to $50. Her butter cream icing is homemade with real butter! Sheet cakes and cupcakes are also available.

Occasional Creations
817-430-1546 or 817-798-8062

Specializing in homemade and gorgeously decorated cakes, Occasional Creations cakes "melt in your mouth," according to baker and owner Susan Moskal's fans. Cakes can be custom designed or you can choose from her theme and designer collection, perhaps a butterfly or castle adorned with thick satin ribbon and a tiara for the birthday gal. A designer cake that serves approximately twenty-eight, starts at $35. Want something grander? A three-tiered rectangular cake, garnished with decorated sugar cookies (your color and theme of choice), is $125.

Romano's Bakery
6465 East Mockingbird Lane
Dallas 75214
214-821-5056
www.romanosbakery.com

Romano's Bakery creates gorgeous custom cakes for any occasion. Their special designs include a fairy tale castle cake, a fire truck cake or an Alice in Wonderland tilted cake. Even if you want a simple nine-and-a-half-inch round, priced at about $35, Romano's Bakery's attention to detail is perfection. You may choose from over forty different flavors. Kelli's son Joshua's first birthday cake was fantastic, and our friends who have used Romano's are equally pleased with their quality. Delivery is available to Dallas and the surrounding areas for an additional charge.

Stein's Bakery
12829 Preston Road
Preston Valley Shopping Center, Suite 417
Dallas 75230
972-385-9911

Stein's is best known for their extra sweet and sugary petit fours—perfect for a baby shower and $16 per dozen. They do character cakes, starting at $34, that feed twenty to twenty-five people.

Two Women Baking
214-738-0855
www.twowomenbaking.com

Two Women Baking is two talented friends, Misty Canale and Jennifer Crosby, who left the corporate world behind to make fabulous food, candy, and cakes. Their designs are amazing and creative, and they are fun to work with. We have used them to cater a party and our guests all wanted their card. So whether it is butterfly-and-frog-shaped party sandwiches, portabello quesadillas, or a three-dimensional frog sitting on a lily pad—all made from cake and sugar cookie dough—they have a passion for what they do and it shows. Delivery is free per quantity ordered.

CAKE BAKING AND ACCESSORIES

We are big fans of making our own cakes. Don't let it sound hard or intimidating—we promise that even if your first attempt turns out lopsided, your baby will never know! So we encourage you to try it, even if it is a boxed cake mix and a simple small one for your family—turn that double eight-inch round into a mini carousel or pond by dying the icing and topping with a decorated sugar cookie. We have included some stores to help you stock up for your baking and decorating needs.

Sur la Table

4527 Travis Street, Suite A
Dallas 75205
214-219-4404

5809 Preston Road, Suite 580
Plano 75093
972-378-5532
www.surlatable.com

Sur la Table is a favorite of ours for cookie cutters, baking pans, and accessories. The staff is friendly and can help you with just about any question.

Williams-Sonoma

Multiple locations
800-541-2233
www.williams-sonoma.com

Beyond bakeware, Williams-Sonoma is a great place for gourmet vanilla and decorating pens for cookies.

Wilton Industries

800-794-5866
www.wilton.com

This is a great Web site for decorating ideas, recipes, and party-planning tips. Wilton shows you that you really can make fun and cute cakes and cupcakes for your little one. You can purchases pans, icing bags, tips, and so much more. Kim has used the candy molds and melting chocolates to make candy favors for baby showers.

CHAPTER THIRTEEN:
PHOTOGRAPHERS

Capturing those first few moments of life, those smiles, the first milestones, and holiday moments are a part of our everyday life as parents. Our homes are filled with photos taken every step of the way since our children were born. We are quite sure yours will be too. The camera bug is contagious and even if you have a fast finger and are great with the shutter, we feel it is worth your while to leave some of the photography to the professionals.

Many parents we know have told us that getting that perfectly posed smile just isn't going to happen. Nor does it reflect the child's true nature—especially if she is a curious toddler. From our experiences, it is the unexpected moments that capture the most intimate of expressions that will vividly remind you of a certain period in your child's life.

The majority of the photographers we have listed have a gallery viewing on their Web site to help you decide what you want out of a photo shoot. Most require an appointment and have sitting fees. Remember to have fun. Do not go into a shoot worried that your darlings may cry or run in the other direction. Leave that up to the professional and your child. Nearly all photographers will provide you with some guidelines or tips for your shoot, such as;

* Nap time is not a good time for your appointment.

* Don't dress your child or yourself in dated clothing.

* Bring familiar toys or special loveys so your child feels comfortable in the different environment.

* Just in case you run late, or to calm your child, bring a bottle or a snack and a drink (stay away from sugar and juice), even if it is not snack time.

* Don't try to overprepare your older child for a picture session because it can cause anxious moments for all involved and "shut off" the natural and fun-loving character of childhood.

* Milestones are a great time to photograph your baby: smiles, pushing up on their tummy, sitting up, crawling, walking. . . .

Oh, and another thought . . . be sure to ask your photographer of choice if he or she backs up your images with an archival format or if they do a multiple method: a hard copy, negatives, or CD-ROM. As for your home photography, a smart tip is to do the same.

PROFESSIONALS

Stacy Bratton (SD/SK Studio)
2114 Farrington Street
Dallas 75207
214-741-7666
www.stacybratton.com

Stacy Bratton's ability to connect with children is magical. She specializes in black and white photography for newborns, toddlers, and pregnant women. Stacy's signature is her personality series in which multiple images of three or more unique expressions of personality are grouped together. She has a gift of capturing the mysterious depth and breadth of a child's soul. Whether you choose the studio, or a location such as the park or your backyard, Stacy spends time with the baby or child before each shoot, making him feel comfortable and at home. Both black and white and color photos are wonderful. She offers birth announcements and greeting cards, too. Sitting fees range from $50 to $275. Stacy's husband, Kyle, a former photographer, does in-house framing.

John Derryberry
5757 West Lovers Lane, Suite 310
Dallas 75209
214-357-5457
www.johnderryberry.com

Known as one of the country's top portrait photographers specializing in black and white, John Derryberry's work is classic and unique with a documentary feel. In the studio, John and his staff combine "cutting edge technology with classical techniques to produce the highest quality archival, museum grade prints." He is an attention-to-detail guy who takes clothing, poses, and lighting into consideration for each shoot. His work has appeared in *Texas Monthly, Town and Country,* and many others. He is pricey—the studio sitting is $300 and the location sitting is $350 for one or two persons ($100 for each additional person). There is a minimum print order of $750.

James French Photography

3001 Fairmount Street
Dallas 75201
214-720-0990
www.jamesfrenchphotography.com

James's love for capturing the traditional children's photograph makes his work truly classic—looks out for the pink feather! Don't let his long list of distinguished subjects intimidate you (President Bush to George Burns). Beyond his twenty-five years of experience, he is gifted at capturing the moment. Assistant Laurie Powell is now taking photos and is great with kids of all ages—she really catches their personalities. If you are looking for a piece to hang front and center in your living room, James is the guy. He specializes in color, and works in his studio and on location. There are special portrait offers throughout the seasons, such as Easter at the park or in the studio with live bunnies. These specials usually offer a complimentary sitting coupled with reduced portrait prices.

John Haynsworth

86 Highland Park Village
Dallas 75205
214-559-3700

John Haynsworth takes a formal or fun classical portrait in his studio or on location. He specializes in family and children, and his color photography can be converted to black and white. John's sitting fees are $150 and he shoots until he gets what you want. Proofs are available in about six days for in-studio viewing, or for a deposit, you can take them home for a few weeks to show friends and family.

Sally Larroca People Photography

6626 Aintree Circle
Dallas 75214
214-363-2598
www.sallylarrocaphotography.com

Sally Larroca loves to work with kids in the outdoors because it is "less of a distraction without the lights and equipment," she says. She specializes in location shoots, either in color or black and white photography. Sitting fees start at $95 for an individual and include a minimum of thirty-six images. There is an increase if services such as taking both color and black and white are added. Proofs are available for pickup in approximately ten days.

Jennifer Lipshy Photography

4424 West Lovers Lane
Dallas 75209
214-358-6822
www.lipshy.com

Jennifer Lipshy specializes in handpainting black and white and sepia toned portraits with oil paints using a special and unique technique. These are also available on canvas—her masterpiece canvas portraits and pricing starts at $315 for a 5x5. Jennifer does most of her photography outdoors and recommends a consultation to learn about your lifestyle and your desires for the portrait. We've been told by parents that Jennifer's "A Year in the Life" program, in which she photographs the infant in four portrait settings, is a great way to capture your child's first year. Her sitting fee is $200 for up to four people.

Milburn's PortraitArt

3417 West 7th Street
Fort Worth 76107
817-882-8600
www.milburnsportraitart.com

Keith Milburn's photography captures children's intimate and natural expressions, either in the studio or at an outdoor location (your home or perhaps the Botanical Gardens in Fort Worth). Milburn's offers black and white or color, and several different styles such as on-canvas or a "Masters" that is touched up or colored. Packages range from $289 to $1,295.95. An 8x10 portrait without a package is $95. Appointments are required. Friends say this is *the* Fort Worth locale for the "formal children's keepsake portrait."

Morgan Studio

5930 East Mockingbird Lane
Dallas 75206
214-821-0811
www.morganphotography.com

Phil and Janet Morgan, a husband and wife team, are great at making you and yours feel comfortable and relaxed from the get-go. Their portraits are beautiful and natural. They've been taking pictures for over thirteen years, specializing in color, black and white, and hand tinting. Sitting fees are $40 for studio shots (which includes their own "mini private garden" located outside their studio home) or $100 for location shoots. Proofs are ready in three to four days either on their Web site or in the studio. Morgan Studio offers custom framing, announcements, and holiday cards.

Debra O'Brien Portraiture

8411 Preston Road, Suite 670
Dallas 75230
214-373-1703
www.debraobrien.com

Debra O'Brien has been taking wonderful children's portraits for over twenty years. She specializes in black and white images taken in her private studio and will take color upon request. Her "traditional sitting" fee for up to three subjects is $195, and $525 for location shoots. Either option includes three to four rolls of film with your proofs ready for viewing in one week. Appointments may be made for Tuesdays through Saturdays.

Poetic Portraits by Charla

5633 Bent Tree Drive
Dallas 75428
972-407-9382
www.colormehappy.com

The word "poetic" literally describes the work of Charla Reed, who specializes in children, families, and expectant mothers. Her work includes black and white portraiture, sepia tone, color, hand tinting (for a vintage feel), fine art, watercolor prints, and black and white fiber prints. She can shoot indoors or outdoors.

Stacy Sims Photography

214-684-4648
www.stacysimsphotography.com

Stacy, a mother of two, is a former corporate marketing wiz who realized that her longtime hobby of photographing families is her "calling." In the past two years (after professional courses and schooling) Stacy has developed a unique technique of capturing the timelessness of childhood and the family relationship or the "precious present" as she calls it. Her prices are very reasonable, and our friends were captivated by the relationships she instantly forms with the children. Stacy's sitting fee for indoors or outdoors is $125 and includes retouching and an on-line proof book. She also offers cards, collages, and framing.

Nichole Capatino Stephens Photography

2540 A Elm Street
Dallas 75226
214-542-2051
www.nicholestephens.com

Nichole Capatino Stephens is a natural at striking a cord with little ones and capturing their nature. This mother of two specializes in children done in either black and white or color. Her work is refreshing and is a fantastic alternative to the posed portrait. Clients say her trick is to let the child just be; then she captures his soul. The minute you view Nichole's work on her Web site, you'll be sold. Whether in the studio or on location, a sitting fee is $175 and includes one roll of black and white or color or even half of each. Nichole offers museum prints, holiday cards, and custom prints. Her custom work includes the addition of names and the date printed on them, or a print with a series of photos. Proofs take about ten days.

Amy Twomey Photography

214-435-9763
www.amytwomeyphotography.com

This photojournalist captures the personal moment in each shot without creating one. Amy Twomey has been taking children's and family portraits since 1993 and is a mother who knows how to relate to all. She shoots primarily on location using natural settings such as White Rock Lake, the Greenbelt, and the East Dallas area. A sitting fee is $155 and includes one roll of film and proofs, which have a three-to-four working-day turnaround. The Pregnancy Journal is her own unique concept of taking photos of mom-to-be (and daddy too, if desired) throughout the entire pregnancy. She also offers invitations, shower announcements, and holiday cards.

Angela Weedon Photography

972-496-6696
www.weedonphoto.com

Angie Weedon, a marine scientist by trade, does striking photography of expectant moms, newborns, children, and families. She specializes in black and white and hand tinted portraiture. Along with her photojournalist husband Matt, Angie also offers underwater portraits for older children—a perfect fit for this duo who shares a profession and passion for photographing underwater marine life. Her sitting fees are $200 for a studio or park shoot. Locations are an additional charge. Weedon Photography offers birth announcements, special occasion cards, and holiday cards.

Kimberly Wylie Photography
4231 Travis Street, Suite 27
Dallas 75205
214-219-7003
www.wyliephotography.com

Kimberly Wylie specializes in classic and hand-tinted black-and-white photography of pregnancy, children, and their families. Her photos are some of the most breathtaking we have seen. Her shots (as seen throughout this book and on the cover) encapsulate the emotion and personality of the child—even the newborn shots! Whether in her studio or at her favorite park location, Kimberly's talent, coupled with her love of children (she's a new mom herself), is evident in her intimate and classic works. No detail is overlooked, and Kimberly and her best friend and business partner, Jessica Alexandersson, are a delightful team to work with. She charges $175 for a sitting fee of one to four people, which includes a proof presentation book for you to keep. There are several series or "portfolio" options as well, such as the Newborn Portfolio, which is $450 for the sitting, 100 birth announcements designed by Kimberly (you may have seen her gift cards in stores), and a free 5x7 black-and-white fine-art print. This is a great way to save some money. Gift certificates, custom framing, announcements, invitations, and holiday cards are available.

CHAIN PORTRAIT STUDIOS

For quick and less expensive alternatives, many choose chain studios versus the private professionals. You can usually walk away with photos ready to hand out to friends and family.

Fetal Fotos
3241 Preston Road, Suite 6
Frisco 75034
214-387-9966
www.fetalfotosusa.com

For expectant parents, this is an ultrasound that provides a 4-D, 3-D, and 2-D look at your baby. Our friends who have done this (at about twenty-six weeks of gestation) loved it, as it provided a close-up of their little miracle. Founded in 1994 by a board-certified obstetrician, Fetal Fotos offers packages starting at $100 for 2-D imaging in a video set to music, four still photos, and gender identification. The 3-D and 4-D ultrasounds provide more detailed images, such as movement and facial features, and are taken at specific times in the pregnancy. These packages are $150 to $200. Not all of the technicians are licensed or registered ultrasound technologists.

Kiddie Kandids

Multiple locations throughout the area
www.kiddiekandids.com

This is a chain of studios across the country and the Dallas-Fort Worth area (most locations are inside area Babies "R" Us stores) that specializes in children's photography—ideal for older infants and toddlers. They offer various props and a selection of backgrounds. The studio shots are digital, allowing for immediate viewing and selection, and instant take-home satisfaction. Other options include custom borders, text, and the ability to create an "old-fashioned" look with black and white or sepia tones. Kiddie Kandids offers an abundance of gift items, from custom calendars to mugs to mouse pads and magnets and birth announcements. There is no sitting fee, and each page of photos you order from their various size options is $15. Packages start at $79 and go to $153. Prices may vary per location.

Picture People

Collin Creek Mall
811 North Central Expressway
Plano 75075
972-422-4711

Town East Mall
2220 Town East Mall
Mesquite 75150
972-270-6686
Valley View Center
13331 Preston Road, Suite 2242
Dallas 75240
972-385-7055

Vista Ridge
2401 South Stemmons Freeway
Lewisville 75067
972-315-7553

www.picturepeople.com

Props, props, and more props—this chain "entertainment retail store" specializes in portrait packages and offers a variety of gifts and frames created from your child's photographs. Sitting fees are a bargain at $9.95 for one person or $19.95 for three or more, and include five different poses. Your color or black-and-white portraits are available to take home in about one hour. Larger prints, such as a 16x20, may take up to three weeks. All prices and services may vary per store.

The Studio at Target

Multiple locations

888-887-8994

www.target.com

This fun and easy portrait chain studio is inside many local SuperTarget stores. There are several backgrounds and props to choose from, and seasonal specials keep everyone smiling. You may choose from several package deals with the basic one starting at $8.99 with no sitting fee, one 8x10, one 5x7, four 3½x5s, twelve wallets, and three billfolds. They offer a Portrait Savings Card, greeting cards, and many specials and coupons. Hours and prices vary per location.

CHAPTER FOURTEEN:
HAIRCUTS

It can't be that difficult to cut your little one's hair, can it? Think again. Kelli's husband, A.J., gave it a try and has since regretted it—when he was done, young Joshua was nearly bald!

We suggest that you leave the "snip, snips" to the professional, but know you could head home with a first curl and a cute picture or not. Know that it is common for children to have a fear of getting a haircut, which is not unreasonable considering a complete stranger is hovering around their head with a pair of scissors. We've had both good and bad haircutting and trimming services with our children and learned you might have to keep trying a different salon that suits you and your child—probably like you have for yourself. Some women take their children to their own hairdresser and it can be pricey, but we encourage you to ask them for a special rate. A fearful child might find extra comfort in knowing you trust this person to cut your hair.

Hair cutteries that cater to children seem to be the trend, and how could they not be? So leave it to the kid-friendly stylists and let the kiddos relish in the child-friendly décor, such as a Barbie jeep chair. All but one of the businesses listed recommend appointments but do accept walk-ins. If you decide to take your chances, try to go during a weekday morning before the older set gets out of school.

Cartoon Cuts
Stonebriar Centre
2601 Preston Road, Suite 1000
Frisco 75034
972-712-4247
www.cartooncuts.com
Hours: Monday-Saturday, 10 a.m. to 9 p.m.; Sunday, noon to 6 p.m.

Though geared to children under twelve years, Cartoon Cuts also offers adult services. Stations feature video games, cartoons playing on built-in televisions, and a play area in case you have to wait. A shampoo and cut for children under twelve is $13.99, and the "Family Plan" for $27.95 includes one child and one adult haircut. Adult haircuts are $15.99. Ear piercing is also available.

Chop Shop

10129 Shoreview
Dallas 75238
214-348-8862
Hours: Monday-Friday, 8 a.m. to 6 p.m.; Saturday, 8 a.m. to 5 p.m.

The Chop Shop is an old-fashioned barber shop found in Lake Highlands, and several people we know take their sons here. Haircuts are a bargain at $12 and the staff goes out of their way to make it a pleasurable experience for kids.

Cool Cuts for Kids

Locations in Allen, Arlington, Carrollton, Flower Mound, Fort Worth, Mesquite, North Richland Hills, Plano, Richardson, and Southlake

4425 Lovers Lane
University Park 75225
214-252-9800

www.coolcuts4kids.com
Hours: Monday-Friday, 10 a.m. to 7 p.m.; Saturday, 9 a.m. to 7 p.m.

Cool Cuts is the largest children's hair salon chain in the United States. Kids will enjoy sitting on seats shaped like cars or motorcycles, watching their favorite video, or playing a video game—all while getting a haircut. Friends say cuts are good and prices are reasonable at $14.95. The stylists go out of their way and are extremely friendly and patient.

The Grooming Room at Culwell and Sons

6319 Hillcrest
Dallas 75205
214-522-7030
www.culwell.com
Hours: Monday-Friday, 9 a.m. to 6 p.m.; Saturday, 8 a.m. to 5 p.m.

Located across the street from SMU, this men's clothing store also includes a dry cleaner, a boys' store, and a charming, old-school barber shop. The barbers and stylists are patient with the kids and work quickly. There are plenty of toys to keep the children occupied, and baskets of lollypops come in handy if you need a bribe. Prices are $14 or $20 depending whether it's a dry or wet cut and how much hair has to be trimmed. Friends say this is "the perfect place for a little man's cut."

Kids B Kids Haircuts for Children

Pepper Square
14902 Preston Road, Suite 406
Dallas 75254
972-233-2112
Hours: Monday-Friday, 10 a.m. to 6 p.m.; Saturday, 9 a.m. to 6 p.m.

Independence Square
3100 Independence Parkway, Suite 106
Plano 75075
972-596-8979
Hours: Monday-Friday, 10 a.m. to 6 p.m.; Saturday, 9 a.m. to 5 p.m.

Your children may not want to leave because of the television stations, chairs shaped like cars and motorcycles, and large play area. Haircuts are $14 for children, $18 for mom and dad, and baby's first cut comes complete with a certificate and is $10.95.

Kids Kuts

6434 East Mockingbird Lane, Suite 109
Dallas 75218
214-874-0800
Hours: Monday-Friday 10 a.m. to 6 p.m.; Saturday, 9 a.m. to 5 p.m.

Kids Kuts, a cousin to Cool Cuts for Kids, is clean and has a large waiting area with lots of toys and a fish tank to help pass time in case you have to wait. During a haircut, videos and games entertain young customers. The price is $14.95. They also offer a "Princess Birthday Party" for up to twelve girls.

Le Duke Hair Dressing

4487 Bryant Irvin Road
Fort Worth 76132
817-377-8778
Hours: Tuesday-Friday, 10 a.m. to 5 p.m.; Saturday, 9 a.m. to 5 p.m.

D Magazine rated this salon the "Best Kids' Cuts" in the Fort Worth area. They swear that Arthur Pruitt can work magic on the most obstinate or fussy kids. The price is around $10 for young children.

Lovers Lane Barbers and Manicurists

4331 Lovers Lane at Douglas Avenue
Dallas 75225
214-522-6595
Hours: Tuesday-Friday, 7 a.m. to 6 p.m.; Saturday, 7 a.m. to 3 p.m.

This barber shop has been a Highland Park institution since 1938. Comprised of three barbers, five nail technicians, and a shoe shine; both young and old stop by here to get a terrific haircut. The barbers love the kids, as do the friendly "groupies" who have been stopping by daily for years to chat—envision a Norman Rockwell picture, complete with an old-fashioned barber pole out front. Walk-ins only and prices start at $11.

Amy Rowlett

Salons in the Park
6301 Abrams Road
Dallas 75231
214-503-3560
214-315-3796 (Cell)
Hours: Monday-Friday, 9 a.m. to 6 p.m.

A.J. has gone to Mrs. Rowlett for haircuts since her days at a local barber shop. Though she also styles hair for adults, Amy's specialty is children's cuts. Her studio is small and uncluttered—no TVs, games, or racecars here. What she lacks in entertainment, she makes up for with her personality, patience, and easygoing manner. She's a mother of two so the interest she shows in your child is genuine. The haircuts she has given Joshua have been the best he has gotten. A child's cut is $12.

Sport Clips Haircuts

Locations in Allen, Carrollton, Flower Mound, Garland, Grapevine, Las Colinas, Lewisville, North Richland Hills, and Plano
3001 Knox Street, Suite 101 A
Dallas 75205
214-219-5900

1664 South University Drive, Suite C
Fort Worth 76109
817-332-3020

Multiple locations
800-872-4247
www.sportclips.com
Hours: Monday-Friday, 9 a.m. to 8 p.m.; Saturday, 9 a.m. to 6 p.m.; Sunday, noon to 5 p.m.

If dad and son need a haircut, why not bond at Sport Clips Haircuts? Sorry, moms—this sports-themed haircutting chain caters only to men and boys. With TVs turned to sports at every styling station and a big screen up front, does it matter how good the haircuts are? But don't worry, their stylists are well trained. Prices start at $11.95.

Stride Rite Hair Salon

6129 Luther Lane at Preston Road
Dallas 75225
214-373-1124
Hours: Monday-Friday, 10 a.m. to the last appointment taken at 5:15 p.m.; Saturday, 9:30 a.m. to the last appointment taken at 5:15 p.m.

Billed as the only shoe store in Dallas with a hair salon, many of our friends confirm that Stride Rite's Ms. Ginger gives a great cut. It is recommended that you make an appointment.

Sweet & Sassy

Southlake Town Square
1246 Main Street
Southlake 76092
817-251-6353
www.sweetandsassy.com
Hours: Monday-Saturday, 10 a.m. to 7 p.m.; Sunday, noon to 5 p.m.

If you enjoy being pampered, then you will feel right at home when you bring the kids to Sweet & Sassy. This salon is as plush as some "adult" salons we have been to. Some of the services they offer are haircuts, highlights, mini-manicures and facials, and ear piercing. If you are cutting your baby's hair for the first time, they have a package which includes a lock of hair and a special certificate with the child's photo for $19.95. Prices for haircuts start at $14.95 and mini-manicures are $11.95. They have several birthday party packages (see chapter 11, Birthday Cheer, Party Locations section).

CHAPTER FIFTEEN:
SCRAPBOOKING

One of the hottest trends when it comes to preserving memories is scrapbooking. Scrapbooking is a fun and creative way to document and preserve photographs in a meaningful way. The Dallas-Fort Worth area is filled with stores that cater to this craft and there are several popular Web sites as well. Most of the stores we have listed offer classes for beginners and for those who want to take their craft to the next level. Kelli's friend shared the scrapbooks she created for her son and they are incredibly unique and personal—all while preserving your child's milestones. A helpful hint: we have had many mothers tell us that they put together their baby's first scrapbook while they were pregnant. That way, after your child is born and you are too tired to think straight, the hard work is out of the way. All you have to do is add pictures. We have listed some locales that are great resources for classes and supplies.

Creative Memories
800-341-5275
www.creativememories.com

Jo-Ann Fabric and Crafts
810 Preston Forest Shopping Center
Dallas 75230
214-369-9699

6330 East Mockingbird Lane
Dallas 75214
214-821-4520

7523 Grapevine Highway
Fort Worth 76180
817-485-6048

2930 Preston Road
Frisco 75034
972-712-4009

700 Alma Drive
Plano 75075
972-424-0011

Multiple locations throughout the Dallas-Fort Worth area
888-739-4120
www.jo-ann.com
Hours: Most stores are open Monday–Saturday, 9 a.m. to 9 p.m.; Sunday, 10 a.m. to 6 p.m.

Michaels

5500 Greenville Avenue
Dallas 75206
214-461-9491

5959 Alpha Road
Dallas 75240
972-239-2800

6401 West Plano Parkway, Suite 130
Plano 75093
972-473-7313

801 West 15th Street, Suite A
Plano 75075
972-691-1355

4921 Overton Ridge Boulevard
Fort Worth 76132
817-423-1727

2901 East Highway 114, Suite 100
Southlake 76092
817-749-2300

Multiple locations throughout the Dallas-Fort Worth area
800-642-4235
www.michaels.com
Hours: Most stores are open Monday-Saturday, 9 a.m. to 9 p.m.; Sunday, 9 a.m. to 6 p.m.

Recollections . . . The Scrapbook Experience
Old Town Center
5500 Greenville Avenue, Suite 203
Dallas 75206
214-572-1112

South Frisco Village
2930 Preston Road, Suite 500
Frisco 75034
972-377-4069

www.recollectionsonline.com
Hours: Monday-Saturday, 10 a.m. to 9 p.m.; Sunday, noon to 6 p.m.

Scrapbook Barn
2760 Trinity Mills Road, Suite 110
Carrollton 75006
972-418-8600
www.thescrapbookbarn.com
Hours: Tuesday-Saturday, 10 a.m. to 8 p.m.; Sunday and Monday, noon to 6 p.m.

Scrapbook Page
6921 Granbury Road
Fort Worth 76133
817-346-2100
888-682-6685
www.scrapbookpage.com
Hours: Monday, Wednesday, Friday, and Saturday 10 a.m. to 6 p.m.; Thursday, 10 a.m. to 8 p.m.;
Sunday 1 p.m. to 5 p.m.

Scrapbook Supercenter
3000 Custer Road at Parker, Suite 180
Plano 75075
972-673-0641

6505 West Park Boulevard at Midway, Suite 220
Plano 75093
972-673-0690

www.scrapbooksupercenteronline.com
Hours: Monday-Saturday, 10 a.m. to 8 p.m.

Scrapbook Warehouse
5611 Colleyville, Suite 140
Colleyville 76034
817-656-4905
Hours: Monday-Saturday, 10 a.m. to 9 p.m.; Sunday, noon to 6 p.m.

2440B South Stemmons Freeway
Lewisville 75067
214-488-1700
Hours: Monday-Saturday, 9 a.m. to 9 p.m.; Sunday, noon to 6 p.m.

www.scrap-bookwarehouse.com

Scrappin' Memories
1913 Justin Road, Suite 117
Flower Mound 75028
972-874-2767
Hours: Monday-Thursday, 10 a.m. to 6 p.m.; Friday-Saturday, 10 a.m. to 9 p.m.

PART FOUR:
OUT AND ABOUT

CHAPTER SIXTEEN:
TIRED CHILD, HAPPY PARENT

What a wonderful feeling it is to take your bundle of joy out of the house and embark on what you believe will be their path to Harvard, becoming a professional musician, or simply learning to do something other than sleep and eat. Get out and enroll your child in a class. We began with one class early on and learned it is not only beneficial for the child, but for you too. It is an invaluable opportunity to expose your little one (and you!) to new and different experiences. It can also be a breath of fresh air for a new mom who just needs someone to talk to or share stories with. When we enrolled our kids in their first class we didn't just walk, we ran!

As with many situations in life, the instructors make the experience. If you are unhappy with a particular teacher, don't assume that all the classes are that way. Ask to switch to another class, and see if everyone is happier and getting more out of it. Remember this is supposed to be fun. If your child isn't enrolled in music class by the age of eighteen months, it doesn't mean she won't be the next Beethoven. Which brings us to our next piece of advice—you don't have to enroll in every activity within a ten-mile radius by the time Junior is one year old. Keep it simple in the beginning and add a class when you feel your child is ready.

BEFORE YOU ENROLL IN ANY CLASS MAKE SURE TO ASK THE FOLLOWING:

- Can I take a trial class? Most of the places listed here will let you try out a class free of charge before you spend the money and make a commitment. This is a great way to see if you and your child will enjoy the experience. Remember, there can be a period of adjustment. Kelli's son didn't warm up to Little Gym until his fourth class, and now he can't wait to get there. Be patient. If you feel the instructors and the environment will be beneficial to the development of your little one then just ride with it.

- What is the sick policy? Will they allow me to make up a class if my child is sick or out of town?

- The time of day and location can be crucial. Most of our children respond best when they have a nap and a snack. Before enrolling, think about the child's schedule and fit the class around it, not the other way around.

THE ARTS

ART-A-RAMA
1610 Avenue J
Plano 75074
972-423-4554

7158 Main Street
Frisco 75034
972-377-9900

www.art-a-rama.com
Ages: 2 years to adult

Your child can enjoy a hands-on experience in a variety of art mediums at Art-A-Rama. Classes are designed for little artists as young as age two up until they are five. Art-a-Rama was voted by *Dallas Observer* readers as "Best Art Classes for Kids" in 2003. Younger children will strengthen their fine motor skills by experimenting with the wonderful world of Play-Doh, while older kids dabble with watercolors and charcoals and develop their inner artist.

Tuition: Monthly tuition is $75, plus a one-time $25 registration fee. They offer discounts if you sign up for one year's, six months', or three months' worth of classes. If you get another child to sign up, you receive two weeks' free tuition the next session.

Artysmarties
4915 West Lovers Lane
Dallas 75209
214-352-0747
Ages: 4 to 10 years

Barbe Cree has created a program that our friends and their children rave about! Artysmarties is unique in that kids work at their own pace and create whatever their heart desires. It's an open space divided into twelve stations consisting of wood working, jewelry making, sewing, music, drama, clay, painting, and drawing. If one week your child wants to make a necklace and the next week is in the mood to paint, she is not "restricted" to a teacher's plan. This freedom is meant to raise a child's self-confidence and heighten the imagination.

Tuition: The fall schedule is sixteen weeks and costs $400, the spring semester is twenty weeks and costs $500. All supplies and materials are provided.

Artzy Smartzy
8440 Abrams Road at Royal Lane
Dallas 75243
214-341-0053
www.artzysmartzy.com
Ages: 2 years to adult

Owner, artist, native Texan, and SMU grad Debbie Alspaw opened Artzy Smartzy to create a casual and encouraging environment for children to discover their creativity. The littlest artists can start off in the Mommy & Me class (two to five years) and begin to explore different mediums such as drawing, painting, and playing with clay. As kids become older, they move up and begin to learn techniques and create masterpieces!

Tuition: Twenty weeks of instruction (one class per week) is $275 for a one-hour class and $335 for a one-and-a-half-hour class. There is an installment plan where you can pay in two payments and they offer a 10 percent discount if tuition is paid in full before the start of the class session.

Capers for Kids
12306 Park Central Drive
Dallas 75251
972-661-ARTS
www.capersforkids.com
Ages: 3 to 18 years

This special school, founded in 1978, specializes in children's creative art and drama classes. The specially designed studio includes props, costumes, and controls for music and lights which the children operate. Preschool classes include Creative Drama and Visual Arts (children must be toilet trained). Older kids study painting and sculpture or they can take a musical theatre class.

Tuition: There is an annual registration fee of $30. Classes are held once a week for two hours. Sixteen weeks of classes are $400 and eighteen weeks of classes are $450. Missed classes cannot be made up or refunded.

Creative Arts Theatre and School (CATS)
1100 West Randol Mill Road
Arlington 76012
817-265-8512
www.creativearts.org
Ages: 4 to 18 years

Creative Arts Theatre and School (CATS), which has been around since 1977, is the only youth theatre in the Dallas-Fort Worth area where the students perform in front of their peers and also run the lights, sound, and crew. Four- to five-year-olds participate in Creative Drama, which focuses on imaginative play, creating characters, acting out stories, and using pantomime to stimulate body awareness. Older children can take classes such as Acting, Musical Theatre, Technical Theatre, Ballet, Tap, Jazz, and Modern Dance.

Tuition: From $50 a month to $130 per month, depending on how many hours of classes your child participates in per week. There is a $30 nonrefundable registration fee for first-time students.

Dallas Children's Theatre—The Rosewood Center for the Arts
5938 Skillman
Dallas 75231
214-978-0010
www.DCT.org
Ages: 3 years and older

If you have a child who has a flair for drama (and what child doesn't?), then consider enrolling him in a Dallas Children's Theatre class. Children as young as three can channel their energy into becoming a dinosaur or acting out their favorite fairy tale. All classes are taught by DCT professionals and run through the summer. Prices are reasonable and the staff is friendly. The Dallas Children's Theatre is a staple in our art community and with a new location, the Rosewood Center for the Arts, it continues to provide fun for the entire family. Be sure to inquire about their family-oriented performances (Please see chapter 17, Indoor and Outdoor Activities)

Dallas Museum of Art
1717 North Harwood Street
Dallas 75201
214-922-1200
www.dallasmuseumofart.org
Ages: 3 years to adult

The Dallas Museum of Art is not just a great place to check out beautiful pieces of art, they also offer classes for children three to twelve years of age and their families. A sampling of activities offered are late nights at the museum for families and kids to enjoy special performances or storytelling (kids can even come in their pajamas), drop-in art (free hands-on art activities for children), summer art camps, workshops for kids, and art exploration classes for three- to five-year-olds accompanied by a grownup. Registration is required and spaces are limited. Prices vary per class and event.

Fort Worth Museum of Science and History

1501 Montgomery Street
Fort Worth 76107
817-255-9300 or 888-255-9300
www.fortworthmuseum.org
Ages: 3 to 5 years and 1st through 5th grade

Housing a planetarium, state-of-the-art theatre, and interactive exhibits, this is a great place for children to learn about the world around them. From September to May, children study age-appropriate lessons in history, art, music, literature, and natural and physical sciences. The Museum School has become a national model for other programs. Classes meet once a week, and children must be toilet trained to participate.

Tuition: The year-long program costs $550.

Lakewood Arts Academy

1911 Abrams Parkway
Dallas 75214
214-827-1222
www.lakewoodarts.com
Ages: 2 years to adult

Classes, such as "Art Classes for Boys," "The Art of Cartooning," and "Mommy or Daddy & Me" have given Lakewood Arts its well deserved reputation as being a cutting edge and nurturing environment for children to become hooked on art. The Mommy or Daddy & Me class starts when the child is two years of age, and during each hour-long class, you will help your child create projects like clay portraits and mosaic flower panels. You might even discover that you have a flair for art!

Tuition: Fall sessions are sixteen weeks and cost $335 for a one-and-a-half-hour class and $445 for a two-hour class. The spring session is nineteen weeks of instruction and $410 for a one-and-a-half-hour class and $510 for a two-hour class. A 5 percent discount is offered if tuition is prepaid in advance. Summer classes and camps are also offered.

Pigment School of the Arts

4410 West Lovers Lane
Dallas 75209
214-352-ARTS
www.pigmentarts.com
Ages: 3 to 13 years

Director Tori Webb Pendergrass has created an art school that our friends and others are raving about. Children ages three to thirteen learn self-discovery while being challenged to explore and study their environment through art instruction. Innovative classes such as "Samurais to Sushi" let older children study Japanese life and art and conclude with a traditional Japanese tea ceremony. Young children can enjoy "Shimmering Stars" to gain a better understanding of their place in the environment while creating things with clay and papier-mâché.

Tuition: During the fall, classes run for fifteen weeks and cost $300. In the spring, classes last for twenty weeks and cost $400. Each class session lasts for an hour and a half.

The Purple Crayon

1108 West Parker, Suite 130
Plano 75075
972-516-4915
www.thepurplecrayon.org
Ages: 2 years to adult

An arts studio for kids as young as two years, the Purple Crayon helps your child gain self-confidence through ceramics or art classes that also teach drawing, painting, and sculpting. Their program is a great way to develop your child's hand-eye coordination, concentration, creativity, and skills. We have had many of our friends tell us that this is a great place.

Tuition: Art tuition is $65 per month and ceramics is $70 per month. There is a quarterly supply fee of $25.

Storybook Children's Theatre

4101 East Park Boulevard, Suite 160
Plano 75074
972-516-1653
www.dancedepot.net
Ages: 3 to 18 years

Owner Mary Ann Morrow has joined her love of dance and theatre and created a 2,500-square-foot studio to teach children both of these arts. Dance is taught through Dance Depot (see p.224) and drama is taught at Storybook Children's Theatre. Little ones, ages three to five years, are introduced to acting at preschool drama. The children act out different stories each week, using pantomime, improvisation, and their imaginations. Fairy Tale Theatre, for kindergarten to second graders, is similar to preschool drama but empowers children by giving them more individual responsibility. As children get older, they begin to work on plays for production. Past productions have included Jack and the Beanstalk and the Magical Land of Oz.

Tuition: Prices start at $50 per month/one class per week and go up to $155 per month/five classes a week. Sibling discounts are offered.

Van Grow: Studio for the Arts
3434 West 7th Street
Fort Worth 76107
817-348-0505
www.vangrowstudio.com
Ages: 2 to 18 years

Husband and wife Maarten and Hanna Vanderstoel have lovingly taught children about the world of art since buying Van Grow in 2002. Hanna has a fine arts degree and Maarten is an artist, so you know your child will be in talented hands. Their Mommy & Me classes (ages two to four years) are one hour, once a week, and offered in the morning or the evening four days a week. Children work on different projects every week and experience clay, stamps, and collage, and learn shapes, numbers, letters, and more.

Tuition: Registration is $20 and classes cost $55 per month. If you need to skip a month you can just pick up and take classes the following month. Call for registration.

COMPUTERS

High Tech Kids, Inc./The Science Place
4411 NorthPark Center
Dallas 75224
214-696-5437 or 866-230-5437
www.htku.com
Ages: 3 to 12 years

Sponsored by The Science Place, HTK teaches your child digital media, paleontology, Web design, and Lego robotics. Classes begin for children aged three and up and last thirty to forty-five minutes. Who knows, your little one may become the next Bill Gates after taking a class at High Tech Kids, Inc.

Tuition: Price for the preschool program is $14.95 an hour.

DANCE

Arabesque Studio of Dance
176 Spring Creek Village
Dallas 75248
972-233-2532
Ages: 2 years to adult

Boys and girls from twenty-four to thirty-six months will sing, tumble, and dance in the Creative Movement class. These classes are small for lots of individual attention. Kids will improve their stamina, coordination, imagination, and self-esteem and will learn to share and take instruction. Classes are offered Monday through Saturday at various times; they fill up quickly so don't put off registration until the last minute.

Tuition: The fall semester is eighteen weeks and costs $193; the spring semester is twenty weeks and costs $214. There are additional costs for a dance concert in May.

Carter Dance Academy
6333 East Mockingbird Lane, Suite 270
Dallas 75214
214-823-8933
Ages: 2½ years to adult

Owner Jana Carter's experience and love for dance led her to create a studio that many of our friends adore. The academy is a nurturing place for children to learn to dance, a contrast to many traditional dance studios. Children as young as two and a half can begin with ballet and tumbling. Carter Dance Academy offers a variety of classes beyond ballet such as jazz, hip-hop, Irish step dancing, and cheer tumble.

Tuition: Tuition varies depending on the time of year, but, for example, during the fall, tuition works out to $55 per month plus additional fees for a recital.

Chamberlain School of Ballet
3003 West 15th Street
Plano 75075
972-985-1374
www.chamberlainschoolofballet.com
Ages: 3 years to adult

Since 1977, founder and director Kathy Chamberlain has been teaching children to dance. The Chamberlain School of Ballet begins teaching little ones in a Creative Movement class (ages three to five years) and Pre-Ballet beginning at age four. The Creative Movement class teaches younger children about taking turns, sharing the attention of the instructors, and developing friendships.

Tuition: Monthly tuition for Creative Movement and Pre-Ballet is $50 per month, and a discount is offered if tuition is paid in full. There is also a $25 nonrefundable registration fee. Classes meet once a week.

Cherrilane School of Dance
1902 Abrams Parkway
Dallas 75214
214-821-2066
Ages: 3½ years and up

Nestled in Lakewood, Cherrilane School of Dance has been teaching little feet to dance for over twenty years. They have five programs that help students progress from infant to preprofessional. The predance class teaches both tap and ballet and is designed for children three and a half years to nine years old.

Tuition: Predance is a forty-five-minute class held once à week, and it costs $55 per month. A $35 nonrefundable registration fee is required.

Dance Depot
4101 East Park Boulevard, Suite 160
Plano 75074
972-516-1653
www.dancedepot.net
Ages: 3 years to adult

Owner Mary Ann Morrow was a theatre arts teacher in the Plano ISD for more than thirteen years and has lots of experience when it comes to teaching dance to children. Dance Depot offers traditional dance classes such as ballet, tap, and jazz, and then there are more unusual choices like hip-hop, traditional Mexican dance, and musical dance theatre. Creative Movement, a combination ballet and tap class, uses creative imagery and exercises to learn basic skills and is offered to students ages three to four years. These students must be out of diapers and have reached their third birthday by the beginning of the school year. Dance Depot is part of Storybook Children's Theatre, where children take drama classes (see p. 222). Tuition: Prices start at $50 per month/one class per week and go to $155 per month/five classes a week. Sibling discounts are offered.

Dancing Angels Ministry
P.O. Box 180837
Dallas 75218
214-712-6914
For further information: dancingangels@att.net
Ages: 18 months to 10 years

Director Tammy Owens, a longtime ballet, tap, and jazz student and performer, founded Dancing Angels to teach the gift of dance through God's eyes. Sawyer and her friends have enjoyed her instruction and love the summer camps. Tammy has Mommy & Me classes starting at eighteen months. Classes are held at various local churches such as Park Cities Baptist Church and Lovers Lane United Methodist Church. Ballerina birthday parties are also available.

Tuition: Classes meet once a week and cost approximately $40 per month.

Gotta Dance

3131 Custer Road, Suite 195
Plano 75075
972-769-0017
www.gottadanceplano.com
Ages: 3 years to adult

Plano's Gotta Dance offers a combination preballet/tap class (ages three to five years) as an introduction to dance and its magic. This studio is also home to the Plano Metropolitan Ballet, a nonprofit organization that gives dancers ages nine to eighteen years a chance to become more serious about dance.

Tuition: There is an annual registration fee of $30 and the cost is $48 per month for the preballet/tap combo class. A discount is offered if tuition is paid early.

Preston Center Dance

6162 Sherry Lane
Dallas 75225
214-739-1737
www.pcdance.net
Ages: 3 years to adult

Co-owners Densil Adams and Janis Rosenthal's school of dance is a professional and fun place to start your child in dance. Introduction to ballet is more than ballet—they sing, work on rhythm, and focus on the very basic and fundamental positions. Parents don't get to watch the class, but there is a parent visitation day. The recitals are for the older ones. Preston Center Dance offers preballet and preballet/tumbling classes for children who are at least age three, complete with a dress code: ballet slippers, leotard, and footless tights. They offer yoga, which is great for Mom while your child is having her class. Classes are offered year-round.

Tuition: Payments are made on a quarterly basis and vary per class.

Southlake Dance Academy

409 North Carroll Avenue
Southlake 76092
817-251-1849
www.southlakedanceacademy.com
Ages: 3 years to adult

Southlake's Dance Academy is a fun, light-hearted, and professional school for dancers of all ages. Three-year-olds will love the variety of fun in the Ballet, Tap & Jazz Class. Students will work on ballet, tap, and tumbling skills each for twenty minutes. A pink leotard, ballet slippers, and tap shoes are required. The academy offers ballet, tap, and jazz classes up to age thirteen, and adults will enjoy tap, jazz, or hip-hop.

Tuition: There is a $25 registration fee for each child. The fifty-minute class is $50. There are extra fees for the end-of-year recital and costumes.

GYM

Gymboree Play and Music

9723 North Central Expressway
Dallas 75230
214-341-2386

3261 Independence Parkway
Plano 75075
214-341-2386

420 East Round Grove Road, Suite 610
Lewisville 75067
972-459-0934

1639 Northwest Highway
Grapevine 76051
817-424-3932

8700 Main Street, Bldg. B, Suite 200
Frisco 75034
214-387-9106

3043 South Cooper Street
Arlington 76015
817-419-3512

www.gymboree.com
Ages: newborn to 5 years

Known for their specially designed play classes, newborns to children age five can take part in a Gymboree Play and Music class. As children become more physically and developmentally sophisticated, they learn more advanced skills that help their self-esteem and further develop motor skills. It's also a great way to learn socialization skills. Classes last forty-five minutes. Gymboree Play and Music is operated as a franchise, so prices vary location to location. Check the Web site to find the class nearest you, the pricing and policies, and to sign up for a free trial class.

Gym Kids Sports Center
510 Parker Square
Flower Mound 75028
972-355-9988
Ages: 6 months and older

Gym Kids classes are fun and filled with energy. Parent and child classes begin at six months and there are also classes for two-and-a-half-year-olds. This state-of-the-art facility has a large waiting area with chairs for parents to watch their child in action. There is also a play area to keep siblings entertained.

Tuition: A full semester (five months) of classes is $285 per child. There is a small discount for siblings. Classes can also be purchased per "term" (anywhere from six to seven weeks) for $105 for the first child. Makeup classes are offered as long as tuition is current.

My Gym Children's Fitness Center
Bardin Place Shopping Center
4654 South Cooper Street
Arlington 76017
817-937-5552

3241 Preston Road, Suite 1
Frisco 75034
972-378-9000

910 West Parker Road, Suite 108
Plano 75075
972-578-6630

www.my-gym.com
Ages: 3 months to 9 years

My Gym Children's Fitness Center is a nationwide franchise with top quality equipment in a clean and cheerful atmosphere. In the lobby, parents and caregivers can watch their children, and many locations have a play area for those not in class. There are parent participation classes (if you have a child from three months to three and a half years), and "independent" classes (for kids between three and a half years to nine years of age). The gym's floor space is rearranged each week to keep kids challenged and stimulated.

Tuition: The cost varies from gym to gym depending on the season and age. Prices range from $135 to $160 for a ten-week session. Since each gym is independently owned, make sure to call or check the Web site for current pricing and sibling discounts.

The Little Gym

204 South Central Expressway, Suite 43
Allen 75013
972-396-7705

740 Southwest Green Oaks Boulevard, Suite 202
Arlington 76017
817-465-9296

2662 Josey Lane, Suite 229
Carrollton 75007
972-446-1122

6441 East Mockingbird Lane, Suite 410
Dallas 75214
214-515-0800

11919 Preston Road at Forest
Dallas 75230
972-644-7333

6295 Granbury
Fort Worth 76133
817-346-9655

4017 Preston Road, Suite 522
Plano 75093
972-985-4545

Multiple locations
www.thelittlegym.com
Ages: 4 months to 12 years

We love the Little Gym! Our children have been mesmerized by its music, activities, bubbles, and especially Mr. Joel. It is a highlight of the week and routine to the kids. Little Gym classes begin with caregiver/child classes (forty-five minutes) to develop a child's social and motor skills. At three years, they "graduate" to the one-hour classes (without an adult) to expand and fine tune more sophisticated skills. Gymnastics and karate are also offered for children (six to twelve years old). Their holiday and summer camps (for ages three and up) are very popular. It is a franchise, so we can't speak for all of the locations, but if they are anything like the locations we have been to, your child will have a blast.

Tuition: Because each location is independently operated, prices vary.

WOGA

6859 Arapaho Road
Dallas 75248
972-866-9642
www.woga.net

The fun never ends at WOGA. Little ones (walking to three years) and parents can work on basic motor skills through play. And three-year-olds will start with the fundamentals of gymnastics and practice their skills on the balance beam, vault, trampoline, and more. Classes are also offered to four- and five-year-olds and on, up to nine. There are free trials, but once you meet the friendly staff and see their love of what they do, parents and kids return every semester and even form their own group for a private class! Choose from one to two classes a week, and don't worry if you forget your leotard—their small apparel shop has adorable gym wear.

Tuition: One class a week for Cubs and Ducklings is $56 per month or $96 for two classes. Chipmunks are $68 for one class per month or $125 for two. There is an annual registration fee of $30 per child.

ICE SKATING

Americas Ice Garden

Plaza of the Americas
700 North Pearl Street at San Jacinto
Dallas 75201
214-720-8080
www.icesk8aig.com
Ages: 2½ to adult

Children as young as two and a half can learn to skate, the proper way to fall down, how to march in place and glide on the ice. Lessons are thirty minutes and include free skate rental and three-hour parking validation. Hockey lessons begin for four-year-old children who have passed previous ice skating requirements. At the time we were going to press, they were talking about adding a Mommy & Me skating class, so check back for more information.

Tuition: $90 for an eight-week session and reenrollment discounts are offered.

Dr Pepper StarCenter

2601 Avenue of the Stars
Frisco 75034
214-387-5600

4020 West Plano Parkway
Plano 75093
972-758-7528

12700 North Stemmons Freeway
Farmers Branch 75063
214-432-3131

1700 South Main Street
Duncanville 75137
972-283-9133

1400 South Pipeline
Euless 76040
817-267-4233

211 Cowboys Parkway
Irving 75063
972-831-2453

www.drpepperstarcenter.com
Ages: 3 years to adult

Do your kids want to learn to ice skate or to play hockey? At the Dr Pepper StarCenter they can. Lessons begin for three-year-olds to familiarize them with the ice and basic techniques. Ice hockey starts for four-year-olds, teaching kids to skate, the fundamentals, and opportunities to "play."

Tuition: Tuition varies at each location.

KARATE

Chamberlain Studios of Self-Defense
2739 Bachman Drive
Dallas 75220
214-351-5367
www.dallaskenpo.com
Ages: 4 years to adult

Dr. Nick Chamberlain (an 8th Degree Black Belt) has created a unique karate program which features Three Steps to a Great Kid. This is a martial arts character development program that incorporates respect for instructors and peers—a lifelong lesson. The program is taught at many of the well respected schools in the area, such as Hockaday, St. Mark's, Greenhill, and ESD. Karate is not only terrific exercise for children, but it builds confidence and allows kids to set and reach obtainable goals. Call for class locations.

Fee: One class a week is $70 per month; two classes a week is $120 a month; and $170 is for unlimited classes for the month. They also offer private instruction.

MUSIC

Dallas Music
3415 Milton
Dallas 75205
214-363-4980
Ages: 3 months and older

One of the first classes Sawyer and Joshua took was the Music, Mommy & Me class (ages three months to eighteen months) at Dallas Music, located in Snider Plaza in University Park. Children enjoy singing, movement, and "playing" instruments. Our kids still get excited when they see jingle bells or hear one of the songs they learned there. Dallas Music has a thirty-minute class for kids ages three months to three and a half years. They also offer Kinder Keys for kindergarten children (age five). Private lessons for piano, violin, guitar, and Suzuki flute are offered for older children.

Tuition: A ten-week session starts at $150. Makeup sessions are allowed.

East Dallas Children's Music
Classes held at First United Lutheran Church
6202 East Mockingbird
Dallas 75214
214-324-2224
www.eastdallaschildrensmusic.com
Ages: newborn to 9 years

These classes are based on the Musikgarten principles, which promote a child's love of music while developing his self-esteem and cognitive skills. Class sizes are intimate with only six to twelve children per class. Family Music for Babies (newborn to sixteen months) involves parents in activities such as singing, peek-a-boo, and musical instruments. Family Music for Toddlers is a similar format, but with more age-appropriate exploration.

Tuition: One class a week for fifteen weeks is $150-$160 for children newborn to three and a half years old. There is also a minimal registration fee that includes a songbook, a CD, and a music gift.

Gymboree Play and Music
9723 North Central Expressway
Dallas 75230
214-341-2386

3261 Independence Parkway
Plano 75075
214-341-2386

420 East Round Grove Road, Suite 610
Lewisville 75067
972-459-0934

1639 Northwest Highway
Grapevine 76051
817-424-3932

8700 Main Street, Bldg. B, Suite 200
Frisco 75034
214-387-9106

3043 South Cooper Street
Arlington 76015
817-419-3512

Multiple locations
www.gymboree.com
Ages: 6 months to 5 years

Let your child explore the world of music through a variety of dances, games, and instruments. Quarter Notes, Half Notes, and Whole Notes are classes for kids six months to five years of age. Their imaginations and skills will grow and before you know it, their babbling might become a song!

Tuition: Since Gymboree Play and Music operates as a franchise, check the Web site or call the location nearest you for pricing and policies.

Kindermusik
Dallas/Park Cities
214-363-6542

Dallas/Lakewood
214-680-7464

Coppell, Flower Mound, Las Colinas and Southlake
972-401-0150

Carrollton
972-292-3626

Plano/Stonebriar Mall area
972-712-8359

Frisco
972-262-6534

Grand Prairie
972-262-6534

Plano
972-596-4742

800-628-5687
www.kindermusik.com
Ages: newborn to 7 years

Kindermusik is dedicated to teaching children about the world around them through dance, music, and imagination. The program has been around for over twenty-five years and is geared toward newborns to seven-year-olds. Parents participate with children in the newborn to age three classes. After age three, kids venture into more independent stylized classes. Kindermusik helps children with language, literacy, peer play, and movement, in a unique way that will give them a love for music that will last throughout their lives. Kim and Ford couldn't get enough of this fun and unique method of music. Kindermusik independently trains their teachers and provides them with the tools to instruct their own classes. Classes run forty-five minutes for children up to the age of five and then are sixty to seventy-five minutes.

Tuition: Prices range around $200-$275 for sixteen classes, depending on the age of your child. Makeup classes are not guaranteed.

Music Together of Dallas, Inc.
972-960-1975
Locations in Plano, Frisco, North Dallas, Richardson, Preston Hollow/Northpark, and at Southern Methodist University.
www.musictogetherdallas.com
Ages: newborn to 5 years

Unlike most music programs, Music Together does not divide children into classes based on their ages. Their focus is on adult/child interaction, and they encourage the younger children to see what the older children are doing. Classes are forty-five minutes long and appropriate for newborns to five-year-olds. If your child loves music, singing, dancing, and musical instruments, he or she will be sure to have a great time. Kim's daughter still sings the songs—along with the CD or not! Children are entitled to three makeup classes per session (two in the summer), and other grown-ups, such as visiting grandparents, are welcome to attend classes.

Tuition: Between $140 and $180, depending on whether you register for spring, fall, or summer (each season offers a different number of classes), and returning families receive a small price break. They offer sibling discounts. A songbook and a CD of the music used during the semester are included in the tuition.

TCU Early Childhood Music Program
Texas Christian University School of Music
Ed Landreth Hall
Fort Worth 76129
817-257-6134
www.music.tcu.edu/early_childhood.asp
Ages: newborn to 7 years

TCU's Early Childhood Music Program "teaches children to sing in tune and keep a steady beat—preparation for learning an instrument when they are older," says coordinator Jennifer Heavyside. The Mommy & Me classes for children newborn to three years old meet once a week for thirty minutes. Preschool music (for children two and a half to four and a half) is forty-five minutes of movement, stories, and instrument play for toddlers. Music Makers (for ages four to seven) is sixty minutes of vocal play, creative movement, and dramatization with music. All classes are taught by two teachers and are limited to ten students. TCU offers classes from 9 a.m. to 7 p.m., Monday through Friday, and on Saturday mornings. It's a great opportunity for parents who work to take a class with their little ones.

Tuition: Sixteen classes, including materials, cost between $200 and $280.

SWIM

Baby Bear-a-Cudas at Baylor Fitness Center
411 North Washington
Dallas 75246
214-820-7870
www.baylortomlandryfitnesscenter.com
Ages: 6 months to 36 months

Both parents and children get wet at Baby Bear-a-Cudas. Several of our friends have given this swim program their stamp of approval. Teachers Yvette Carson and Rachel Johnson, both mothers, are advocates of early introduction into the water, and they are sympathetic to the obstacles you and your child may face.

Tuition: $40 per session for Baylor Tom Landry Fitness Center members and $60 for nonmembers. Sessions consist of three fifty-minute classes.

Dolfin Swim School
Owner: Linda DeSanders
214-361-4542
www.dolfinswimschool.com
Ages: 3 months to 12 years

The "Baby Dolfin" (three months to two and a half years) classes are parent/child classes; when your child is comfortable in the water, he will learn strokes, diving, and breath control. Kelli signed up Joshua for these classes; before Ms. Rebecca, he would cling to Kelli in sheer terror when entering a pool. He now swims to the bottom of the pool and jumps off the side after only six days. Classes are conducted at the private residence of swim school parents and during the summer and throughout the rest of the year at an indoor pool. Makeup lessons are only given for school cancellations due to threatening weather conditions.

Tuition: $168 per session for the first child; the second registered child is $152. Registration is only done by mail. Additional sessions are $148 per session.

Emler Swim School

2201 Lavern Street
Arlington 76013
817-275-7946

6125 Colleyville Boulevard
Colleyville 76034
817-481-7946

4621 West Park Boulevard, Suite 104
Plano 75039
972-599-7946

www.iswimemler.com
Ages: 6 months to 8 years and older

Emler Swim School teaches children to swim in a fun, nonthreatening environment. Water Acclimation (ages six months to thirty-five months) uses parent participation to introduce children to underwater submersion. Waterbaby classes (six months to two years) involve parents in games, songs, and teaching their little ones underwater breath control. Emler has its own indoor pool facilities, making it convenient for swim lessons all year.

Tuition: One class a week for ten weeks is $154; one class a week for eleven weeks is $159.50; one class every day for two weeks is $155. There is a $25 annual registration fee.

Fish Factory Swim School at Baylor Fitness Center

411 North Washington
Dallas 75246
214-820-7870
www.baylortomlandryfitnesscenter.com
Ages: 3 years and older

This class is suited for toddlers who have had some swimming experience. Classes are conducted in a group setting in one of the two heated indoor pools. The teacher/student ratio is low.

Tuition: $80 for Baylor Tom Landry Fitness Center members and $100 for nonmembers.

Infant Aquatics

Dallas/Bev Steinfink: 214-890-7946
Frisco/Richard Wescott: 972-712-5704
Ages: 6 months to 6 years
www.infantaquatics.com

"Survival Swimming" is the premise of this highly praised swim program. Lessons are one-on-one and babies as young as six months can begin to learn how to swim. This program is more than children learning how to do the breaststroke. Infant Aquatics teaches infants what to do if they were to fall into the water, thus providing a foundation to learn more advanced swim techniques. Classes meet four days a week for as long as it takes a child to master the skills, usually sixteen to twenty-four lessons.

Tuition: This is not a "typical" swim program. The price varies because your child continues taking classes until he or she has mastered the skills. Plan on budgeting approximately $300 for this class.

Parent & Tots Swim Class at Premier Club

Premier Athletic Club
5910 North Central Expressway
Dallas 75206
214-891-6619
Ages: 6 months to 2 years

For over eight years, Rachel Logan has been teaching little ones how to hold their breath under water, survival techniques, and strokes—all instruction age appropriate and individualized to fit your child. By taking a class once a week, you can begin to build your child's confidence around water. Sawyer has enjoyed playtime and singing songs with Miss Rachel while mastering her skills. Private or group classes are also available with Peron Jones.

Tuition: $10 per child per class. Private instruction is available for children and adults.

Swim Kids Swim School

510 Parker Square
Flower Mound 75028
972-355-9988
Ages: 1 to 10 years and older

Sing and play games while introducing your infant to the water with Swim Kids Swim School. Youngsters learn to float and breathe, gentle underwater submersion, and survival skills—in a low-pressure environment. As your child gets older, he learns more advanced techniques, but with the same attention to fun and respect for his comfort level. This swim school is part of Gym Kids and the pool is located next door at The Health and Athletic Center in Flower Mound.

Tuition: $72 for a six-week session or $195 per semester. There is an annual registration fee of $30 for non-Gym Kids members.

Swimmers by Jessica

Instructor: Jessica Kramer
214-360-9037
swimmersbyjessica@hotmail.com

For over eighteen years, Jessica Kramer, a local mom of two daughters, has been teaching children swimming during the summer. Water safety basics and stroke form are taught to the small groups of kids. Jessica and her close friend Adrienne, who has taught with her for over twelve years, love kids and teach ages two and a half to ten. Parents have been known to wait over two hours in line to sign their child up for a session (two consecutive weeks, forty-five minutes a day). Parents are not allowed to stay and watch. Ask about the art classes available after selected class sessions. Jessica was coowner of Kids Next Door, a clothing boutique for kids, and now offers yummy pajamas on her Web site www.kidcrazy.biz (see chapter 7, Kid Style). Kim's daughter Sawyer would go to bed each night and wake up in the morning asking not only about swimming but about when she could see Ms. Jessica and Ms. Adrienne—they have a special touch, and Sawyer now goes under with confidence and finds her way to the side—an amazing feat for a little girl who was once terrified of the pool.

Tuition: Camps cost $160 and art camp is $10 per class.

YOGA

Let's Play Yoga

972-618-3079
www.letsplayyoga.com
Ages: 2 to 6 years

Karen Prior is the creator of this unique yoga program for children. Her goal is for children to develop a love for yoga that they will carry into their adult lives. Instructors use music, games, puppets, and storytelling to challenge children while helping them to develop the fundamental skills for yoga. Unlike adult yoga classes, these are animated and noisy, so there is no need to worry if your child doesn't yet know how to find his or her inner peace. Classes are taught at Natural Trends, Oak Point Recreation Center in Plano, and Joe Farmer Recreation Center in Allen. Check the Web site for current class locations and prices.

Mommy & Me Yoga at Bend Studio

5014 McKinney Avenue
Dallas 75205
214-841-9642
www.bendstudio.com
Ages: 5 years and younger

Mara Black incorporates her twenty-nine years of experience as a doula and working in children's education to teach Mommy & Me yoga at this uptown studio.

Fees: Prices range from a $15 drop-in fee to a yearly membership for $1,350.

Mommy & Me Yoga at Dallas Yoga Center

4525 Lemmon Avenue, Suite 305
Dallas 75219
214-443-9642
www.dallasyogacenter.com
Ages: 6 to 20 months

Serving Dallas for the past fifteen years, Dallas Yoga Center is owned by David Sunshine and offers Mommy & Me yoga classes for mothers and infants. Babies help their moms to strengthen and tone their body by serving as resistance; basic infant massage and baby yoga are also introduced.

Fees: The eight-week Mommy & Me series is $108.

Sunstone Yoga

11661 Preston Road, Suite 206
214-373-7999
www.sunstoneyoga.com
Ages: 4 to 8 years

Jennifer Chitwood teaches children many of the same yoga principles adults learn, but she tailors it for little ones. Jennifer incorporates storytelling and games into teaching children yoga poses and how each pose benefits their body. She also introduces mediation to the kids, and discusses nutrition and anatomy. Our friends, who have kids taking this class, rave about Jennifer!

Fees: Classes cost $115 for an eight week session.

YMCA Downtown Dallas

601 North Akard Street
Dallas 75201
214-954-0500
www.downtowndallasymca.org
Ages: 6 weeks to 18 months

Yogababies is a parent and child postnatal fitness class offered to all Dallas-Fort Worth YMCA members. It is open to parents of all fitness levels who have babies between six weeks and eighteen months. New, exhausted, or underactive/overfed parents can get in shape and learn to relax while bonding with their babies.

Fees: Check your local YMCA as prices may vary.

MISCELLANEOUS FUN

Baby Sign Language
Presbyterian Hospital of Dallas
8200 Walnut Hill Lane
Dallas 75231
800-477-3729

Presbyterian Hospital of Plano
6200 West Parker Road
Plano 75093
800-477-3729

www.texashealth.org

Most of us can use help when it comes to communicating with our infant. This one-time class shows parents the basic concepts needed to teach their children sign language. From learning the signs for "more" to "help," Kim found sign language to be a helpful and simple way to increase communication with her children. It is for adults only, but it is recommended that parents take the class when their baby is six to nine months old.

Fee: $35 per couple.

Baby Signs
Harris Methodist Fort Worth Hospital
1301 Pennsylvania Avenue
Fort Worth 76104
888-4-HARRIS
www.texashealth.org

Harris's Baby Signs teaches parents and caregivers how to interact with babies using sign language. The information learned in the two-hour workshop is meant to be brought home and practiced with your infant and can be taught to grandparents and siblings. This class is free; all you have to do is call ahead to register.

Infant Massage

Presbyterian Hospital of Dallas
8200 Walnut Hill Lane
Dallas 75231
800-477-3729
www.texashealth.org
Ages: newborn to 9 months

Anyone who has been around a baby long enough has probably wished at some time or another she knew how to relax and calm an uptight infant. Taught by an infant massage instructor, this class is for parents with babies from newborn to nine months of age. Parents will practice massage and learn about such benefits as helping your baby to sleep, increasing circulation, and helping parents and baby bond.

Fee: $25 per family.

Infant Massage by Monica Hamer

214-642-0242
www.monicahamer.com
Ages: newborn to 3 years

Monica Hamer truly believes in the powerful benefits of massage and specializes in massage for women and infants. She shares her knowledge with other parents through an infant massage class. It not only strengthens the bond between parent and child, but it also helps with sleeping and with reducing colic. This is a great way for adoptive parents to bond with their new baby! Classes are held at Monica's home or the Lover's Lane Birth Center and are limited to four families per session.

Tuition: $135 for three sessions that last between sixty and ninety minutes and are taught by a certified infant massage instructor.

Mis Amigos

3409 Rosedale in Snider Plaza
Dallas 75205
214-265-0981
www.misamigosdallas.com
Ages: 18 months to adult

Mis Amigos, owned and founded by Highland Park mom Mary Meier, is Dallas's newest Spanish language enrichment school. Children as young as eighteen months can join the Mommy or Daddy & Me class. Kids-only classes start when los niños (see, we are already practicing) turn three years old. Mis Amigos introduces Spanish to children through art, music, Spanish culture, and vocabulary acquisition. Classes are fifty minutes with up to twelve children in a class, and the classes meet in the mornings once a week. The afternoons are for children in kindergarten through fourth grade.

Tuition: A semester costs $250-$300, depending on the age of your child. Be sure to ask about their sibling discounts and courses for adults.

Play and Learn

Preston Doctors Center
8215 Westchester, Suite 112
Dallas 75225
214-368-7765

2415 Coit Road, Suite D
Plano 75093
972-596-4949

www.play-and-learn.net
Ages: 10 months to 5 years

Play and Learn helps parents to develop their child's language and cognitive skills through play and social interaction. Play and Learn believes that interaction with familiar loved ones is a child's best teacher and that a shared learning experience bolsters a child's confidence. All classes are taught by a degreed, licensed language specialist who makes learning exciting through age-appropriate experiences. For instance, a ten-month-old may begin to learn basic vocabulary skills with puppets while a four-year-old will use them to learn letter-sound association. Classes are for parents and children ten months through five years.

Tuition: $210 for fourteen one-hour sessions.

CHAPTER SEVENTEEN:
INDOOR AND OUTDOOR ACTIVITIES

Little ones thrive on exploring and engaging in activity, especially if they get to learn interesting things. Take a trip to the farmer's market, the zoo, or the mall—you can't go wrong. We have found that through little adventures, our children have developed so much, and as they have gotten to the toddler years, their language, motor and sequencing skills have flourished. Who knew that gathering twigs and leaves at the Dallas Arboretum would lead to fun art projects and a discussion of how trees grow and change? Even at six months, they love feeling new objects and different textures.

So now that you feel that getting out of the house just might be doable, pack your bag and enjoy yourself. There are so many great places in our area for children to experience the world around them. Let's face it, though, during the summer months many of us can't bear to even walk outdoors in Dallas, so we have also included a list of favorite places to find refuge from the heat. In addition to the local parks, we are fortunate enough to have lots of excellent outdoor options that go beyond the ordinary.

Just don't stray too far from your babe's routine—then nobody will have a good time. With that said, are you ready to experience the world again, but through your child's eyes? It is pretty amazing!

INDOOR ACTIVITIES

Angelika Film Center & Cafe
Mockingbird Station
5321 East Mockingbird
Dallas 75206
214-841-4700 (recorded information)
214-841-4712 (office)

The Shops at Legacy
7205 Bishop Road
Plano 75024
972-444-FILM (recorded information)
972-943-1300 (office)

www.angelikafilmcenter.com

Going to the movies with the baby in tow—seriously? Oh yes, moms (dads are welcome too), each Tuesday at 1:30 p.m., Wednesday at 1:30 p.m., and Saturday morning at 11:00 a.m., the Angelika Film Center presents the "CryBaby Matinee at the Angelika." The lights are dimmed, the sound volume is down, and a baby changing table is provided in the theater. Admission is $5.50, and children under five get in free.

The Dallas Aquarium at Fair Park

1462 First Avenue & MLK Boulevard
Dallas 75226
214-670-8443
www.dallas-zoo.org
Hours: Daily from 9 a.m. to 4:30 p.m.

Get to know thousands of reptiles and aquatic animals at the Dallas Aquarium at Fair Park. It is managed by the Dallas Zoo and while not as impressive or as large as the Dallas World Aquarium, it is less expensive so you don't feel obligated to spend the entire day. Admission is $3 for adults, $1.50 for children three to eleven years, and free for children under three.

Dallas Children's Museum

308 Valley View Center
Dallas 75240
972-386-6555
www.dallaschildrens.org
Hours: Monday-Friday, 9 a.m. to 6 p.m.; Saturday, 11 a.m. to 6 p.m.; Sunday, noon to 6 p.m.

The Dallas Children's Museum is a local jewel! It is 6,500 square feet of climate-controlled fun, including an indoor play and learn center designed to teach children ages two to ten about different cultures, science, imaginary play, creative arts, and so much more. Many of our friends love that their kids get a hands-on look at adult responsibilities, like shopping, as they scan and pay for groceries at the store sponsored by Kroger. There are seasonal events such as summer camps, Spanish classes, and Hands in Hand (a story, art, and playtime that kids, parents, and caregivers enjoy). Admission is $3 for adults, $4 for children two to twelve years of age, free for children under twenty-four months, and $2 for senior citizens.

Dallas Children's Theatre—The Rosewood Center for the Arts

5938 Skillman
Dallas 75231
214-740-0051 (Box office)
www.DCT.org
Performance Times are Fridays, 7:30 p.m.; Saturdays, 1:30 p.m.; Sundays, 1:30 p.m. and 4:30 p.m.

If you can't wait to introduce your child to the theatre, then don't skip the Dallas Children's Theatre. The the-atre is a staple in our art community and with a new location, the Rosewood Center for the Arts, it continues to provide fun for the entire family. Performances for the 2004/2005 season will include *Stuart Little*, *If You Give a Mouse a Cookie*, *To Kill a Mockingbird* and *The Velveteen Rabbit*. If you are unsure whether your child is age-appropriate for a particular play, check the Web site, which lets you know the ages for which the play is intended. Tickets are $13 for children and $15 for adults. DCT also offers classes for children (Please see p.213).

Dallas Museum of Art

1717 North Harwood
Dallas 75201
214-922-1200
www.dallasmuseumofart.org
Hours: Tuesday-Sunday, 11 a.m. to 5 p.m.; Thursday, 11 a.m. to 9 p.m.

This is one of our all-time favorites, not only because we are art fans, but because our children get a breath of culture and a vision that anything is possible. The DMA is a family-friendly venue for strolling with your tiny infant, or for year-round activities from bedtime stories to concerts on the grounds to art and family days. There are many things to do with the kiddos and the DMA Web site is a great place to keep up with all the activities and events. Be sure to visit the Gateway Galleries, where children and adults can explore hands-on art activities. We have friends who come here every weekend with their three babes and discover something new each time.

Dallas Museum of Natural History

3535 Grand Avenue in Fair Park
Dallas 75210
214-421-3466
www.dallasdino.org
Hours: Monday-Saturday, 10 a.m. to 5 p.m.; Sunday, noon to 5 p.m.; Closed on Thanksgiving Day, Christmas Day, and New Year's Day

With 200,000 items housed within 45,000 square feet, we could never tire of the Dallas Museum of Natu-ral History. The live animal room contains an ever-changing variety of animals, including mammals, reptiles, amphibians, fish, and insects. Dioramas of birds, animals of the wetlands, a life-sized robotic dinosaur, and tons of mammals make this both a fun and educational trip. The museum also offers family festivals through-out the year which are jam-packed with entertainment, arts, crafts, games, and live animals. Admission is $7 for adults, $4 for children three to twelve years, and free for children under three.

Dallas Symphony Orchestra

2301 Flora Street
Dallas 75201
214-692-0203
www.dsokids.com

The Dallas Symphony Orchestra's Family Concerts will be sweet music to your family's ears. Seventy-minute intermission-free concerts are for adults and children ages six and up. The DSO chooses unique and creative stories set to music to draw young ones into the performances. Whether it's through dance, getting the kids to help lure an elephant to the concert hall, or by some other creative means, the Family Concerts are a casual and playful way to introduce children to classical music.

The Dallas World Aquarium

1801 North Griffin
Dallas 75202
214-720-2224
www.dwazoo.com
Hours: Daily from 10 a.m. to 5 p.m.

Ever wonder what a howler monkey looks like? What might you see in a rainforest? Get your answers firsthand without leaving Dallas city limits. The Dallas World Aquarium is a multilevel exhibit (making the navigation of a stroller difficult) that houses both aquatic and land creatures from the world over. Visit when you have time to spend because there is so much to see and experience, especially the new shark tunnel. Admission is $15.95 for adults, $8.95 for children three to twelve years, and free for children under two.

Fort Worth Museum of Science and History

1501 Montgomery Street
Fort Worth 76107
817-255-9300
www.fortworthmuseum.org
Hours: Monday-Thursday, 9 a.m. to 5:30 p.m.; Friday and Saturday, 9 a.m. to 8 p.m.; Sunday, 11:30 a.m. to 5:30 p.m.

Where else can your child go fishing, paint daddy's face, learn to use an ATM, perform in a puppet show, dig for dinosaurs, and much more? This is an amazing place to learn, play, and experiment as a family—no matter the age of your little ones. We recommend heading to the hands-on-science KIDSPACE area first and then enjoying a snack at the café. You could really spend a day here if you didn't have to head home for naptime. They even offer a school, summer programs, classes, and birthday parties. Also worth a visit: the Noble Planetarium and the Omni Theater. This is a popular field trip location, so afternoons are your best bet. Nonmember prices for a combination ticket for the museum, theater, and planetarium are $13 for adults and $10 for children and seniors.

Fort Worth Stockyards Championship Rodeo

Cowtown Coliseum
121 East Exchange Avenue
Fort Worth 76106
817-625-1025
www.StockyardsRodeo.com

Bull riding, barrel racing, calf roping, music, and more. These are just some of the exciting events at the Wild West show and rodeo that takes place almost every weekend at the Cowtown Coliseum. This is a show not to be missed and the historic coliseum, built in 1908, is worth a visit. Matinee times are 2:30 p.m. and 4:30 p.m. on Saturday and Sunday. Tickets are $4.50 for children ages three to twelve and adults are $8. Visit their Web site for a printable $1 coupon.

The Livestock Exchange, the location for the world's only daily cattle drive, the Fort Worth Herd, is next door to the Coliseum.

Frontiers of Flight Museum

6911 Lemmon Avenue
Dallas 75209
214-350-3600
www.flightmuseum.com
Hours: Monday-Saturday, 10 a.m. to 5 p.m.; Sunday, 1 p.m. to 5 p.m.

Kids of all ages are fascinated by the wonders of flying, and the Frontiers of Flight Museum doesn't disappoint! They offer a wonderfully safe and clean play area and hold numerous activities for the little ones, including a small theatre (which plays select Jay Jay the Jet Plane videos), a pretend plane complete with a back slide and pilot's seat, and a climbable pretend control tower. Housed in a reconstructed 1950s hanger, the open and fun 100,000-square-foot facility is not for kids only. This is a great adventure for Dad or Grandfather, who will enjoy seeing an Apollo 7 Command Module, vintage uniforms, photos, and restored vintage planes. We have had a ball here and enjoy Pacuigo gelato from the snack bar after climbing aboard the cockpit of a Southwest Airlines 737. Birthday parties and event space are available. Tickets are $8 for adults and $5 for children ages three to seventeen.

Galleria Dallas

I-635 at Dallas North Tollway
Dallas 75001
972-702-7100
www.galleriadallas.com
Hours: Monday-Saturday, 10 a.m. to 9 p.m.; Sunday, noon to 6 p.m.

Texans love to shop. Not surprisingly, there's no shortage of shopping malls in the area. The Galleria Dallas offers some of the finest shopping for adults. Kids know it well for its fabulous ice rink. The holiday decorations are worth the car ride alone—our children continue to ask us where the giant teddy bear is every time we walk through the doors. At press time, major renovations were under way. You'll see the improvements soon, and so will the kids.

Interskate 1 Roller Rink

1408 South Business Highway 121 at I-35E
Lewisville 75067
972-221-4666
www.interskate.net

Roller skating with little ones? Is this a joke? Not at all! Interskate I in Lewisville is a great place to reserve for a private skate time with friends and toddlers in their riding toys (no bicycles please). This place is a blast—and a blast from the past. There is a full-service snack and beverage bar. Don't forget your socks! Two hours of exclusive rink use starts at $295 for up to fifty people. They also have Toddler Skate & Scoot once a week. Call for an updated schedule.

Kimbell Museum of Art

3333 Camp Bowie Boulevard
Fort Worth 76107
817-332-8451
www.kimbellart.org
Hours: Tuesday-Thursday and Saturday, 10 a.m. to 5 p.m.; Friday, noon to 8 p.m.; Sunday, noon to 5 p.m.

From works by Monet to African Art and Egyptian mummy masks, there is something for all to learn, and the Kimbell Museum of Art makes it fun. Upon arrival, stop by the information desk and tell them you'd like to do a treasure hunt. With a brochure, writing board, and map, off you go to discover new things not only about the art itself, but what your child sees and feels about various works and pieces. There are several scheduled events throughout the year, such as the Saturday Family Festival from I p.m. to 4 p.m. with local performers, music, films, and hands-on art activities. If Mom and Grandma want a quiet Friday afternoon, join the Kimbell for the superb adult workshops. The discussion and related art craft is $15. Strollers are not allowed in the exhibition areas during peak times.

Launa's Little Library

9549 Spring Branch
Dallas 75238
214-348-4384
Hours: Tuesday-Thursday, 10:30 a.m. to 5:30 p.m.

Launa's Little Library is a neighborhood children's lending library in the home of founder and supervisor Arthiss Kliever. Known to the kids as Mrs. K, she is a former library specialist at Southern Methodist University and volunteer for the Dallas Public Library. With all of her experience in library work and her special love for children's books, Mrs. K started this brilliant neighborhood treasure back in 2001. At last count, Launa's Little Library carries over four thousand titles including picture books, board books, beginner readers, several Caldecott and Newberry Medal Winners, and over one hundred children's videos. There are library cards and overdue fines just like the public library. Launa's Little Library was written up in *People* magazine in 2004.

Legends of the Game Baseball Museum

Ameriquest Field
1000 Ballpark Way, Suite 400
Arlington 76011
817-273-5600
www.texas.rangers.com
Hours: Game days April-September, 9 a.m. to 7:30 p.m.; on non-game days, hours are Monday-Saturday, 9 a.m. to 4 p.m., and Sundays, 11 a.m. to 4 p.m.; October–March, the museum is open Tuesday-Saturday, 10 a.m. to 4 p.m.

It's impossible not to catch baseball fever at Legends of the Game Baseball Museum. At the museum learning center, both young and old learn about history, math, geography, and physical exercise—all through baseball. Do you have a future big-leaguer in the making? Bring your three- to five-year-old to the monthly story time, which includes a baseball-related preschool story, discussion, crafts, time in the Learning Center and Museum, and visits to different areas of Ameriquest Field. Also check out the special events scheduled throughout the year, like the Field of Dreams sleepover (older kids get to run the bases, bat and pitch, then sleep on the field under the stars). Admission is $10 for adults, $6 for children four to sixteen years, and children under four years get in free. Admission includes a tour of the ballpark.

Library Events

Carrollton Public Library
972-466-4800
www.cityofcarrollton.com/library

Dallas Public Library
214-670-1400
www.dallaslibrary.org

Flower Mound Public Library
972-874-6200
http://library.flower-mound.com

Irving Public Library
www.irvinglibrary.org

McKinney Memorial Public Library
972-547-7323

Plano Public Library
www.planolibrary.org

University Park Public Library
214-363-9095
www.uplibrary.org

www.guidelive.com

It is never too early to read to your little one, so take advantage of your local area library for story times, music, crafts, and performances. Each week there are different times and activities, so visit the library closest to you or consult the *Dallas Morning News'* Guide. We have had fun learning to borrow books and videos with each visit. The library is a place to learn life lessons, interact quietly with others, and is always a smart outing for hot, cold, or rainy days.

Loews Cineplex Reel Moms

Cityplace 14
2600 North Haskell Avenue
Dallas 75204
214-828-6008
www.enjoytheshow.com

Tuesday is the day for a real big-screen experience as you watch the latest releases with Junior and some junior mints! The lights are dimmed and the bathrooms are equipped with changing stations. The movie begins at 11:00 a.m. Doors open early so moms can socialize and get settled. It is geared for newborns to one-year-olds and crying is perfectly acceptable—even expected for the babies (and the parents, depending on the movie).

Meadows Museum at Southern Methodist University

5900 Bishop Boulevard
Dallas 75275
214-768-2765
www.meadowsmuseumdallas.org

If you and your child have read some of the Baby Einstein art board books, they just might recognize the Miró or Picasso at SMU's Meadows Museum. This is the gorgeous new home to SMU's expansive Spanish art collection and more, and can be as brief an outing as you desire. Plus, minimal crowds and no shushing! We just love to run around and look at the various sculptures in the front courtyard. When asked what she had learned here, Kim's daughter replied, "to walk like a little lady, talk softly, not to touch, and to tell mommy what I saw in the pictures." The underground parking is easy, as is access via elevator to the museum level with a stroller. Culture vultures: this museum is as convenient as can be, and totally up your alley!

NorthPark Center

1030 NorthPark Center
Dallas 75225
214-361-6345
www.northparkcenter.com
Hours: Monday-Saturday, 10 a.m. to 9 p.m.; Sunday, noon to 6 p.m.

NorthPark is much more than a collection of retail stores. Watch the turtles and ducks in front of Neiman Marcus and then stroll to the large water fountain in front of Dillard's. Make your way toward Foley's, and for $1.00, take the kids on a miniature train ride. On a given day you will find a sea of mothers pushing strollers from one end of the mall to the other, which says something about how much kids enjoy this mall. La Madeleine French Bakery & Café is a great choice for a family-friendly meal when you need a break from all there is to do.

The Parks at Arlington

3811 South Cooper
Arlington 76015
817-467-0200
www.theparksatarlington.com
Hours: Monday-Saturday, 10 a.m. to 9 p.m.; Sunday, noon to 6 p.m.

As the name implies, this is more than just a mall. Two dollars get your child a delightful trip around and around the carousel. Or maybe she's into climbing and jumping on the soft play equipment while you chill out, supervise, and cheer her on! You can also cool off and take a spin around the NHL-sized ice skating rink. Admission to the rink is $6 plus $2 for skate rental. There are family restrooms, convenient nursing areas, and a food court, so make a day of it.

Pepsi Kid's Zone at The Shops at Willow Bend

6121 West Park Boulevard
Plano 75093
972-202-4900
www.shopwillowbend.com
Hours: Monday-Saturday, 10 a.m. to 9 p.m.; Sunday, noon to 6 p.m.

Up, down, all around and then Junior takes a long nap. This is the routine for many, including Joshua and Kelli, who make the pilgrimage to Plano. Pepsi Kid's Zone is a spacious, enclosed play area with oversized, soft, play equipment for children to climb and explore. Young ones can run around a large grapefruit, climb into a tea cup, and slide down a spoon. There is comfortable seating for the adults around the perimeter of the play space, with a clear view of the entire area from any seat. There is one small entrance so the chances of your child escaping are slim, especially given the abundance of other adults in the vicinity. A topnotch food court and large, clean family restrooms make this a great place for an outing—especially when the weather outside isn't so great.

Pottery Barn Kids Story Time

3228 Knox Street
Dallas 75205
214-522-4845

Whether you need to do a little shopping or not, this is a great place for story time. Outstanding staffer Brandon Kendrick loves reading to the little ones. Call for times or to schedule a reading for your playgroup—a cool summer idea!

Ridgmar Mall

I-30 at Green Oaks Road
Fort Worth 76116
817-731-0856
www.ridgmar.com
Hours: Monday-Saturday, 10 a.m. to 9 p.m.; Sunday, noon to 6 p.m.

You can enjoy an afternoon at the newly redone Ridgmar Mall and shop at Neiman Marcus, Dillard's, Foley's, Old Navy, The Children's Place, and many more stores. Then let the kids run off energy in the toddler play area located in the Kids District. Häagen Dazs is a great treat after lunch at Chili's, and if the kiddos are good, a reward from KB Toys is fair game.

The Science Place & TI Founders IMAX Theater

Fair Park
1318 Second Avenue
Dallas 75210
214-428-5555
www.scienceplace.org
Hours: Tuesday-Friday, 9:30 a.m. to 4:30 p.m.; Saturday, 9:30 a.m. to
5:30 p.m.; Sunday, 11:30 a.m. to 5:30 p.m.
June 1-August 15: Monday-Saturday, 9:30 a.m. to 5:30 p.m.; Sunday, 11:30 a.m. to 5:30 p.m.

We can't begin to give enough praise to the Science Place. Your children can spend hours at the Kids Place (up to age seven) building a sandcastle in the oversized sandbox, watching boats float in the Waterworks, studying how farms affect our lives at the Urban Farm, and pretending to cook dinner in the play kitchen—and that's just for starters. Highlights include an electric theater in which demonstrations and hands-on activities help demystify electricity for youngsters, three moving and roaring dinosaurs, and the TI Founders IMAX Theater and a planetarium. The Science Place also boasts a highly regarded school (preschool to second grade) and also offers classes and workshops. Admission starts at $7.50 for adults and $4.00 for children three to twelve years. IMAX and the planetarium are additional. If you think you might go the Science Place with any regularity, check out the memberships, which make it a terrific bargain.

Slappy's Puppet Playhouse
Galleria Dallas/Third level
I-635 at Dallas North Tollway
Dallas 75001
214-369-4849
www.slappysplayhouse.com

With imagination, music and puppets, any child will be captivated by a show at Slappy's Puppet Playhouse. Kids and adults will watch a forty-five-minute European-style marionette show, such as the Little Mermaid or Rumplestiltskin. Afterwards, your child can see how the marionettes work! Your family will also enjoy the variety and clown shows. Show times vary, so call or check the Web site for upcoming shows and times. Prices are $7 for children and seniors and $8 for adults.

Stonebriar Centre
121 & Preston Road
Frisco 75034
972-668-MALL
www.shopstonebriar.com
Hours: Monday-Saturday, 10 a.m. to 9 p.m.; Sunday, noon to 6 p.m.

Kids can go crazy at the CoServ KidZone playground. Play equipment is sculpted from foam and children love to explore its soft surfaces, bounce to their heart's content on a giant polka-dot chair, and fly down a telephone slide - all in this brightly-colored, one thousand-square-foot play area. While it may not be as child friendly for younger children as other mall play areas, the full-size carousel is a bonus and is only $1. Stonebriar Centre also has an NHL-sized ice arena and is the largest rink in any Dallas area mall. The rink is located on the lower level near Sears—a great opportunity to learn to skate. Ask about classes, as schedules change seasonally. Stadium and table seating on the upper level offer a great view of all the skating and hockey action. Public skate admission is $6, plus a $2 per pair skate rental.

Storybook Children's Theatre
4101 East Park Boulevard, Suite 160
Plano 75074
972-516-1653
www.dancedepot.net

To be, or not to be, that is the question—at least when we are talking about Storybook Children's Theatre. Your child can either audition to be in one of the plays, or simply sit back and enjoy the performance. Storybook Children's Theatre, part of Dance Depot, holds auditions for children ages five years and older to perform in productions such as *Charlotte's Web, The Lion, the Witch, and the Wardrobe, The Three Little Pigs, Cinderella,* and *Alice in Wonderland*. If there are enough preschoolers interested, they might have a chance to put on a small play. Ticket prices are $5 for children and $7 for adults.

Tots Towne

816 West McDermott Road
Allen 75013
214-495-TOYS (8697)
Hours: Monday-Saturday, 9 a.m. to 8 p.m.

Preston Oaks Shopping Center
10720 Preston Road
Dallas 75230
214-363-9929
Hours: Monday-Saturday, 9 a.m. to 8 p.m.; Sunday, noon to 5 p.m.

www.totstowne.com

It is obvious that a marketing mastermind is behind Tots Towne—while playing with toys before you buy them sounds like a great idea (and it is), watch out because you may leave with a few new playthings if you don't put your foot down! While the kids play and try out all of the Little Tikes products in the Tots Towne fun area, you can sit in a comfortable chair and chat with friends or take notes for the next gift-giving holiday. Don't worry if you have forgotten snacks, because you can purchase enough for all, such as pretzels, Goldfish, and a variety of crackers. If kids have trouble leaving, the free balloons are sure to quash the exiting tantrums. The verdict is still out on the degerming, but sources say they sanitize periodically. Tots Towne also carries products by Baby Einstein and the Learning Journey International. This rainy-day or any day play town is also available for birthday parties and playgroups.

The Trains at Children's Medical Center Dallas

1935 Motor Street
Dallas 75235
214-920-2000
www.childrens.com

Kim and Nevin first saw the trains in the atrium of Children's Medical Center Dallas while they were taking Sawyer to a doctor's appointment. At age one, she was amazed and didn't know where to look next, as there are several trains, scenes, and whistles to enjoy. This is a great rainy-day activity and the valet parking makes it so easy! Be sure to also visit the Bright Building just across the street to see a large ultralight glider in a four-story atrium.

Valley View Center
13331 Preston Road
NW Corner of LBJ Freeway & Preston Road
Dallas 75240
972-661-2424
www.shopvalleyviewcenter.com
Hours: Monday-Saturday, 10 a.m. to 9 p.m.; Sunday, noon to 6 p.m.

Learn to speak Spanish like a native, marvel at the Victorian carousel, or go for a drive in a big red car—all under one roof. Valley View Center offers something for all children, including dad! The Children's Museum (see listing in this chapter) offers art, language classes, imaginary play opportunities, and much more. For high-energy times, there is a small play area with soft foam equipment. After the kids work up an appetite, you can visit the food court! Or when it's time to wind down before a nap, there's always time for a spin on the carousel. We have found that older children can sometimes dominate the play area, making it more difficult for the little ones to navigate, so just keep your eyes open.

OUTDOOR ACTIVITIES

Adventure Landing
17717 Coit Road
Dallas 75252
972-248-4966
wwww.adventurelanding.com
Hours: seasonal, so call for a current schedule.

Adventure Landing is a fun-filled place to take the kids and spend some time in engaging in friendly family competition. There are three eighteen-hole miniature golf courses, nine batting cages, a laser tag arena, a mega-arcade with over one hundred games, and a state-of-the-art go-kart track. Prices depend on the attractions you choose.

Barnyard Buddies
3316 North Central Expressway, Building C
Plano 75074
972-633-9779
www.fairview-farms.com/barnyard.htm
Hours: Monday-Friday, 10 a.m. to 2 p.m.; Saturday, 10 a.m. to 6 p.m.; Sunday, 1 p.m. to 5 p.m.

Barnyard Buddies is a family favorite and a great choice for a preschool fieldtrip. You really don't notice that this petting zoo/pumpkin patch/farmer's market is tucked in between busy city restaurants and retailers. Parents and kids alike will enjoy feeding horses, pigs, goats, and chickens. Hayrides, the pumpkin patch, and farmer's market constitute a fun fall event with plenty of pumpkins, decorations, and fruits and veggies to choose from. Prices start at $2 for hayrides and $5 for a pony ride. There is a picnic area, but be sure to call ahead or go early—this is a busy place, as they also juggle birthday parties and school and church trips.

Burger's Lake

1200 Meandering Road
Fort Worth 76114
817-737-3414
www.burgerslake.com
Hours: Open daily from 9 a.m. to 7:30 p.m., Mother's Day through Labor Day.

What better way to spend a sunny day than lounging at the beach, tending to your barbecue, or swinging from a twenty-five-foot trapeze? You don't have to go to an exotic resort to get all of this. Burger's Lake is a legendary one-acre spring-fed lake and a great place to spend a hot summer day—complete with lifeguards. Admission is $10 for adults and children over six years. Children six and under are free.

Cedar Ridge Preserve

7171 Mountain Creek Parkway
Dallas 75249
972-293-5150
www.audubondallas.org
Hours: Tuesday-Sunday sunrise to sunset.

Cedar Ridge Preserve was formerly known as the Dallas Nature Center until the Audubon Society began managing it in 2003. The preserve offers 633 acres of picnic areas, trails for hikers with all levels of experience, and a butterfly garden. Some trivia for you here: it's the highest point in the Dallas-Fort Worth area. There is a suggested donation of $3 per visit.

Dallas Arboretum and Botanical Garden

8617 Garland Road
Dallas 75218
214-327-8263
www.dallasarboretum.org
Hours: 10 a.m. to 5 p.m. daily.

Escape city life at the Dallas Arboretum and Botanical Garden. Sixty-six acres of waterfalls, gardens, and expansive grassy areas provide a peaceful getaway for children to explore. Mommy & Me Mondays are packed with special activities just for children and are perfect for playgroups or meeting friends, especially during Dallas Blooms in the spring. Around Christmastime, Afternoon with Santa is a big hit, as children can have their picture taken and check out a one-horse open sleigh! First through sixth graders can develop a green thumb by taking a class at the Trammell Crow Education Pavilion. Classes like "City Critters" and "Butterflies and Blossoms" bring flora to life for our urban children. The gift shop carries some original and adorable gifts for children. We love to pack a picnic and a camera for monthly outings when the weather is great, especially for Cool Thursdays, with music on the lawn. This is a great place to go pumpkin shopping close to Halloween!

The Dallas Farmers Market

1010 South Pearl Street
Dallas 75201
214-670-5880
www.dallasfarmersmarket.org
Hours: Monday-Sunday, 7 a.m. to 6 p.m.

In our opinion it's never too early to get children to help choose, prepare, and of course enjoy the area's best produce. The Dallas Farmers Market is the perfect place for burgeoning taste buds to savor the freshest fruits and vegetables grown within 150 miles of the city. No matter the time of year, there's something in season. Don't forget to check out the meat and seafood markets and the international marketplace for jewelry, pottery, furniture, and more. The plant and landscape area is tailor-made for families shopping for pumpkins, Christmas trees, and perennials. The market area is covered, so don't let rain keep you away. Trying to get a parking space on the weekends can be difficult but during the rest of the week it's a breeze. The narrow sidewalks and brisk attendance let you practice your stroller skills.

Dallas Zoo

650 South R.L. Thornton Freeway
Dallas 75203
214-670-5656
www.dallas-zoo.org
Hours: Monday-Sunday, 9 a.m. to 5 p.m. *Check for seasonal hours.

Animal sounds usually come first in a child's repertoire of impressions, and what better place than the Dallas Zoo for kids to observe elephants, monkeys, giraffes, and lemurs, and to ride through the wilds of Africa on the monorail? Second to the animals, our little ones love a ride on the carousel. Be sure to keep some cash handy to purchase tokens. The Lacerte Family Children's Zoo is a favorite of ours, and a weekend ritual. Feeding goats, playing, sliding around in the sand at the Tot Spot, feeding fish, and hopping through the creek (be sure to bring dry clothes) are just some of the highlights that keep it a busy family place. Before leaving, you can grab a quick lunch or snack inside the Children's Zoo or opt to drive through the playfully zoo-ey McDonald's on the way home for a pre-nap surprise! Prices are $8 for twelve to sixty-four years of age, $5 for children three to eleven, and $4 for senior citizens. Annual memberships are the best deal and include free parking!

Elves Christmas Tree Farm

601 Harvey Lane
Denison 75020
903-463-7260
www.elveschristmastreefarm.com
Hours: Seasonal, please call for times.

This mom-and-pop shop is decidedly old school and definitely all about family. What a great tradition it is to select and cut your own Christmas tree! The first Friday after Thanksgiving kicks off the season, and it goes until the trees are sold out. Be sure to bring a camera, pack a picnic, and enjoy fun activities. Starting in October, dress the kiddos up and head out for a hayride, a trip to the petting zoo, and a walk by their huge pumpkin patch, which usually boasts over fifty thousand pumpkins! Proprietors Marshall and Sharlote Cathey make the big city feel a million miles away. Keep this one in mind for a fall birthday party or family reunion.

Forest Park Miniature Train Ride

1989 Colonial Parkway
Fort Worth 76106
817-336-3328
Hours: Seasonal and weather dependent. Please call for further information.

What child doesn't love the sights, sounds, and motion of trains? All aboard for a fun ride on the longest miniature train route in the United States. The wait is not bad, since trains run hourly during the week and more frequently on the weekends. This is a forty-minute ride between the zoo and the Trinity Park Duck Pond. Children (ages one to twelve) and seniors ride for $2.50, and adults (ages twelve to sixty-five) ride for $3.

Fort Worth Botanic Garden

3220 Botanic Garden Boulevard
Fort Worth 76107
817-871-7689
www.fwbg.org
Hours: Monday-Sunday, 8 a.m. to sundown.

Visit the oldest gardens in Texas and the 109 acres of splendor while enjoying a Thursday evening with the Fort Worth Symphony. The fireworks and light shows are huge hit with the kids if they can stay up for concert hours (8 p.m. to 10 p.m.). During the day, this is a great spot to stroll and stop for Kodak moments among lush, colorful backgrounds, like the Japanese and rose gardens and the Kids Corner. If you have time, their Web site has a printable nature walk that maps your route as curious little ones wander the grounds in search of turtles, flowers, and a plant that smells like a pizza pie! There are several scheduled events throughout the year such as Grandparent's Day. The Botanic Garden also hosts summer camps and various classes for adults such as yoga and watercolor painting.

Fort Worth Rail Market

1401 Jones Street
Fort Worth 76102
817-335-6758
www.fortworthrailmarket.com
Hours: Monday-Thursday, 10 a.m. to 7 p.m.; Friday and Saturday, 10 a.m. to 9 p.m.; Sunday, 11 a.m. to 5 p.m.

If you have had trouble getting your little one to try new fruits or veggies, this may be the place for them. At the Fort Worth Rail Market and Farmers Market, housed in the historic Santa Fe Freight

House, you can sample the season's best and take some home, too. Don't miss the outdoor Farmers Market on Fridays, Saturdays, and Sundays, at the Intermodal Transportation Center (ITC)—it is all open from 7:30 a.m. to 3 p.m. throughout the spring and summer. There is usually a concert, a cooking demonstration, and a host of child-friendly activities. We have some friends whose children love going here to pick out their veggies for the week rather than having mom serve "yucky stuff"! Their menu that first week consisted of corn on the cob, corn on the cob, and, well, corn on the cob. There is a Safari Shuttle now running from the ITC to the Fort Worth Zoo; check for times and schedule.

Fort Worth Zoo
1989 Colonial Parkway
Fort Worth 76107
817-759-7050
www.fortworthzoo.org

Voted by *USA Today* and *Family Magazine* as one of the nation's top zoos, the Fort Worth Zoo is a place not to be missed. Worth the drive for Dallasites since the day it opened in 1909, this zoo is home to almost every animal your child could imagine, and more. Kim's daughter Sawyer recognized the zoo entrance from her *Barney at the Zoo* video and kept on the lookout for the purple dinosaur all day! Besides the wildlife, the carousel, the play barn with baby animals, and the train are just a few of the highlights. The shaded areas, refreshment stands, and cool restrooms were a much-welcomed hideaway from the summer heat. Stroller and wagon rentals are available. Tickets are $9.75 for adults, $7.25 for children ages three to twelve, and $6.25 for seniors. Tickets are half price on Wednesdays. Parking is $5. There is a shuttle to and from the Fort Worth Farmers Market and if you still have energy, the Forest Park Miniature Train, located across from the zoo, is a forty-minute ride up the Trinity River.

Fossil Rim Wildlife Center
2155 CR 2008
Glen Rose 76043
214-897-2960
www.fossilrim.com
Hours: Check for seasonal changes. Monday-Sunday, 8:30 a.m. to 5:30 p.m.

Have you ever wanted to hand feed a giraffe? Here is your chance. Just fifty miles southwest of Ft. Worth, Fossil Rim is a haven for endangered species such as zebras, cheetahs, black rhinos, and Attwater's prairie chickens. You can take a guided tour or drive your car through a ten-mile scenic reserve. For over twenty years, Fossil Rim has been protecting and researching endangered animals, so not only is this an appealing activity, it also supports a great effort for the environment. Kim's nephew still raves about the giraffe that licked his hand, and that was five years ago! Be sure to visit the Children's Animal Center, where young animal enthusiasts brush sheep and walk the nature trails. There is a lodge for overnight stays and early morning safaris. Admission is $16.95 for adults, $10.95 for ages three to eleven, and free for kids under three. Wednesdays are half price from April through November. Call ahead if the weather is questionable.

The Heard Nature Science Museum and Wildlife Sanctuary

One Nature Place
McKinney 75069
972-562-5566
www.heardmuseum.org
Hours: Monday-Saturday, 9 a.m. to 5 p.m.; Sunday, 1 p.m. to 5 p.m.
Closed on major holidays

Families young and old love to pack a picnic and visit the Heard. The 289-acre site features beautiful hiking trails, live animals, a native plant garden, and natural science exhibits. Little hands and feet will love the textures, sights, smells, and sounds in a "huge changing exhibit that is different each and every day of the year." Admission to the grounds and exhibits is $8 for adults and $5 for children three to twelve years.

Log Cabin Village

2100 Log Cabin Lane
Fort Worth 76109
817-926-5881
www.logcabinvillage.org
Hours: Tuesday-Friday, 9 a.m. to 4 p.m.; Saturday and Sunday, 1 p.m. to 5 p.m.; closed Mondays and holidays

Celebrating Texas Heritage since 1966, Log Cabin Village is home to six cabins that date back to the 1800s. This is a unique place that lets visitors get a real feel for pioneer life. The blacksmith shop, herb garden, and schoolhouse are as authentic as can be. The friendly staff—decked in period wear—bring the frontier days to life for young history buffs. Children ages seven to twelve can spend the day living as pioneer children, doing chores and attending school as they did in the 1800s. Reservations must be made for special programs. Log Cabin Village is open year round. Admission for adults is $2.50, and for children four to seventeen and senior citizens admission is $2.

McKinney Avenue Trolley

Between the Dallas Arts District and Uptown
Dallas 75204
214-855-0006
www.mata.org
Hours: Monday-Sunday, 10 a.m. to 10 p.m.

If you can't get to San Francisco for a visit, hop on the McKinney Avenue Trolley. This historic electric cable car takes you back to the turn of the century, complete with bells, handrails, and the spirit of a simpler time. While enjoying your ride, you can visit the abundant restaurants and stores that line the route. Children will love the sights and sounds. All aboard!

Nasher Sculpture Center

2001 Flora
Dallas 75201
214-242-5100
www.NasherSculptureCenter.org
Hours: Tuesday and Wednesday, 11 a.m. to 6 p.m.; Thursday, 11 a.m. to 9 p.m.; Friday-Sunday, 11 a.m. to 6 p.m.

This little retreat in the middle of downtown Dallas exhibits over three hundred modern sculptures by artists such as Picasso, Calder, Moore, and Matisse. The Nasher Sculpture Center, which opened in October 2003, is a great learning and cultural outing for even the wee ones. Children can wander the outside gardens and explore the different shapes and sizes or they can stroll inside as well. Enjoy a lovely lunch of soups, salads, and sandwiches at the Café Mansion while the kids eye the lily pond and fountains. This is a peaceful place our kids really enjoy. Tickets are $10 for adults, and children under twelve are free. The Dallas Museum of Art is just across the way. Parking is available at several area lots or at the DMA for Center members.

The Playground at Scottish Rite Hospital for Children

2222 Welborn Street
Dallas 75219
214-559-5000
www.tsrhc.org

The playground at Scottish Rite Hospital for Children is a special place and a clean, bright, and fun play area with restrooms and an area for a picnic lunch or snack—all in front of the hospital. You may think first to go to the park, but give this area a try and you'll find shade and tot-sized play equipment too. Parking is easy and if you have the urge for popcorn, volunteers sell it by the bag on the lower level of the hospital. Look up—in this area, the kids can cool off and enjoy the aerial art and planes.

Southern Methodist University Football

214-SMU-GAME
www.smumustangs.com

Even the smallest fans and cheerleaders will have trouble leaving the Kid's Corral to catch a glimpse of SMU play football at the amazing new Ford Stadium. Before the game, your family can meet up with friends on the Boulevard and enjoy the food and entertainment. Even if you did not attend the university, this is a fun afternoon for the entire community. The Kid's Corral is located at the south-east corner of Ford Stadium at SMU. Due to warm afternoon temperatures, game times are typically in the early evening. We love to hit the Boulevard, feed our children, and let them run around and make friends right before the first half of a game. Coming home for bedtime during the second half is just fine—it was the perfect amount of time for all before we melted! Parking can be a hassle, but SMU offers shuttle parking from Mockingbird Station all day.

Southlake Town Square

North Carroll between Highway 114 and FM 1709
Southlake 76092
817-329-5566
www.southlaketownsquare.com

Grab the stroller and spend an afternoon window shopping at "small-town downtown." Open since 1999, Southlake Town Square has become a popular destination, especially for families. Children will enjoy watching the fountains at the center of the square and then grabbing a bite to eat at kid-friendly restaurants such as Corner Bakery or Café Express. Don't forget to bring your wallet—it will be hard to pass up buying an outfit at Animal Crackers or Gymboree (or a treat for yourself). Check out the annual celebrations—Art in the Square in April, Oktoberfest, and an Independence Day fireworks show (see chapter 19, Seasonal Events).

Texas Discovery Gardens

3601 Martin Luther King Jr. Boulevard at Fair Park
Dallas 75210
214-428-7476
www.texasdiscoverygardens.org
Hours: Tuesday-Saturday, 10 a.m. to 5 p.m.

This is the first public garden in the state of Texas to be certified organic! Little ones will love to watch (and try to catch) butterflies in a garden habitat. All five senses are stimulated at the Scent Garden and kids love to soak up the surroundings at the Circular Lawn and Reflecting Pool. The fee is $3 for adults, $1.50 for children three to eleven years, and free for children under three.

Texas Sculpture Garden

6801 Gaylord Parkway
Hall Office Park
Frisco 75034
972-377-1152
www.texassculpturegarden.org
Hours: Outside artwork is open from dawn until dusk. Interior artwork is open weekdays from 8 a.m. to 6 p.m. and Saturday mornings from 9 a.m. to noon.

Art is accessible to everyone at the Texas Sculpture Garden. This private collection of sculptures by Texas artists, such as Mac Whitney and James Surls, is the largest ever made available to the public, both outdoors and indoors. Lakes, fountains, and lushly landscaped walking trails make this an idyllic setting to enjoy this unique collection of art. Just remember to keep the kids from climbing or touching. They have indoor drinking fountains, and the bathrooms are clean and make a cool refuge from the heat.

CHAPTER EIGHTEEN:
CHILD-FRIENDLY EATERIES

Eating out with the little ones is an adventure! Whether you have a new baby or toddler, don't let it be intimidating. We have found that if you go into the outing with an open mind, knowing your child is not going to be quiet or sit all of the time, then you will do fine. Just remember that there are times food may fly and then there are times when taking them to an upscale locale is doable. We have had to walk out of places with drinks spilled in our laps and rice in our hair, but letting our kids experience the various kinds of cuisine and different atmospheres is worth it to us. And while you may think your days of eating at four-star restaurants are over, please don't forgo them—we have found several to be more child-friendly than those you dine at every day!

So get ready for fine dining and create an eating out "bag of tricks" filled with stickers, markers, mini Play-Doh, crayons, and anything else new, exciting, and age appropriate to keep the kids entertained. We have also found that asking your server for extra spoons and napkins can make an entertaining toy for your child!

HELPFUL TIPS

- Dine out at your baby's normal eating hour if possible.
- Try to order for your child right after you are seated, then look over the menu for yourself.
- Don't forget the bag of tricks.
- Dine out with friends and other families. Not only is it an opportunity for learning and socialization, it is instant entertainment!
- Take a break and don't be afraid to go for a walk while waiting for your food or bill.

BAKERIES

Bread Winner's Bakery & Café

3301 McKinney Avenue
Dallas 75204
214-754-4940

5560 West Lovers Lane
Dallas 75209
214-351-3339

www.breadwinnerscafe.com

Yummy! is all we can say, and for the McKinney Avenue location—crowded! But it is worth the wait to sit on the small patio of either locale. Friends love their Lovers Lane location for the playful wait-staff that is eager to please and play peek-a-boo with the little ones. Salads, sandwiches, and break-fast fare are tasty and fresh. Kids' grilled cheese and fruit is big and melts in your mouth—that is, if they let you have a bite! There are great desserts and bakery items to go.

Celebrity Café & Bakery

24 Highland Park Village
Dallas 75205
214-528-6612

Multiple locations, including Dallas, Plano, Lewisville, and Fort Worth.

Celebrity Café and Bakery is now franchised, and each one is special in its own way. They are a great place to grab a salad, soup, or sandwich, and while the children's menus vary per location, the grilled cheese seems to be a favorite everywhere. Fresh fruit and a mini muffin are great sides, or you may choose chips. We forewarn you about their huge iced cookies in fun seasonal shapes that are very visible in the front display cases . . . temptation city for the kiddos.

BARBECUE

Dickey's BBQ Pit

Multiple locations
www.dickeys.com

Dickey's is a simple and fast solution for barbecue lovers. Kim's husband and the kids eat here almost every Saturday. The children's chicken plate ensures leftovers for dinner. The high chairs have a bib and Wet One secured under plastic wrap for extra cleanliness. Soft serve ice cream is a special treat.

Peggy Sue BBQ
6600 Snider Plaza
Dallas 75205
214-987-9188

Peggy Sue's buttery grilled cheeses will satisfy even the pickiest eater. This extremely family-oriented restaurant located across from SMU is so popular it is known for its long wait. One of our friends promises that if you are there by 11:15 a.m., you can have your pick of tables for lunch!

BREAKFAST/BRUNCH

Café Brazil
6420 North Central Expressway
University Park 75206
214-691-7791

Multiple locations
www.cafebrazil.com

If your child is craving pancakes, these are buttermilk and fluffy all the way! Eggs come in many styles, including migas or southwestern style. Flavored coffees are on a serve-yourself system. This spot is a busy one on the weekends.

Dream Café
5100 Belt Line, Suite 208
Addison 75254
972-503-7326

The Quadrangle
2800 Routh Street
Dallas 75201
214-954-0486

Dream Café is fun for kids and parents no matter what time of day, thanks to the outdoor play areas and crayons. Breakfast choices are great and their lunch and dinner menus have savory choices, like a delicious noodle bowl. Kids' food is served from 7 a.m. to 3 p.m. Favorites are the Mickey pancake, kid pizza, and fruit smoothies.

Lucky's
4727 Frankford Road
Addison 75287
972-447-0624

3531 Oak Lawn Avenue
Dallas 75219
214-522-3500

Kelli's parents have been taking Joshua here since he was born and they love it. Crayons, a placemat to color, and a big basket of biscuits and cornbread are a great start. Unless you haven't fed your child for a week, the portions are generous enough for leftovers. The waitstaff is conscientious about placing children's orders as soon as possible. If you go on a weekend, be prepared to wait!

BURGERS

Ball's Hamburgers
3404 Rankin in Snider Plaza
Dallas 75205
214-373-1717

4343 West Northwest Highway & Midway
Dallas 75227
214-352-2525

Ball's is a great place for Dad to take the kids if he is trying to catch a glimpse of a sporting event —they always have something on the TV. The Little Leaguer burgers come three to an order and melt in your mouth. They are the perfect size for tiny hands, as are the chicken fingers. The fries are good, and if you want something on the lighter side, the salads are fair. There is a surprise toy trinket machine for toddler treats and video games for the big kids.

Burger House
6913 Hillcrest
Dallas 75205
214-361-0370

Multiple locations

While there are several locations such as in Garland and Lakewood, the Hillcrest location is one of our school day favorites. These are some of the best salty fries and thickest milkshakes we have ever had. The outdoor seating area or the small diner style bar is fun for kids. To-go orders do make this place even busier, as do SMU students, so try calling your order in as a to-go and then eat there.

Chip's Old Fashioned Hamburgers
4501 Cole Avenue
Dallas 75205
214-526-1092

4530 Lovers Lane
Dallas 75225
214-691-2447

Chip's offers a no-frills delicious burger. Kids can choose a hamburger, cheeseburger, corn dog, or fried chicken fingers, complete with fries and a small drink. Parents, be sure to try the shredded pork sandwich—The Pig sandwich. The chocolate sorbet and banana milkshakes are a thick and creamy delight.

Gazebo Burger

5950 Royal Lane
Dallas 75230
214-368-3387

Gazebo Burger is a neighborhood favorite and is always lively. The kids' menu is the typical burger joint fare, and portions are big enough for two. Turkey burgers are a hit for grownups (99 percent fat free). Be sure to try their pico de gallo, from the toppings bar, on your burger or salad.

Who's Who Burgers

69 Highland Park Village
Dallas 75205
214-522-1980

Located in Highland Park Village, this small, multilevel restaurant also offers covered outdoor dining complete with a quaint water fountain—great for penny wishes. The second floor cow statue, thick milkshakes, and Kobe beef burgers make this a weekly favorite of many, and making new friends is part of the fun too. You can write your name on the walls for a $100 donation to Hunger Busters, a charity for feeding the homeless. Who's Who Burgers is a Phil Romano concept.

CASUAL

Café Express

Multiple locations
www.café-express.com

From Southlake to Addison to University Park, Café Express offers wonderful salads, pastas, soups, burgers, and sandwiches in a self-serve café atmosphere. Once you place your order, let the kiddos hold the receiver that lights up and vibrates when your order is ready. The children's menu has shell pasta with cheese or marinara sauce, and the child-size burgers have soft homemade buns. You can choose fries or fruit for the side. Some locations have outdoor dining with a fountain.

Chili's Grill and Bar

Multiple locations

www.chilis.com

Chili's, a national chain, has a huge children's menu. Sides range from the healthy steamed broccoli and corn on the cob to the fried food extravaganza. A great activity book will entertain kids. The friendly staff overcomes the not-so-clean high chairs.

Einstein Bros.

Multiple locations

www.einsteinbros.com

There has never been a time that we have not seen moms and children enjoying lunch or families having a weekend bagel breakfast. Favorite choices beyond Sawyer's favorite of a cinnamon sugar bagel with butter are pannini sandwiches, yogurt parfait, bagel dogs, homemade soups, and fresh fruit.

Highland Park Pharmacy

3229 Knox Street

Dallas 75205

214-521-2126

This ninety-six-year-old pharmacy eatery makes you feel like a regular and is a place your parents and grandparents would enjoy. The diner setting is in the middle of a drug store and serves old fashioned sodas, milkshakes, malts, an oozing grilled cheese, a traditional pimiento cheese sandwich, and much more. If you can find a seat at the counter between the regulars for breakfast, then be sure to order the crisp bacon and waffles. There are no runny eggs here and the waitstaff is super friendly.

Luby's

Multiple locations

www.lubys.com

Friends say they love Luby's for their great "home cooked" food served cafeteria style. Kids will love to choose from the numerous selections, but Jell-o and mac and cheese seem to be favorites. Luby's has clean high chairs with wheels that make it easy to go through the line hands free and fast! They even have activity packs with Teddy Grahams, crayons, stickers, a placemat, and a plastic bib.

McAlister's Deli

3432 East Hebron Parkway

Carrollton 75010

972-248-8288

This place has a friendly staff that is all about catering to the customers. McAlister's is a favorite of Nevin's not only for this reason, but for their fresh and quick food, sweet tea, and yummy children's menu. (Cheese pita pizza, hot dog, toasted cheese with ham or turkey—all with chips, fruit, and a drink.) You can tell that this new national chain likes kiddos when you see a bumper sticker that says, "Add a little sweet tea to my sippy cup" on the very clean high chairs.

Mermaid Bar
Neiman Marcus NorthPark
400 NorthPark Boulevard
Dallas 75225
214-363-8311
www.neimanmarcus.com

This place is a treat and perfect for a newborn outing or lunch with your little lady or gentleman. The mosaic mermaid décor and the swiveling bar stools have always mesmerized Sawyer and her friends. The food is signature Neiman's fare. Choose from homemade soups, fresh salads, and sandwiches. Timing can be everything to beat waiting in line.

The Purple Cow
110 Preston Royal Village
Dallas 75205
214-373-0037

5809 Preston Road
Dallas 75205
972-473-6100

4601 West Freeway
Fort Worth 76107
817-737-7177

It is not unusual to find kids looking up at the ceiling here because of the train that circles on a landing above the front eating area. A favorite for the kids is the jukebox and the signature Purple Cow milkshake. There are alcohol-infused shakes for the parents. The 99 percent fat free turkey burgers and salads are great light options for adults, while chicken fingers, grilled cheese, and burgers are big enough to feed two children. The Plano location does have a side room for parties of eighteen or fewer, and the Fort Worth location takes reservations for birthday parties of twenty or more.

Slider & Blues
8517 Hillcrest Road
Dallas 75225
214-696-8632

3033 West Parker Road
Plano 75023
972-867-8666

Slider and Blues is a cheerful and relaxed locale for lunch, a family dinner, a gathering of friends, or a birthday party. Slider and Blues was created fifteen years ago by owner Andy Stassio and his love of family. There is a large menu with great salads and pastas, and the thin crust pizza is light and fresh. There is a game room for kids of all sizes, which includes a miniature boat for the wee ones to ride in.

Snuffer's Restaurant and Bar

14910 Midway Road
Addison 75001
972-991-8811

3526 Greenville Avenue
Dallas 75206
214-826-6850

8411 Preston Road
Dallas 75225
214-265-9911

2408 Preston Road
Plano 75093
469-467-9911

www.snuffers.com

The epitome of a casual burger joint, Snuffer's is popular with everyone. Burgers are a staple, but other fare, such as chicken sandwiches and quesadillas, are always great choices. If you go, you have to try their famous cheddar fries at least once.

Wild About Harry's

3113 Knox Street
Dallas 75205
214-520-3113

11661 Preston Road, Suite 309
Dallas 75230
214-378-5000

While they have incredible custard, people line up for Wild About Harry's real Chicago hot dogs with an abundance of toppings. It's a fun and fast location that is popular with adults even without kids. A child's meal includes a hot dog, chips or fries, milk or soda, and a small serving of custard. Seating is limited at the Knox Street location, so leave the stroller in the car.

CHINESE

Pei Wei Asian Diner
Multiple locations, including Allen, Arlington, Carrollton, Dallas, Fort Worth, Las Colinas, Lewisville and Southlake
www.peiwei.com

Pei Wei's is an inexpensive offspring of P.F. Chang's and is a great quick casual spot with flavorful options. A favorite of Joshua's is the fried rice.

P.F. Chang's China Bistro
225 NorthPark Center
Dallas 75225
214-265-8669

18323 Dallas Parkway
Dallas 75287
972-818-3336

650 Highway 114
Grapevine 76051
817-421-6658

www.pfchangs.com

P.F Chang's serves everything family style and provides enough food for two in one order. This is a great place for kids to experience new foods such as the shrimp and pork dumplings. Surely, you have heard of their yummy and fun-to-eat lettuce wraps. Friendly service accommodates special requests. Be prepared for a wait, but reservations are now accepted.

GOURMET TO GO

Central Market
5750 East Lovers Lane
Dallas 75206
214-234-7000

4651 West Freeway
Fort Worth 76107
817-989-4700

320 Coit Road
Plano 75075
469-241-8300

www.centralmarket.com

Café on the Run has everything from salads, soups, and entrees to a sandwich counter. They serve breakfast, lunch, and dinner seven days a week. The child-sized tables with paper and crayons make this a fun place for kids and adults to eat, and the outdoor patio is a refreshing alternative. After eating, grocery shopping is great and kids love the complimentary purple or green balloons and extra large fruit and vegetable statues out front.

Eatzi's
3403 Oak Lawn Avenue
Dallas 75219
214-526-1515
www.eatzis.com

Eatzi's, a Phil Romano concept, is all about the WOW! factor. What fun it is for the kids to watch the busy staff and crowds while you choose from an enormous selection of gourmet delights. It is fun to eat outside or great to take home. If you are in need of gourmet, prepackaged meals to go or a half gallon of milk Eatzi's is the answer, but they are not a one-stop grocery.

La Madeleine
Multiple locations
www.lamadeleine.com

This is a great place to tempt you child's palate with a mild French-country flair. Quiche, tomato basil soup, and fresh breads and jam are favorites of our kiddies, as are the tasty desserts. High chairs seem clean from location to location—even at the busy NorthPark location.

Whole Foods
4100 Lomo Alto Drive
Highland Park 75219
214-520-7993

Multiple locations
www.wholefoods.com

The Whole Foods on Lomo Alto at Lemmon is a new location and our favorite for a quick healthy lunch or dinner. Kids love to sip on a Jamba Juice after dining, while riding in the red racer grocery carts. For dining in or take out, their prepared food is healthy and fresh. Options are grilled chicken, vegetables, pizza, soups, sushi, sandwiches, salad bar, and to-die-for homemade mac and cheese! Stickers and balloons upon checkout are an added bonus.

ITALIAN

California Pizza Kitchen
8411 Preston Road
Dallas 75225
214-750-7067

Stonebriar Center Mall
2601 Preston Road
Frisco 75034
972-712-0884

The Shops at Willow Bend
6121 West Park
Plano 75093
469-366-0060

1051 State Highway 114
Grapevine 76051
817-481-4255

www.cpk.com

This nationwide chain is always filled with children and it was voted by *Child* magazine in Spring 2004 as one of the top twenty restaurants for families. Kids can choose from a large selection of pizza and pasta, while grown-ups may want one of their many delicious salads, soups, or sandwiches.

Campisi's Egyptian Restaurant
5610 East Mockingbird Lane
Dallas 75216
214-827-0355

1520 Elm Street
Downtown Dallas 75201
214-752-0141

Mulitple locations
www.campisis.com

Campisi's is a Dallas landmark and a favorite of Nevin's while growing up. Whether it is thin crust pizza, a meatball sandwich, pasta, or a hamburger, you can't go wrong. You can choose from pastas and sauces off of the children's menu at the downtown location. There is not a child's menu at the Mockingbird location, but they are very accommodating. The family owned and operated restaurant is a fun place for kids, and they will love the friendly staff and fried ravioli appetizer.

Carrabba's Italian Grill
6130 Luther Lane
Dallas 75225
214-361-2255

17548 Dallas Parkway
Dallas 75287
972-732-7752

1901 Abrams Parkway
Dallas 75214
214-823-8678

3400 North Central Expressway
Plano 75074
972-516-9900

1701 Crossroads
Grapevine 76051
817-410-8461

www.carrabbas.com

Carrabba's is a family restaurant that truly caters to the "bambinis." Kids can dine on cheese ravioli and tomato sauce, grilled chicken breast, spaghetti and meatballs, chicken fingers, and cheese or pepperoni pizza. All children's entrees are $4.99 and include a beverage. Children are presented with a coloring book and crayons at seating and then servers bring them pizza dough for their entertainment. They can make a mini-pizza and bring it to the chefs at the wood-burning grill. Traditional pasta, seafood, and chicken dishes are delicious and come with a generous salad. An added bonus: Carrabba's is dimly lit so if your child drops food on the floor or you don't feel like freshening up your makeup before you leave the house, chances are that nobody will notice.

Pasta Plus

Preston Shopping Center
225 Preston at Royal Avenue
Dallas 75230
214-373-3999

Imagine yourself enjoying a leisurely dinner while your children happily keep themselves busy. Think you are dreaming? Well, it might not be a dream if you take them to Pasta Plus. Located in the same shopping center as kid-friendly Purple Cow, the owners, parents themselves, have made every effort to ease the stress of dining out with kids. In one corner there is a chalkboard, books and games, and quite a few tables that allow you to keep your eyes on them. Children's meals include pasta, fried cheese, scampi, a grilled chicken breast, and cheese pizza, ranging from $3.95 to $8.95. Adults will enjoy their homemade sauces, chicken, seafood, veal, or traditional Italian dishes. Buono Appetito!

Patrizzio's

1900 Preston Road
Plano 75093
972-964-2200

25 Highland Park Village
Dallas 75205
214-522-7878

At Patrizzio's, patio dining is at its best, but not during the summer months. This is another favorite restaurant of Kelli's parents to bring Joshua. Since it can get fairly loud, it's a great choice for kids who forget to use their indoor voices. Pastas, salads, and calzones are served in a hip and fun atmosphere located in Highland Park Village.

Romano's Macaroni Grill

Multiple locations
www.macaronigrill.com

This chain restaurant is all about family and was based on the idea of the family table. Friendly wait-staff and a large menu make it a crowd pleaser. Kids can color on the paper table cover.

Sal's Pizza Restaurant

2525 Wycliff Avenue
Dallas 75219
214-522-1828

The Shops at Legacy
5760 Legacy Drive
Plano 75024
972-943-8600

www.salspizzadallas.com

The original location on Wycliff always seems to have an eclectic group of diners but one thing they have in common is a love for the food at Sal's. Their New York pizza is some of the best we have ever had, and they have delicious pasta entrees to choose from. Children can choose among spaghetti with tomato sauce, meatballs, or meat sauce, and fettuccini alfredo, all regular menu items but just in smaller portions. The newer location in Plano has the same menu as the original.

JAPANESE

Blue Fish
18149 Dallas Parkway
Dallas 75287
972-250-3473

3519 Greenville Avenue
Dallas 75206
214-824-3474

925 West John Carpenter Freeway, Suite 100
Las Colinas 75039
972-385-3474

Blue Fish might not appear to be a place to take children, but since Sawyer was three weeks old, the staff at the Greenville Avenue location has catered to making her feel at home. They offer plenty of warm cloths for cleaning up, and they don't mind rice on the floor. Let your independent toddler help you fill in the sushi menu while munching on edamame. There is not a children's menu, but there are a lot of options—kids love their chicken meatballs, tempura vegetables, and brown rice.

Sushi on McKinney
4500 McKinney Avenue
Dallas 75205
214-521-0969

A fun place to take the kids and sit at the sushi bar, but be sure to ask if they would make an allowance and serve cooked items at the bar. A chilled orange is a treat at the end of your meal.

LATIN

Gloria's
3715 Greenville Avenue
Dallas 75206
214-874-0088

5100 Beltline Road
Addison 75240
972-387-8842

4140 Lemmon Avenue
Dallas 75219
214-521-7576

www.gloriasrestaurants.com

Gloria's delicious El Salvadoran food and the black bean dip they bring with the salsa and chips make this one of our favorite restaurants. Fajitas, quesadillas, and more exotic dishes with plantains and tamales are great for adults. Children's choices include enchiladas, quesadillas, or a chicken breast with rice and beans. Kids of all ages love the tres leches dessert.

La Duni Latin Kitchen & Baking Studio
4264 Oak Lawn Avenue
Dallas 75219
214-520-6888
www.laduni.com

The sister to La Duni Latin Café on McKinney Avenue, this intimate locale has a fun espresso bar area that is perfect for an early morning latte, pastries, and eggs Latin style. On any given evening (open seven days a week), you will see babies snoozing in infant carriers while parents enjoy a glass of wine and a piece of the award-winning cakes, such as the cuatro leches, panque de limon, or Nutella milk chocolate. Lunch and dinner items include sandwiches, salads, and flavorful chicken, pork, salmon, beef, and vegetarian entrees (See chapter 12, Cakes and Treats).

MEXICAN

Cantina Laredo
165 Inwood Village
Dallas 75209
214-350-5227

2031 Abrams Road
Dallas 75214
214-821-5785

Multiple locations
www.cantinalaredo.com

Cantina Laredo is extremely family friendly with a waitstaff who hustles and bustles about making sure that even the smallest of clients is happy. There are savory selections for adults (from chicken fajitas to fresh fish of the day) and for kids (from tacos to quesadillas). The word on the street is that their Carne Asada is worth the wait, as is their brunch. Ask to sit upstairs at the Inwood location where there are kid videos playing on the large screen TV.

Joe T. Garcia's Mexican Restaurant

2201 North Commerce
Fort Worth 76106
817-626-4356
www.joets.com

Whether it is a week night or Sunday brunch, you will have to wait, but friends swear by their intoxicating Mexican fare. Joe T.'s is a family owned and operated business, so they know what to expect. They know children have a melting point. Dining outdoors is ideal, especially with a large group, and it makes the drive from Dallas fun with friends. Just don't let the kids pick the flowers!

Luna de Noche

7927 Forest Lane
Dallas 75230
972-233-1880

Multiple locations

Luna de Noche's friendly atmosphere makes eating out with kids a dream. Our friends say they really cater to you as a family by giving you a large table so you can spread out, and fast service. And if your children don't like Mexican food, they offer other options such as chicken tenders. The little cups and straws are great if you leave the sippy at home.

Mi Cocina

77 Highland Park Village
Dallas 75205
214-521-6426

The Shops at Legacy
5760 Legacy Drive
Plano 75024
972-473-8777

Multiple locations
www.mcrowd.com

Don't worry if you have a crying baby because your neighbors won't be able to hear them on a typical night. Mi Cocina, founded by Michael "Mico" Rodriguez, is a family Tex-Mex hot spot that serves children rice, beans, and a choice of quesadillas, fajita or shredded chicken, and tacos. It is not unusual to have someone nonchalantly sweep up the floor under your children. Sawyer's all time favorite dessert is their flan with two spoons to share with a friend. A favorite place of Nevin and A.J.'s for dining with the kids. Could it be the Mombo Taxi (Mi Cocina's signature margarita)?!

Rafa's Café Mexico
5617 West Lovers Lane
Dallas 75209
214-357-2080

You all might have to take a bath after indulging in the sopapillas and honey, but it is worth it. Rafa's is a great choice for those who also like seafood Mexican style. Kids love to color on the paper tablecloths.

Taco Diner
4011 Villanova Street
Dallas 75225
214-363-3111

Multiple locations
www.mcrowd.com

Taco Diner, founded by Michael "Mico" Rodriguez of Mi Cocina fame, started this upscale taco joint to provide a cheap yet gourmet favorite. The service is friendly, the locale is hip, and it makes you feel like the adult you are, even if the new parent lifestyle has kept you at home for a bit. So try a tasty margarita and munch on chips and a variety of salsas while you wait for your order. The salads are great too.

SEAFOOD

Half Shells Oyster Bar & Grill
6617 Snider Plaza
Dallas 75205
214-691-8165

Half Shells Seafood Grill
5800 Legacy Drive
Plano 75024
469-241-1300

Fish City Grill
2628 Long Prairie
Flower Mound 75022
972-899-1630

Fish City Grill
10720 Preston Road
Dallas 75230
214-891-9979

www.fishcitygrill.com

Half Shells and Fish City Grill are owned by Bill and Lovett Bayne and feature the same menu at all four locations. These are great family restaurants that are very popular, so be ready for a wait. Kim worked at the original Snider Plaza location while in graduate school, and she knows first hand that the owners love families! The children's menu is pretty extensive, and the service typically is fast. We love the Cajun steamer platters or po-boys for adults, and the friend shrimp or catfish basket with fries and a side of steamed veggies for your munchkins.

Picardy's Shrimp Shop
6800 Snider Plaza
Dallas 75205
214-373-4099

You will see grandparents and family groups eating at Picardy's Shrimp Shop, for it is a favorite for eating out with children. If the cups of crayons and fun menus aren't enough entertainment, the crackers on the table and the child-friendly cups with short straws are. Parents can sip on a glass of wine and dine on the fresh catch of the day, while the little ones choose from macaroni and cheese, grilled chicken fingers, and fries.

UPSCALE FOR SPECIAL OCCASIONS

Bob's Steak & Chop House
4300 Lemmon Avenue
Dallas 75219
214-528-9446

5760 Legacy Drive
Plano 75024
972-608-2627

www.bobs-steakandchop.com

Bob's is a great place to take the children for dinner as long as you eat around 5:30 or 6 p.m. We have found the staff extremely friendly and patient. They can find you a table in a corner if your infant is in a car seat or your toddler needs some standing room. Sides are a perfect choice for little diners, and the fresh bread and butter is a great starter.

Café Pacific
24 Highland Park Shopping Village
Dallas 75205
214-526-1170

Café Pacific is all about elegant food and fine dining, but don't be too timid to try dining al fresco for a Saturday lunch or an early dinner. Favored by several of our friends, it is a perfect way to enjoy the art of fine seafood crêpes, salads, or pastas with the wee ones in tow. Just ask your server what the chef can prepare for your toddler.

Capital Grille
500 Crescent Court, Suite 135
Dallas 75201
214-303-0500
www.thecapitalgrille.com

The Grille serves fabulous food in a classy, upscale atmosphere, but any night of the week with the business diners, it can get loud by 6:30 p.m. Capital Grille is doable with a small baby in a car seat and a toddler, for there is always a staff member within arm's reach, ready to get what you or your child needs. Parents can enjoy steaks and seafood while sharing sides such as potatoes or steamed asparagus. When Sawyer was just two years old, our server taught her how to unfold a napkin in her lap and how to sip soup from the side of a spoon—you've got to love that!

Javier's Restaurant
4912 Cole Avenue
Dallas 75205
214-521-4211
www.javiers.net

Javier's makes you feel like family upon each return, so taking your little ones there for a special occasion is a no brainer. The Mexico City gourmet fare is fantastic, as is the service in this cozy locale. There is not a kids' menu, but the staff is always willing to assist you and goes above and beyond, in our book.

Roy's
2480 Dallas Parkway & Parker Road
Plano 75093
972-473-6263
www.roysrestaurant.com

Chef Roy Yamaguchi's Hawaiian fusion cuisine is enough to make anyone drool, but it's their service for children that will make you a repeat customer. It is so well synchronized . . . children are given crayons and a menu upon sitting, within minutes, your server brings a small plate of cheese quesadilla and crudités with peanut butter appetizers. Now while they bring you your drinks, you may order teriyaki salmon with rice, penne pasta with butter and cheese, or chicken fingers for your child's dinner. While you are eating appetizers, you little one is eating dinner and then enjoying an ice cream sundae while you eat your entrée.

CHAPTER NINETEEN:
SEASONAL EVENTS

You know what the experts say: "Children love routine." But when it comes to fun activities, the last thing you want to do is fall into a rut! Fortunately, we live in a city with a dizzying variety of enjoyable and educational activities—year round. We have listed just a few that are specially geared toward children. Two Web sites to check out regularly are the Dallas Convention and Visitors Bureau (www.dallascvb.com) and the Fort Worth Convention and Visitors Bureau (www.fortworth.com). Both Web sites list events and give a brief description and contact information.

JANUARY

Dallas Train Show
2000 East Spring Creek Parkway
Plano 75086
972-422-0296
www.dfwtrainshows.com
Choo-Choo! Model trains in every size will delight children of all ages. The show is held at the Plano convention center and children under twelve get in free.

DINO DASH & Discovery Fest
The Science Place
1318 2nd Avenue
Dallas 75210
214-428-2033
www.dinodash-discoveryfest.org

Run through Fair Park in a 10K, a 5K, or walk/run in a 1K that little ones can enjoy. Following the race, explore the world of science through crafts, games, and entertainment while enjoying good food and music.

Fort Worth Stock Show and Rodeo

Will Rogers Center
3401 West Lancaster
Fort Worth 76107
817-877-2400
www.fwssr.com

The nation's oldest stock show runs for twenty-three days, from mid-January until the beginning of February, and is loads of fun whether you fancy yourself a cowboy or not. A petting zoo, a carnival, live entertainment, and an interactive stock show for children are just a few activities for the family to enjoy.

KidFilm Festival

USA Film Festival
6116 North Central Expressway, Suite 105
Dallas 75206
214-821-6300
www.usafilmfestival.com

For youngsters, this is the oldest and largest film festival in the world, and it features the best new films—domestic and international. It is held each year at the Angelika Film Center toward the end of January. The films are shown on Saturday and Sunday afternoons.

Plano Symphony Orchestra's Family Series

972-473-7262
www.planosymphony.org

"Symphony Sundays" are for children ages four to twelve, but open to any age. It's a wonderful opportunity for young children to begin to appreciate classical music. The interactive concert and the "instrument petting zoo" are big hits. Another highlight is when the musicians explain their instruments and talk about their craft. Each concert is approximately forty-five minutes. Tickets for a series of five concerts can be purchased for as little as $20 per person!

The Texas Art & Rubber Stamp Festival

Grapevine Convention Center
1209 South Main Street
Grapevine 76051
817.410.3459
www.grapevinetexasusa.com

Believe it or not, we had several friends tell us about this festival. Check out rubber stamp art, scrapbooking, paper crafting, calligraphy, and free demonstrations. Children under twelve get in free.

FEBRUARY

Arts, Letters Live Jr.
Dallas Museum of Art
1717 North Harwood
Dallas 75201
214-922-1822
www.dallasmuseumofart.org

For kids ages nine to thirteen and their families, this highly touted event showcases various authors.

MARCH

Easter in the Park
Lee Park
3400 Turtle Creek Boulevard
Dallas 75219
972-380-7390

This Easter, Sunday afternoon tradition combines a pooch parade with owners and pets dressing up in hilarious outfits and a performance by the Dallas Symphony Orchestra. Bring a picnic and enjoy some excellent people watching.

Taste of Plano
Southfork Ranch
3700 Hogge Drive
Parker 75002
469-752-8009
www.tasteofplano.com

Forget about the diet for one night and dine on cuisine from over fifty area restaurants. It is held during the beginning of March at the Southfork Ranch—yes that's right, the "site" of the former television show *Dallas*.

TCU Easter Egg Hunt
2800 South University Drive
Fort Worth 76129
817-257-7803
www.alumni.tcu.edu

Six thousand eggs filled with toys and candy dot the lawn of TCU each Easter. Children are divided into age groups for the egg hunt and can win special prizes. We don't want to forget to mention the life-sized Easter bunny and the SuperFrog who pay a visit.

APRIL

Art in the Square
Southlake Town Square
North Carroll between Highway 114 and FM 1709
Southlake 76092
817-329-5566
www.southlaketownsquare.com
Held at the end of the month, Art in the Square is the perfect way to spend the weekend. Adults can choose the perfect picture to hang over the fireplace while the kids spend time at Kids Korner. Past activities at Kids Korner have included face painting, sugar art, easel painting, creating clay necklaces, and making newspaper hats—plus there is a popcorn and cotton candy tent. Look for other child-friendly entertainment on the entertainment schedule. Best of all, admission is free for everyone.

Earth Fest: Go Wild, Go Native!
Texas Discovery Gardens
3601 Martin Luther King Boulevard
Dallas 75210
214-428-7476
www.texasdiscoverygardens.org

Get in touch with nature at this wonderful festival with plenty of outdoorsy things for the little ones to do.

Family Night at Six Flags Benefiting Children's Medical Center Dallas
214-456-8360
www.childrens.com

Usually held on the first Friday in April, families are invited to enjoy a night of festivities and fundraising. There is so much going on and it is a great time to gather a group of friends. Tickets are available by calling the Office of Development at Children's.

Fort Worth Zoo Fun Run
Fort Worth Zoo
1989 Colonial Parkway
Fort Worth 76110
www.fortworthzoo.org

Are you slow as a turtle or fast as a cheetah? What better place to find out than at the Fort Worth Zoo. There is a 5K run/walk through the zoo grounds, a one-mile stroller walk, and a children's activity area with refreshments.

Main Street Fort Worth Arts Festival

Downtown Fort Worth
817-366-4748
www.msfwaf.org

Nationally recognized artists, crafts, gourmet food, performance artists and live music make this Fort Worth's premier festival. This family-fun event takes place mid-April and admission is free.

Mesquite Championship Rodeo (April–September)

1818 Rodeo Drive
Mesquite 75149
972-285-8777
www.mesquiterodeo.com

Join in some authentic Texas fun at the Mesquite Rodeo. Barrel racing, steer wrestling, and bull riding are just a few of the highlights. Your little cowpokes can enjoy the petting zoo, pony rides, and other activities. Open every Friday and Saturday evening from the first weekend in April to the last weekend of September.

The Rise and Shine Fun Run

Hotel Crescent Court
400 Crescent Court
Dallas 75201
www.riseschool.org

The Rise and Shine Fun Run, benefiting the Rise School, is held at the Crescent in the open lot at the intersection of Pearl Street and McKinney Avenue. The morning event includes the Early Riser Kid's IK, 5K Walk and Run, and also features live entertainment, food, and beverages.

Scarborough Faire/The Renaissance Festival

Outside of Waxahachie
972-938-FAIR
www.scarboroughRenFest.com

There are too many events, food, and entertainment to list here. The little ones will enjoy the wonderful butterfly habitat. Tickets are available on the Web site and at various Tom Thumb stores. It is held from mid-April until Memorial Day and takes place just thirty minutes outside of Dallas-Fort Worth, near Waxahachie.

YMCA Healthy Kids Day

www.ymca.net

Held on the second Saturday of April, Healthy Kids Day celebrates our most special resource—our children and their fitness. All day long, families enjoy entertainment, scale obstacle courses, listen to stories, and join forces in parent/child interaction games. Check your local YMCA to see what they have scheduled.

MAY

Cool Thursdays at the Dallas Arboretum (May–July)
8617 Garland Road
Dallas 75218
214-515-6500
www.dallasarboretum.org
Survive the Dallas heat by enjoying a concert on the breathtaking grounds of the arboretum. Young and old will love the performers. Don't forget to get your kids to help you pack a picnic! Children under three are admitted for free.

Dallas ARTFEST
Addison Theatre and Conference Center
15650 Addison Road
Addison 75001
214-565-0200
www.dallasartfest.com

Held every Memorial Day weekend, ARTFEST is not only a great adventure for adults, but also for children. Young artists can paint and play with Play-Doh while adults shop for art and feast on food and fun.

Mayfest
Trinity Park in Fort Worth
817-332-1055
www.mayfest.org

Mayfest is an annual Fort Worth tradition geared toward families and held during the first weekend in May. Children can spend hours in a specially designated area where they can build sandcastles and enjoy other arts and crafts. The day ends with a fireworks show!

Safari Days
Dallas Zoo
650 South R. L. Thornton Freeway
Dallas 75203
214-670-5656
www.dallas-zoo.org

Two days of entertainment, activities, and crafts for the entire family.

Taste Addison

Addison Arts & Events District
4970 Addison Circle Drive
Addison 75001
800-233-4766
www.addisontexas.net

Savor each bite while you taste favorites from countless restaurants—all at discounted prices during this mid-May weekend festival. There is something for everyone; try carnival rides, wine tasting, a cooking demonstration, Midway games, and children's entertainment. Kids under four years old get in free.

Wildflower!

Galatyn Parkway and US 75
Richardson 75080
972-744-4580
www.wildflowerfestival.com

Wildflower! is Richardson's Annual Arts and Music Festival. It is a true celebration of family, music, and festivities. For over eleven years, held on the last weekend of May, this event has drawn people from all over to hear the talents of artists such as Hank Williams, Jr., the Dixie Chicks, Peter Frampton, and Tanya Tucker. There are a Kidz Korner, café, market, jugglers, and petting zoo. Every hour, the Galatyn Fountain does a little light and dancing show to music.

Zoobilee at the Dallas Zoo

650 South R. L. Thornton Freeway
Dallas 75203
214-670-5656
www.dallas-zoo.org

Open to members of the Dallas Zoological Society, this is a great family event held in the evening at the Dallas Zoo. Live entertainment, activities for the kids, and all kinds of food make this a fun-filled night. Invitations are sent out to members of the zoo, so you will have to join to get in on this "wild" party.

JUNE

Concerts in the Garden
Fort Worth Botanic Garden
3220 Botanic Garden Boulevard
Fort Worth 76107
817-665-6000
www.fortworthsymphony.com

Enjoy the sounds of the Fort Worth Symphony while looking at the beautiful grounds of the Fort Worth Botanic Garden. Music selections range from classical to rock 'n' roll. Both table and lawn seating are available. Concerts are held throughout the month of June and usually conclude on the fourth of July.

Jazz Under the Stars at the Dallas Museum of Art
1717 North Harwood
Dallas 75201
214-922-1200
www.dallasmuseumofart.org

Every Thursday throughout the month of June, enjoy a free evening of jazz at the museum. It's held outside the DMA at Harwood and Ross Avenue. Bring your own picnic or purchase food there. It is hot, so bring lots of water and drinks for the kiddos.

Jewish Music, Art, and Food Festival
Charles W. Eisemann Center for the Performing Arts
959 East Lookout Drive
Richardson 75082
www.jccdallas.com
www.eisemanncenter.com

Enjoy Jewish culture and tradition at this annual festival. Crafts, a fair, puppets, delicious food, and music will be enjoyed by your family.

Juneteenth Celebration
Celebrated at several area locations

Learn about the oldest known celebration of the ending of slavery. June 19 marks the day that black slaves in Texas learned that slavery had been abolished by Abraham Lincoln two years earlier. Many Juneteenth celebrations have activities that can be enjoyed by kids while learning about a significant event in Texas history.

JULY

Fourth of July

Red, white, blue, and firework celebrations can be found almost everywhere. From small neighborhood parades to full-blown firework extravaganzas, there is a patriotic way to celebrate near you. Check out the *Dallas Morning News'* www.guidelive.com; it has a comprehensive list of celebrations all over the city with all the information you will need.

Taste of Dallas

West End Historic District
214-741-7185
www.tasteofdallas.org

Touted as the city's largest free outdoor event, you can feast on the delicious eats from local area restaurants while listening to great music during this early July event. Children's entertainment, arts, and crafts are also featured.

AUGUST

Summer Family Fun Program

NorthPark Center
1030 NorthPark Center
Dallas 75225
214-361-6345
www.northparkcenter.com

Keep the kids cool on Saturdays throughout August, while they enjoy puppet shows, arts and crafts, and educational sessions.

SEPTEMBER

GrapeFest

Grapevine Convention Center
1209 South Main
Grapevine 76051
817-410-3185
www.grapevinetexasusa.com/grapefest

Enjoy great wine and delicious food at the largest wine festival in the southwest. There are mini-train rides for kids under five years of age. Admission is free, and GrapeFest is usually held the weekend after Labor Day.

Greek Food Festival of Dallas

Holy Trinity Greek Orthodox Church
13555 Hillcrest Road at Alpha
Dallas 75240
Festival hotline: 972-233-4880
www.greekfestivalofdallas.com

The Chabrias have attended this event for years and always have a great time. Delicious food, Greek dancing, and live music keep both young and old entertained. Last year was Joshua's first year, and he was mesmerized by the live entertainment! Opa! It takes place mid-September.

The Heard Museum's Outdoor Nature Festival

One Nature Place
McKinney 75069
972-562-566
www.heardmuseum.org

Explore the great outdoors and enjoy some fresh air at this wildlife sanctuary that includes over four miles of nature trails. There are special activities for kids.

Oktoberfest

Addison Arts & Events District
4970 Addison Circle Drive
Addison 75001
800-233-4766
www.addisontexas.net

It's not a mistake! Oktoberfest actually takes place in September, just like in Bavaria. You don't have to sprechen zie Deutsch to take part in this authentic recreation of the Munich Oktoberfest. Adults can enjoy beer and German sausages while listening to yodels and watching the polka. Children's activities include carnival rides, a petting zoo, and pony rides. Admission is free for children three years and under.

Plano Balloon Festival

Oak Point Park
2800 East Springcreek Parkway
Plano 75086
972-867-7566
www.planoballoonfest.org

The largest balloon festival in Texas takes place over three days in September. There are special kids' activities, balloon rides, and live entertainment. Children under thirty-six inches get in free. Look for the festival to take place mid-September.

State Fair of Texas (September–October)
Fair Park
1300 Robert B. Cullum Boulevard
Dallas 75210
www.bigtex.com

You can't miss this legendary Texas event, and neither can your young ones. Here is just a tiny sample of things for you to do: a petting zoo, interactive exhibits, puppet shows, live bands, a chance to ride North America's largest Ferris wheel, and lots of food!

OCTOBER

Boo at the Dallas Zoo
650 South R. L. Thornton Freeway at Marsalis
Dallas 75203
214-670-5656
www.dallas-zoo.org

Trick or treating, arts, crafts, and other Halloween surprises are a safe Halloween alternative for children three to ten years old and their families. This is an annual favorite of our children, their friends, and parents too!

Boo at the Fort Worth Zoo
1989 Colonial Parkway
Fort Worth 76110
817-759-7200
www.fortworthzoo.org

Carnival rides, live entertainment, and trick or treating make this a "spooktacular" Halloween event for families.

Haunted Symphony
Dallas Symphony Orchestra
2301 Flora Street
Dallas 75201
214-692-0203
www.dallassymphony.com

Celebrate a classically ghoulish Halloween evening at the Meyerson Symphony Center. Come in costume and try out musical instruments, have your face painted, and trick or treat in the lobby.

Southlake Oktoberfest

Southlake Town Square
North Carroll between Highway 114 and FM 1709
Southlake 76092
817-329-5566
www.southlakeoktoberfest.com

The Southlake Oktoberfest celebration takes place the first weekend in October and offers fun for the entire family. Arts and crafts exhibitors, lots of food and drink, live entertainment, and a 5K run/1-mile fun run are for the grown-ups. The little ones are not forgotten—a bounce house, rock climbing wall, and face painting are just for the kids.

NOVEMBER

Annual Tree Lighting & Carriage Rides

Highland Park Village
Southwest corner of Mockingbird & Preston Road
Dallas 75205
Threejays Carriages: 214-521-6717

Get in the mood for the holidays during this annual Highland Park tradition. Caroling, carriage rides, a Santa sighting, and of course, the tree lighting make this an elegant and merry way to start the season. Every year, it is held the Friday after Thanksgiving. Carriage rides through the residential area of Highland Park are a chance to snuggle under blankets and sing your favorite holiday songs—a Bannister family tradition. You can choose a thirty-minute or sixty-minute horse-drawn carriage ride. Reservations sell out, so it is best to reserve your carriage starting in late October or early November.

Dallas YMCA Turkey Trot

Downtown Dallas
www.thetrot.com

Don't worry about how much you eat on Thanksgiving Day if you participate in the Turkey Trot in downtown Dallas. It's an eight-mile race or three-mile fun run/walk, which is great for young families since baby joggers are welcome.

Fort Worth Train Show

Fort Worth Convention Center
1201 Houston Street
Fort Worth 76102
www.dfwtrainshows.com

Model trains in every size will delight children of all ages. The show is held at the Amon Carter Hall, and children under twelve get in free.

Tinsel Time
Fort Worth Museum of Science and History
1501 Montgomery Street
Fort Worth 76107
www.ftworthrmh.org

Benefiting the Ronald McDonald House of Fort Worth, the museum, planetarium, and Omni Theatre are open exclusively to families who buy a ticket for this event. Children can have their pictures taken with Santa, and there is a silent auction with lots of toys! The best thing is that the money goes to a wonderful organization.

DECEMBER

Breakfast with Santa
The Adolphus Hotel
1321 Commerce Street
Dallas 75202
214-456-8360 or 214-456-2000 for information

What could be better than having your wide-eyed tykes dine with jolly old Saint Nick? Held at the Adolphus Hotel the first Saturday in December, it precedes the Neiman Marcus Adolphus Children's Parade. There are clowns, balloons, artists, and more. Proceeds benefit Children's Medical Center Dallas.

Christmas in New York at Addison Square Garden
15100 Midway Road
Addison 75001
972-960-7465
www.addisonsquaregarden.com

This is a family event that is not to be missed! Imagine Central Park, thousands of holiday lights, falling snow (from the wall-mounted snow machines), ice skating, and hot cider—all close to home and available 24/7 Monday through Sunday, from the middle of December until New Year's Day.

Christmas in the Stockyards
Stockyard District in Fort Worth
817-625-9715
www.stockyardsstation.com

A variety of holiday entertainment and activities are planned throughout the month, so bring the family and soak up some holiday spirit.

Dickens in Historic Downtown Plano
Haggard Park

901 East 15th Street
Plano 75074
972-941-7250

Go back in time and experience the quaintest Dickensian outing with your wee ones as downtown historic Plano is transformed. Music, carolers, and bands are all part of the experience.

Holiday at the Arboretum

8617 Garland Road
Dallas 75218
214-515-6500
www.dallasarboretum.org

December is winter wonderland time at the arboretum! Special events and entertainment are planned throughout the month.

Jingle Bell Run

www.dallascvb.com

Catch some holiday cheer at this annual evening 5K run/walk. Features include a costume contest, crafts, a Santa Land for kids, and a post-race party. The race begins at the Dallas Convention Center.

Neiman Marcus Adolphus Children's Parade

Downtown Dallas
Dallas 75202
214-456-8383
www.childrensparade.com

Put this event on your calendar because you won't want to miss it: it's usually held the first Saturday in December. Large inflatable balloons, music, floats, and of course Santa Claus entertain children of all ages along the streets of downtown Dallas. The parade is free and bleacher seating is offered for around $15 a seat.

Santa's Village

Richardson City Hall
411 West Arapaho
Richardson 75080
972-744-4580
www.cor.net
Hours: 6 to 9 p.m.

Each weekend throughout the month of December, people from all over visit this adorable little town set up in front of Richardson's City Hall. Children can meet Mrs. Claus and make crafts, sit on Santa's lap for photos, or create e-mail letters to him, and families can dine at the café. Admission is free.

DIRECTORY

A

ACTIVITIES (INDOOR)

Angelika Film Center & Cafe

Mockingbird Station
214-841-4700 (recorded information)
214-841-4712 (office)

The Shops at Legacy
972-444-FILM (recorded information)
972-943-1300 (office)

www.angelikafilmcenter.com

The Dallas Aquarium at Fair Park

214-670-8443
www.dallas-zoo.org

Dallas Children's Museum

972-386-6555
www.dallaschildrens.org

Dallas Children's Theatre— The Rosewood Center for the Arts

214-740-0051
www.DCT.org

Dallas Museum of Art

214-922-1200
www.dallasmuseumofart.org

Dallas Museum of Natural History

214-421-3466
www.dallasdino.org

Dallas Symphony Orchestra

214-692-0203
www.dsokids.com

The Dallas World Aquarium

214-720-2224
www.dwazoo.com

Fort Worth Museum of Science and History

817-255-9300
www.fortworthmuseum.org

Fort Worth Stockyards Championship Rodeo

817-625-1025
www.StockyardsRodeo.com

Frontiers of Flight Museum

214-350-3600
www.flightmuseum.com

Galleria Dallas

972-702-7100
www.galleriadallas.com

Interskate 1 Roller Rink

972-221-4666
www.interskate.net

Kimbell Museum of Art

817-332-8451
www.kimbellart.org

Launa's Little Library

214-348-4384

Legends of the Game Baseball Museum

817-273-5600
www.texas.rangers.com

Library Events

Carrollton Public Library
972-466-4800
www.cityofcarrollton.com/library

Dallas Public Library
214-670-1400
www.dallaslibrary.org

Flower Mound Public Library
972-874-6200
http://library.flower-mound.com

Irving Public Library
www.irvinglibrary.org

McKinney Memorial Public Library
972-547-7323

Plano Public Library
www.planolibrary.org

University Park Public Library
214-363-9095
www.uplibrary.org

www.guidelive.com

Loews Cineplex Reel Moms

214-828-6008
www.enjoytheshow.com

Meadows Museum at Southern Methodist University

www.meadowsmuseumdallas.org
214-768-2765

NorthPark Center

214-361-6345
www.northparkcenter.com

The Parks at Arlington

817-467-0200
www.parksatarlington.com

Pepsi Kid's Zone at The Shops at Willow Bend

972-202-4900
www.shopwillowbend.com

Pottery Barn Kid's Story Time

214-522-4845

Ridgmar Mall

817-731-0856
www.ridgmar.com

The Science Place

214-428-5555
www.scienceplace.org

Slappy's Puppet Playhouse

214-369-4849
www.slappysplayhouse.com

Stonebriar Centre

972-668-MALL
www.shopstonebriar.com

Storybook Children's Theatre

972-516-1653
www.dancedepot.net

The Trains at Children's Medical Center—Dallas

214-920-2000
www.childrens.com

Tots Towne

Allen
214-495-TOYS (8697)

Dallas
214-363-9929

www.totstowne.com

Valley View Center

972-661-2424
www.shopvalleyviewcenter.com

ACTIVITIES (OUTDOOR)

Adventure Landing

972-248-4966
wwww.adventurelanding.com

Barnyard Buddies at Fairview Farms

972-633-9779
www.fairview-farms.com/barnyard.htm

Burger's Lake

817-737-3414
www.burgerslake.com

Cedar Ridge Preserve

972-293-5150
www.audubondallas.org

Dallas Arboretum and Botanical Garden

214-327-8263
www.dallasarboretum.org

The Dallas Farmers Market

214-670-5880
www.dallasfarmersmarket.org

Dallas Zoo

214-670-5656
www.dallas-zoo.org

Elves Christmas Tree Farm

903-463-7260
www.elveschristmastreefarm.com

Forest Park Miniature Train Ride

817-336-3328

Fort Worth Botanic Garden

817-871-7689
www.fwbg.org

Fort Worth Rail Market

817-335-6758
www.fortworthrailmarket.com

Fort Worth Zoo

817-759-7050
www.fortworthzoo.org

Fossil Rim Wildlife Center

214-897-2960
www.fossilrim.com

The Heard Nature Science Museum and Wildlife Sanctuary

972-562-5566
www.heardmuseum.org

Log Cabin Village

817-926-5881
www.logcabinvillage.org

McKinney Avenue Trolley

214-855-0006
www.mata.org

Nasher Sculpture Center

214-242-5100
www.NasherSculptureCenter.org

The Playground at Scottish Rite Hospital for Children

214-559-5000
www.tsrhc.org

Southern Methodist University Football

214-SMU-GAME
www.smumustangs.com

Southlake Town Square

817-329-5566
www.southlaketownsquare.com

Texas Discovery Gardens

214-428-7476
www.texasdiscoverygardens.org

Texas Sculpture Garden

972-377-1152
www.texassculpturegarden.org

AU PAIR

Au Pair in America

800-928-7247
www.aupairinamerica.com

AuPairCare Inc.

800-428-7247
www.aupaircare.com

Au Pair Foundation

866-428-7247
www.aupairfoundation.org

Cultural Care Au Pair

800-333-6056
www.culturalcare.com

EurAupair Intercultural Child Care Programs

800-713-2002
www.euraupair.com

Go Au Pair

888-287-2471
www.goaupair.com

B

BABYSITTING SERVICES

Babysitters of Dallas

214-692-1354
817-960-2174 (24/7 pager)
www.babysittersofdallas.com

Caring Hands

972-259-1184
www.caringhands.net

Coughs & Cuddles

Presbyterian Hospital of Plano
972-981-8585
www.texashealth.org

Kiddin' Around Play Care

Coppell
972-462-1300

Frisco
214-618-5433

www.kiddinaroundplaycare.com

The Little Gym

Allen
972-396-7705

Arlington
817-465-9296

Carrollton
972-446-1122

Dallas/Lakewood
214-515-0800

Dallas/Preston and Forest
972-644-7333

Fort Worth
817-346-9655

Plano
972-985-4545

www.thelittlegym.com

BIRTHDAY
(DECORATIONS & FAVORS)

Birthday Express

800-424-7843
www.birthdayexpress.com

Card & Party Factory

Dallas 214-824-6223

Oriental Trading Company, Inc.

888-875-8480
www.orientaltrading.com

Party City

800-477-4841

BIRTHDAY
(ENTERTAINMENT)

Adventure Railroad

972-293-0634

Mr. Barnaby

972-266-5747
www.mrbarnaby.com

Melody "Afi" Bell

214-374-1192

Bonkers the Clown

214-221-9779

Broadway Babies

972-672-2308

Capers for Kids

972-661-2787
www.capersforkids.com

David Chicken

214-929-4376
www.davidchicken.com

Country Carnival

817-477-5556
www.countrycarnival.com

Critterman & Safari Sue

940-365-9741
www.critterman.com

Emergency Ice

214-747-6746
www.emergencyice.com

Face Painting by Germaine

214-826-5009

Fun on the Farm

972-390-1933

www.funonthefarm.net

Jessica's Princess Parties

214-686-1056

www.jessicasprincessparties.com

MiMi's Pony-Go-Round

214-460-0245

Zooniversity

972-979-9847

www.zooniversity.net

BIRTHDAY (LOCATIONS)

Age of Steam Railroad Museum

214-428-0101

www.dallasrailwaymuseum.com

Artzy Smartzy

214-341-0053

Barnyard Buddies

972-633-9779

www.fairview-farms.com/barnyard.htm

Birthday Avenue

972-333-4150

www.birthdayavenue.com

The Dallas Arboretum and Botanical Garden

214-515-6500

www.dallasarboretum.org

Dallas Zoo

214-943-2771

www.dallas-zoo.org

Emler Swim School

972-599-SWIM

www.iswimemler.com

Fort Worth Museum of Science and History

817-255-9300

www.fortworthmuseum.org

Fort Worth Zoo

817-759-7200

www.fortworthzoo.org

Frisco Fire Station

972-335-5525

www.friscofire.org

Life Time Fitness

972-202-8100

www.lifetimefitness.com

The Little Gym

Lakewood
214-515-0800

Preston/Forest
972-644-7333

www.thelittlegym.com

My Gym

Arlington
817-937-5552

Flower Mound
972-874-5700

Frisco
972-378-9000

Plano
972-578-6630

www.my-gym.com

Playtime

972-781-2244
www.mytimeplaytime.com

Premier Club

214-891-6641

Pump It Up

Frisco
214-387-9663

Dallas
972-792-9663

www.pumpitupparty.com

The Purple Cow

817-737-7177

The Scottish Rite Hospital Playground

214-559-5000
Jeannie.munoz@tsrh.org

Sunshine Glaze Creative Studio

817-424-1417
www.sunshineglaze.com

Sweet & Sassy

817-251-6353
www.sweetandsassy.com

University Park Fire Station

214-987-5383

Van Grow: Studio for the Arts

817-348-0505
www.vangrowstudio.com

Whole Foods Market

214-361-8887

BIRTHDAY (RENTALS)

All-4-Fun

972-234-1700
www.all-4-fun.com

Bill Reed Decorations

214-823-3154
www.billreed.com

Ducky Bobs

Dallas area
972-381-8000

Fort Worth area
817-370-8400

www.duckybobs.com

Just Jump'n

214-634-5867
www.justjumpn.com

M & M Rental Center

214-350-5373
www.mmspecialevents.com

Simply Pretend

972-396-1486
www.simplypretend.com

The Social Bee

972-782-0151

BIRTHING CENTERS

Allen Birthing Center

214-495-9911
www.allenbirthingcenter.com

Birth and Women's Center

214-821-8190
www.birthcenter.net

Lovers Lane Birth Center

214-366-3579
www.dallasmidwife.com

Women's Health Alliance

214-824-3200
www.wha-docs.com

BOOKSTORES

Barnes & Noble

Cedar Hill
972-293-7397

Dallas/Northwest Highway
214-739-1124

Dallas/Preston Road at Beltline
972-661-8068

Frisco
972-668-2820

Fort Worth
817-335-2791

Grapevine
817-251-1997

Irving
972-594-8187

Lewisville
972-315-7966

Plano/West 15th
972-422-3372

Plano/Preston Road at Park
972-612-0999

Richardson
972-699-7844

www.bn.com

Bebe Grand

214-887-9224

Bookstop

214-357-2697
www.bn.com

Borders

Dallas/Lovers Lane
214-739-1166

Dallas/Uptown
214-219-0512

Dallas/Preston-Royal
214-363-1977

Fort Worth 8
817-370-9473

Fort Worth
817-737-0444

Lewisville
972-459-2321

Plano
972-713-9857

www.borders.com

Doubleday Bookshop

214-528-6756

Logos Book Store

Dallas
214-369-3245

Fort Worth
817-732-5070

www.logosbookstore.net

Southern Methodist University Bookstore, Barnes & Noble College

214-768-2435

BREASTFEEDING (LACTATION CONSULTANTS, ORGANIZATIONS, AND BREAST PUMP RENTAL)

The Breastfeeding Center and Boutique Harris Methodist Fort Worth Hospital

817-882-2000
www.harrisfw.org

Confident Beginnings

Jill Walpole
972-390-0812

Lactation Consultant Services

Judy Eastburn
972-931-5578

La Leche League

Dallas County
972-669-5714

Tarrant County
817-588-1006

www.lllusa.org

Medela

www.medela.com

Medical City Hospital

972-566-4580 (Rental Station)
972-566-4811 (Warmline)
www.medicalcityhospital.com

A Mother's Gift

Presbyterian Hospital of Plano
972-981-3788

Mother's Milk Bank at Austin

512-494-0800
www.mmbaustin.org

Natural Beginnings

Sharon Mattes: 972-495-2805
Linda Worzer: 972-699-3921
www.naturalbeginningsonline.com

The Nesting Place

Kay Willis
877-625-6803
www.thenestingplace.net

Simply Mom's, A Breastfeeding Boutique

Baylor Medical Center at Garland
972-487-5154

Baylor University Medical Center—Dallas
214-820-3103

www.bhcs.com

C

CAKES

A and J Bakery

Dallas/Oak Lawn
214-526-0077

Dallas/Pacific Avenue
214-880-0850

Dallas/Coit Road
972-732-7724

www.aandjbakery.com

Amazing Cakes by Tom Lawson

214-521-3456
www.amazingcake.com

Aston's English Bakery & Catering

214-368-6425

Cakes To Go & More

214-357-2488
www.cakestogo.com

Casa Linda Bakery

214-321-0355 or 214-321-0551

Central Market

Dallas
214-234-7000

Plano
469-241-9336

www.centralmarket.com

Dallas Affaires Cake Company

214-826-9409

La Duni Latin Kitchen & Baking Studio

214-520-6888
www.laduni.com

Magnolia Café & Bakery

972-459-3100

Moonlighting Cakeworks

972-418-7663

Romano's Bakery

214-821-5056
www.romanosbakery.com

Stein's Bakery

972-385-9911

Two Women Baking

214-738-0855
www.twowomenbaking.com

CAKE BAKING AND ACCESSORIES

Sur la Table

Dallas
214-219-4404

Plano
972-378-5532

www.surlatable.com

Williams-Sonoma

800-541-2233
www.williams-sonoma.com

Wilton Industries

800-794-5866

www.wilton.com

CAR SEAT INSPECTION

Carrollton Police Department

972-466-3530

Cook Children's-Lewisville Specialty Clinic

682-885-2634

Dr. Babyproofer

972-380-1116

Flower Mound Police Department

972-874-3345

City of Fort Worth Health Department—Car Seat Safety Program

817-871-7240

Harris Methodist Hospital

888-4-HARRIS

Presbyterian Hospital of Plano

972-981-3948

www.phscare.org

Safe for Life

214-497-1650

Seat Check

866-SEAT-CHECK

www.seatcheck.org

CHILDBIRTH EDUCATORS AND COURSES

Confident Beginnings

972-390-0812 or 972-814-7556

Gentle Birth Companions

972-237-1626

Janet Miller

972-475-6556

www.yourpregnancymatters.com

Natural Beginnings

Sharon Mattes: 972-495-2805
Linda Worzer: 972-699-3921
www.naturalbeginningsonline.com

The Nesting Place

877-625-6803

www.thenestingplace.net

Jill Stillwell

817-563-1007

CHILDBIRTH RESOURCES

ALACE (Association of Labor Assistants and Childbirth Educators)

888-222-5223

www.alace.org

Association of Texas Midwives

903-592-4220

www.texasmidwives.com

The Bradley Method of Natural Childbirth

800-4-A-BIRTH
www.bradleybirth.com

Childbirth and Postpartum Professional Association (CAPPA)

888-MY-CAPPA
www.childbirthprofessional.com

Doulas of North America

888-788-DONA
www.dona.org

HypnoBirthing

www.hypnobirthing.com

Intuitive Birthing: The Amazing, Life Changing Benefits of Natural Birth

A book by Kalena Cook
with Margaret Christensen, MD

www.IntuitiveBirth.com

MANA (Midwives Alliance of North America)

888-923-MANA
www.mana.org

Natural Beginnings

www.naturalbeginningsonline.com

Pregnancy Matters

www.yourpregnancymatters.com

Sidelines

888-447-4754

ViaCord

866-668-4895
www.viacord.com

Waterbirth International

800-641-2229
www.waterbirth.org

Women's Health Alliance

214-823-3200
www.wha-docs.com

Women to Women Health Associates

214-823-6500
www.wwha.yourmd.com

CHILDREN'S APPAREL

Animal Crackers

817-416-6246

Babies on the Boulevard

817-737-7171
www.gordonboswell.com

Baby Bean, Vintage Daywear

www.babybeanwear.com

Baby Gap

800-GAP-STYLE
www.gap.com

Babystyle.com

877-378-9537

Bamboo & Bananas

469-366-2084

Bebe Grand

214-887-9224

www.bebegrand.com

The Children's Place

877-PLACE USA

www.childrensplace.com

Chocolate Soup

214-363-6981

Dillard's

Dallas
972-386-4595

Dallas
214-373-7000

Hurst
817-284-4566

Irving
972-258-4968

Plano
972-202-4730

Richardson
972-783-2598

www.dillards.com

Flora and Henri

888-749-9698

www.florahenri.com

For Children

214-363-1651

Good Night Moon

214-691-9393

www.gnm.com

Gymboree

877-4GYMWEB

www.gymboree.com

Hanna Andersson

800-222-0544

www.hannaandersson.com

Haute Baby

214-357-3068

www.hautebaby.com

Hip Hip Hooray!

214-369-2788

Janie & Jack

Frisco
214-618-6430

Plano
469-366-0707

www.janieandjack.com

Keedo

972-867-6100

Kid Biz

214-692-5437

Kidcrazy.biz

214-696-6287

www.kidcrazy.biz

Korshak Kids at Stanley Korshak

214-871-3668

Life Size at Fred Segal

310-458-1160

www.lifesizekids.com

Little Bo-tique Children's Apparel

972-899-8787

www.littlebotiquewest.com

Marshalls

888-MARSHALLS

www.marshallsonline.com

Mini Boden

866-206-9508

www.miniboden.com

Neiman Marcus

Plano
972-629-1700

Dallas/Downtown
214-741-6911

Dallas/Northpark
214-363-8311

888-888-4757

www.neimanmarcus.com

Nordstrom

Dallas
972-702-0055

Frisco
972-712-3794

www.nordstrom.com

Oilily Dallas

214-692-5173

www.oilily-world.com

Old Navy

800-653-6289

www.oldnavy.com

Orient Expressed

888-856-3948

www.orientexpressed.com

Papo d'Anjo

888-660-6111

www.papodanjo.com

Safari Kids

972-473-3336

www.safarikidsplano.com

St. Michael's Woman's Exchange

214-521-3862

Stein Mart

www.steinmart.com

Strasburg Children

Plano
469-366-0099

Dallas
972-934-2074

www.strasburgchildren.com

Target and Super Target

www.target.com

Ten Monkeys

214-350-2888

www.ten-monkeys.com

TJ Maxx

800-2TJMAXX

www.tjmaxx.com

You and Me Babe

972-669-2110

www.youandmebabe.com

CHILDREN'S APPAREL (RESALE)

Kids Kloset

214-369-2243

www.kidskloset.com

Kidswap

214-890-7927

Kid to Kid

Allen
972-390-1117

Plano
972-781-2543

Mudpuppy . . . Gently Housebroken Kidswear

817-731-2581

Once Upon a Child

Flower Mound
972-874-0779

Plano
972-618-5800

www.ouac.com

CHILDREN'S HEALTH RESOURCES

American Academy of Medical Acupuncture

www.medicalacupuncture.org

American Chiropractor Association

800-986-4636

www.amerchiro.org

International Chiropractic Pediatric Association

610-565-2360

www.icpa4kids.com

International College of Applied Kinesiology

www.icak.com

The International Dyslexia Association—Dallas

972-233-9107

www.interdys.org

Learning Disabilities Association of Texas

800-604-7500

The National Center for Complementary and Alternative Medicine

www.nccam.nih.gov/health/practitioner/index.htm

The Upledger Institute, Inc.

561-622-4706

www.upledger.com

CLASSES

THE ARTS

ART-A-RAMA

Plano
972-423-4554

Frisco
972-377-9900

www.art-a-rama.com

Artysmarties

214-352-0747

Artzy Smartzy

214-341-0053
www.artzysmartzy.com

Capers for Kids

972-661-ARTS
www.capersforkids.com

**Creative Arts Theatre and School
(CATS)**

817-265-8512
www.creativearts.org

**Dallas Children's Theatre—The
Rosewood Center for the Arts**

214-978-0010
www.DCT.org

Dallas Museum of Art

214-922-1200
www.dallasmuseumofart.org

**Fort Worth Museum of
Science and History**

817-255-9300 or 888-255-9300

www.fortworthmuseum.org

Lakewood Arts Academy

214-827-1222
www.lakewoodarts.com

Pigment School of the Arts

214-352-ARTS
www.pigmentarts.com

The Purple Crayon

972-516-4915
www.thepurplecrayon.org

Storybook Children's Theatre

972-516-1653
www.dancedepot.net

Van Grow: Studio for the Arts

817-348-0505
www.vangrowstudio.com

COMPUTER

High Tech Kids, Inc./The Science Place

214-696-5437 or 866-230-5437
www.htku.com

DANCE

Arabesque Studio of Dance

972-233-2532

Carter Dance Academy

214-823-8933

Chamberlain School of Ballet

972-985-1374
www.chamberlainschoolofballet.com

Cherrilane School of Dance

214-821-2066

Dance Depot

972-516-1653

www.dancedepot.net

Dancing Angels Ministry

214-712-6914

Gotta Dance

972-769-0017

www.gottadanceplano.com

Preston Center Dance

214-739-1737

www.pcdance.net

Southlake Dance Academy

817-251-1849

www.southlakedanceacademy.com

GYM

Gymboree Play & Music

Dallas and Plano
214-341-2386

Lewisville
972-459-0934

Grapevine
817-424-3932

Frisco
214-387-9106

Arlington
817-419-3512

Fort Worth
817-263-2386

www.gymboree.com

Gym Kids Sports Center

972-355-9988

The Little Gym

Allen
972-396-7705

Arlington
817-465-9296

Carrollton
972-446-1122

Dallas/Mockingbird
214-515-0800

Dallas Preston-Forest
972-644-7333

Fort Worth
817-346-9655

Plano
972-985-4545

www.thelittlegym.com

My Gym Children's Fitness Center

Arlington
817-937-5552

Frisco
972-378-9000

Plano
972-578-6630

www.my-gym.com

WOGA

972-866-9642

www.woga.net

ICE SKATING

Americas Ice Garden

214-720-8080
www.icesk8aig.com

Dr Pepper StarCenter

Farmer's Branch
214-432-3131

Frisco
214-387-5600

Plano
972-758-7528

Duncanville
972-283-9133

Euless
817-267-4233

Irving
972-831-2453

www.drpepperstarcenter.com

KARATE

Chamberlain Studios of Self-Defense

214-351-5367
www.dallaskenpo.com

MUSIC

Dallas Music

214-363-4980

East Dallas Children's Music

214-324-2224
www.eastdallaschildrensmusic.com

Gymboree Play & Music

Dallas/Plano
214-341-2386

Lewisville
972-459-0934

Grapevine
817-424-3932

Frisco
214-387-9106

Arlington
817-419-3512

www.gymboree.com

Kindermusik

Dallas/Park Cities
214-363-6542

Dallas/Lakewood
214-680-7464

Coppell, Flower Mound,
Las Colinas, and Southlake
972-401-0150

Carrollton
972-292-3626

Plano/Stonebriar Mall area
972-712-8359

Frisco
972-262-6534

Grand Prairie
972-262-6534

Plano
972-596-4742

800-628-5687
www.kindermusik.com

Music Together of Dallas, Inc.

972-960-1975

www.musictogetherdallas.com

TCU Early Childhood Music Program

817-257-6134

www.music.tcu.edu/early_childhood.asp

SWIM

Baby Bear-a-Cudas at Baylor Fitness Center

214-820-7870

www.baylortomlandryfitnesscenter.com

Dolfin Swim School

214-361-4542

www.dolfinswimschool.com

Emler Swim School

Arlington
817-275-7946

Colleyville
817-481-7946

Plano
972-599-7946

www.iswimemler.com

Fish Factory Swim School at Baylor Fitness Center

214-820-7870

www.baylortomlandryfitnesscenter.com

Infant Aquatics

Dallas/Bev Steinfink: 214-890-7946

Frisco/Richard Wescott: 972-712-5704

www.infantaquatics.com

Swim Kids Swim School

972-355-9988

Swimmers by Jessica

214-360-9037

Tots Swim Class at Premier Club

214-891-6619

YOGA

Let's Play Yoga

972-618-3079

www.letsplayyoga.com

Mommy & Me Yoga at Bend Studio

214-841-9642

www.bendstudio.com

Mommy & Me Yoga at Dallas Yoga Center

214-443-9642

www.dallasyogacenter.com

Sunstone Yoga

214-373-3999

YMCA Downtown Dallas

214-954-0500

www.downtowndallasymca.org

MISCELLANEOUS FUN

Baby Sign Language

Presbyterian Hospital of Dallas
800-477-3729

Presbyterian Hospital of Plano
800-477-3729

www.texashealth.org

Baby Signs

Harris Methodist Fort Worth Hospital
888-4-HARRIS
www.texashealth.org

Infant Massage

Presbyterian Hospital of Dallas
800-477-3729
www.texashealth.org

Infant Massage by Monica Hamer

214-642-0242
www.monicahamer.com

Mis Amigos

214-265-0981
www.misamigosdallas.com

Play and Learn

Dallas
214-368-7765

Plano
972-596-4949

www.play-and-learn.net

COMPLEMENTARY MEDICINE

Greenville Avenue Chiropratic and Applied Kinesiology

214-823-1323

Kinesiology Clinic, Integrated Healing Sciences

214-521-4873

Nancy Miller, DC

214-473-8188

COMPLEMENTARY MEDICINE RESOURCES

American Academy of Medical Acupuncture

www.medicalacupuncture.org

American Chiropractor Association

800-986-4636
www.amerchiro.org

International Chiropractic Pediatric Association

610-565-2360
www.icpa4kids.com

International College of Applied Kinesiology

www.icak.com

The International Dyslexia Association—Dallas

214-890-8151
www.interdys.org

Learning Disabilities Association of Texas

800-604-7500
www.ldat.org

The National Center for Complementary and Alternative Medicine

www.nccam.nih.gov/health/practitoner/index.htm

The Upledger Institute, Inc.

561-622-4706
www.upledger.com

CPR EDUCATION

American Heart Association

214-748-7212 or 877-242-4277
www.americanheart.org

American Red Cross

214-678-4800
www.redcross.org

Arlington Memorial Hospital

817-548-6500
www.arlingtonmemorial.org

Baylor Healthcare System

800-4BAYLOR
www.bhcs.com

Dallas Association of Parent Education (DAPE)

972-699-0420
www.dallasparents.org

Frisco Fire Department

972-335-5525
www.friscofire.org

Harris Methodist Hospital

888-4-HARRIS
www.harrishospitals.org

Medical Center of Lewisville

972-420-1000
www.lewisvillemedical.com

Medical Center of Plano

972-596-6800
www.medicalcenterplano.com

The Nesting Place

877-625-6803
www.thenestingplace.net

Presbyterian Healthcare System

800-4PRESBY
www.phscare.org

YMCA

www.ymcadallas.org

D

DOOR TO DOOR DELIVERY SERVICES

BABY GEAR

Baby's Away

www.babysaway.com

DRY CLEANER

Avon Cleaners

469-621-2656

Bibbentucker's

www.bibbentuckers.com

FOOD DELIVERY

Albertson's
www.albertsons.com

Central Market
Dallas
214-361-2169

Plano
469-241-8386

www.centralmarket.com

The Chefmeister
972-539-1887
www.thechefmeister.com

Diet Gourmet
972-934-0900
www.dietgourmet.com

Feastivities, Gourmet-to-Go
817-377-3011
www.feastivitiesinc.com

Rehoboth Ranch
903-450-8145
www.rehobothranch.com

BEAUTY SERVICES

Alice Hughes
214-343-7021

NLook
469-241-9744

DIAPER DELIVERY

Albertson's
www.albertsons.com

The Baby Outlet
877-693-BABY
www.babyoutlet.com

DFWgrocer.com
972-267-4440
www.dfwgrocer.com

DryBottoms.com
866-drybottoms
www.drybottoms.com

Metroplex Diaper Service
972-780-9801
www.metroplexdiapers.com

PET SERVICES

Marsha's Pampered Pet Sitting
214-341-4350
www.marshaspets.com

Park Cities Pet Sitter
214-828-0192
www.parkcitiespetsitter.com

PHARMACIES

Dougherty's Pharmacy
214-363-4318

Drugstore.com
800-378-4786
www.drugstore.com

E

EARLY CHILDHOOD PTA

Allen ECPTA

www.aecpta.com

Bradfield Elementary Preschool Association

214-780-3200

Carrollton ECPTA

www.cecpta.org

North Carrollton ECPTA

www.ncecpta.org

Collin County ECPTA

www.ccecpta.com

The Colony ECPTA

www.inthecolony.com

Coppell ECPTA

www.myschoolonline.com

North Dallas ECPTA

www.ndecpta.com

Far North Dallas ECPTA

972-732-6574

Farmers Branch ECPTA

www.myschoolonline.com

Garland ECPTA

www.earlychildhoodpta.com

Hyer Elementary School Preschool Association

214-361-9658

Lake Highlands ECPTA

www.lhaecpta.org

Lakewood ECPTA

www.lecpta.org

Greater Lewisville ECPTA

www.myschoolonline.com

Mesquite ECPTA

972-613-7607

Preston Hollow ECPTA

www.phecpta.com

Richardson ECPTA

www.town-hall.net/Education/ptsa.html

Texas PTA

Nationwide: 1-800-TALKPTA

University Park Preschool Association

214-750-1233

F

FITNESS (PROGRAMS AND STUDIOS)

Arlington Memorial Hospital

817-548-6575
www.texashealth.org

Strollerfit!

Allen, Dallas, and Frisco:
Darlene Davis: 214-394-5101

Plano and Richardson:
Victoria Patel: 469-633-1151

www.strollerfit.com

YMCA Downtown Dallas

214-954-0500
www.downtowndallasymca.org

Yoga for Life

972-392-9642
www.yfldallas.com

FITNESS (PERSONAL TRAINERS)

Delivering Fitness

214-679-7871
www.deliveringfitness.com

Executive Personal Training

Chad Krisher
214-581-5299

Future Mommy Fitness

972-985-0363
www.futuremommy.com

Muscle Moms

Laurie Stein: 214-340-2199

FURNITURE & GEAR

Babies "R" Us

Lewisville
972-459-9333

Arlington
817-784-2229

Plano
972-735-1229

Addison
972-247-4229

Mesquite
972-682-1450

Fort Worth
817-423-8829

www.babiesrus.com

be-dazzled!

972-378-3211
www.bedazzledplano.com

Bellini

214-352-2512
www.bellini.com

Cargo Kids

Hurst
817-595-1225

Frisco
214-387-0109

www.cargokids.com

Designs for Children

817-732-6711

Haute Tot

818-448-8467
www.hautetot.com

The Land of Nod

800-933-9904
www.landofnod.com

Frisco
972-335-5222

Richardson
972-234-2552

www.usababy.com

H

HAIRCUTS

Cartoon Cuts

972-712-4247
www.cartooncuts.com

Chop Shop

214-348-8862

Cool Cuts for Kids

214-252-9800
www.coolcuts4kids.com

Crop Shop

214-348-8862

The Grooming Room at Culwell and Sons

214-522-7030
www.culwell.com

Kids B Kids Haircuts for Children

Dallas
972-233-2112

Plano
972-596-8979

Kids Kuts

214-874-0800

Le Duke Hair Dressing

817-377-8778

Lover's Lane Barbers and Manicurists

214-522-6595

Amy Rowlett

214-503-3560 (Office)
214-315-3796 (Cell)

Sport Clips Haircuts

Dallas
214-219-5900

Frisco
972-668-5324

Fort Worth
817-332-3020

800-872-4247 (Customer Service)
www.sportclips.com

Stride Rite Hair Salon

214-373-1124

Sweet & Sassy

817-251-6353
www.sweetandsassy.com

HEALTH RESOURCES (SPECIALTY)

Early Childhood Intervention

800-250-2246
www.eci.state.tx.us

Lakewood Pediatric Therapy, Inc.

The Sensory Integration Center of Dallas
214-821-9083

The Sensory Integration Center of Coppell
972-745-8087

www.sensoryintegration.com

The Language, Speech, and Hearing Clinic

Shelton School
972-774-1772
www.shelton.org

HOSPITALS

Arlington Memorial Hospital

817-548-6100 (General)
817-548-6500 (Classes)
www.texashealth.org

Baylor All Saints Medical Center—Fort Worth

817-926-2544 (General)
www.baylorhealth.com

Baylor Medical Center at Garland

972-487-5000 (General)
972-487-5154 (Simply Mom's Breastfeeding Boutique)
www.baylorhealth.com

Baylor Medical Center at Irving

972-579-8100
www.baylorhealth.com

Baylor Regional Medical Center—Grapevine

817-481-1588
www.baylorhealth.com

Baylor University Medical Center—Dallas

214-820-0111 (Main)
800-422-9567 (Classes)
214-820-3103 (Simply Mom's Breastfeeding Boutique)
www.baylorhealth.com

Denton Community Hospital

940-898-7000
www.dentonhospital.com

Harris Methodist/Fort Worth

817-882-2000 (General)
817-882-BABY (Breastfeeding Resource Center)
888-4-HARRIS (Classes)
www.texashealth.org

Las Colinas Medical Center

972-969-2000
www.lascolinasmedical.com

Medical Center of Lewisville

972-420-1000 (General)
972-420-1086 (Classes)
www.lewisvillemedical.com

Medical Center of Plano

972-596-6800 (General)
972-519-1251 (Classes)
www.medicalcenterofplano.com

Medical City Hospital

972-566-7000 (General)
972-566-7153 (Parent Education)
www.medicalcityhospital.com

Methodist Charlton Medical Center

214-947-7777 (General)
214-947-7199 (Labor and Delivery)
www.methodisthealthsystem.org

Methodist Dallas Medical Center

214-947-8181 (General)
214-947-3000 (Maternity)
www.methodisthealthsystem.org

Parkland Memorial Hospital

214-590-8000 (General)
214-631-BABY (University Neonatal Services)
www.pmh.org

Presbyterian Hospital of Dallas

214-345-6789
www.texashealth.org

Presbyterian Hospital of Plano

972-981-8000 (General)
972-981-3788 (A Mother's Gift for Lactation)
www.texashealth.org

HOSPITALS (CHILDREN)

Children's Medical Center Dallas

214-456-8360
www.childrens.com

Cook Children's

682-885-4000
www.cookchildrens.com

Our Children's House at Baylor

Allen
972-727-5312

Coppell
972-304-6062

Dallas
214-820-9850

Grapevine
817-305-5800

Irving
972-790-8505

Waxahachie
972-938-7040

www.bhcs.com

North Texas Hospital for Children at Medical City

972-566-8888
www.jacknjill.com

Texas Scottish Rite Hospital for Children

214-559-5000
www.tsrhc.org

M

MASSAGE

Baylor Tom Landry Fitness Center

214-820-7870
www.baylortomlandryfitnesscenter.com

Body Essentials

972-596-2470

The Greenhouse

817-640-4000
www.thegreenhousespa.net

Rhonda Grubb

214-327-1013

Monica Hamer

214-642-0242
www.monicahamer.com

Sandra Honea

469-358-8960

Lori Larsen-Hart

214-213-5111

The Riviera Spa

214-521-2112
www.rivieraspadallas.com

The Spa at the Cooper Aerobic Center

972-392-7729

The Spa at the Crescent

Hotel Crescent Court

214-871-3232
www.crescentcourt.com

MATERNITY CLOTHING

A. Hooper & Co.

817-348-9911
www.ahooperco.com

Babystyle

877-378-9537
www.babystyle.com

Bella Band

415-642-2879
www.ingridandisabel.com
www.bellaband.com

BellaBlu Maternity

888-678-0034
www.bellablumaternity.com

Belly Basics Pregnancy Survival Kit

www.babystyle.com
www.babycenter.com

BellyDance Maternity

888-802-1133
www.bellydancematernity.com

Destination Maternity

972-788-4115
www.maternitymall.com

elements

214-987-0837
www.elementsclothing.com

Gap Maternity

972-776-4750
www.gapmaternity.com

Japanese Weekend

469-366-4474
www.japaneseweekend.com

Liz Lange Maternity

888-616-5777
www.lizlange.com

Mimi Maternity

Frisco
469-633-1465

Hurst
817-284-0475

Fort Worth
817-332-7223

www.mimimaternity.com

Naissance Maternity

800-505-0517
www.naissancematernity.com

A Pea in the Pod

Dallas
214-346-9140

Plano
469-366-1018

www.apeaninthepod.com

Pickles & Ice Cream

Dallas
214-361-1898

Plano
972-781-1898

www.picklesmaternity.com

Target and Super Target

www.target.com

MISSING CHILDREN

The Federal Bureau of Investigation's Missing and Exploited Children's Program

www.fbi.gov/kids/crimepre/abduct/abdmiss.htm

McGruff the Crime Dog

www.mcgruff-safe-kids.com

National Center for Missing and Exploited Children

800-843-5678
www.missingkids.com

National Child Identification Program

214-630-5895
www.childidprogram.com

N

NANNY (AGENCIES)

Domestically Yours

972-669-5059
www.domesticallyyours.com

MBF Agency (Mom's Best Friend)

972-446-0500 or 866-26-NANNY
www.momsbestfriend.com

Park Cities Home Staffer

972-774-4550

NANNY (TAXES)

Breedlove & Associates

888-273-3356
www.breedlove-online.com

HomeWork Solutions

800-626-4829
www.4nannytaxes.com

Household Employment Tax Services

www.nannytaxusa.com

Internal Revenue Service

800-829-1040 (Asking tax questions)
800-829-3676 (Ordering forms)
www.irs.ustreas.gov

Nanny Tax, Inc.

888-626-6982
www.nanytax.com

Texas Workforce Commission

800-832-9394
www.twc.state.tx.us

NANNY (REFERENCE CHECK)

The Integrity Center

972-484-6140 or 800-456-1811
www.integctr.com/CheckNanny/

NEWSPAPERS

The Dallas Morning News

214-977-8924 or 877-932-2390
www.dallasnews.com

Fort Worth Star-Telegram

817-332-3333 or 800-222-3978
www.dfw.com

People Newspapers

214-739-2244

Star Community Newspapers

972-422-7355
www.dfwcn.com

NUTRITION

American Dietetic Association

800-877-1600
www.eatright.org

O

ORGANIC (HOME & YARD)

Baker Environmental Services

469-443-0990
www.bakeresi.com

Blackmon Mooring Steamatic

877-730-1948
www.blackmonmooring.com

**Children's Health Environmental
Coalition (CHEC)**

609-252-1915
www.checknet.org

The Dirt Doctor

www.dirtdoctor.com

Earth Friendly Products

www.ecos.com

Ecosafe Pest Control

214-358-5201 or 800-710-4545
www.ecosafepest.com

green living

214-821-8444
www.green-living.com

Jackson Mosquito Control

214-350-9200 or 800-340-6747
www.jacksonmosquitocontrol.com

Mosquito Nix

972-934-2000 866-934-2002
www.mosquitonix.com

Rhode's Nursery and Nature Store

972-864-1934 or 800-864-4445
www.beorganic.com

RID-All Pest Control

214-340-6969
www.ridall.biz

Soils Alive

972-272-9211
www.soilsalive.com

Walton's Lawn & Garden Center

214-321-2387

P

PARENTING CLASSES AND SEMINARS

Baby & Me Week

The Greenhouse Spa
817-640-4000
www.thegreenhousespa.net

Dallas Association for Parent Education (DAPE)

972-699-0420
Warmline (Monday-Friday, 9 a.m. to 3 p.m.):
972-699-7742
www.dallasparents.org

Dr. Jan Dunn, LPC, LMFT

214-890-6637
www.drjandunn.com

Love and Logic

800-338-4065
www.loveandlogic.com

Natural Beginnings

Sharon Mattes: 972-495-2805
Linda Worzer: 972-699-3921
www.naturalbeginningsonline.com

The Nesting Place

Kay Willis, RN
877-625-6803
www.thenestingplace.net

St. Alcuin Montessori School

972-239-1745
www.saintalcuin.org

Touch Points for Toddlers

888-4-HARRIS

PARENTING GROUPS

Cradle Roll at Temple Emanu-El

214-706-0000
www.tedallas.org

Homebirth Association of North Dallas (HAND)

214-521-9310
www.homebirthdallas.org

Incredible Infants

Harris Methodist Southwest Education Center
888-4-HARRIS
www.texashealth.org

Jewish Community Center

214-739-2737
www.jccdallas.org

Moms & Babies Newborn and Crawlers Groups

Presbyterian Hospital of Dallas
214-345-8568
www.phscare.org

MOMS Club

www.MOMSClub.org

MOPS (Mothers of Preschoolers)

www.gospelcom.net/mops

Mothers & More

National Headquarters
630-941-3553
www.mothersandmore.org

Plano
972-994-1118
www.mothersandmoreplano.org

Lewisville
www.greaterlewisvillemothersandmore.org

Hurst/Euless/Bedford
817-424-8858
www.ahconnect.com/mothersandmore

New Dad Group

Presbyterian Hospital of Dallas
214-345-8568
www.phscare.org

New Moms and Babies Support Group

Highland Park United Methodist Church
214-523-2202

New Moms Support Group

Contact: Monica Hamer
214-642-0242
www.monicahamer.com

Parents of Little Ones (POLO)

Church of the Incarnation
214-522-0160

PHOTOGRAPHERS

Stacy Bratton (SD/SK Studio)

214-741-7666
www.stacybratton.com

John Derryberry

214-357-5457
www.johnderryberry.com

James French Photography

214-720-0990
www.jamesfrenchphotography.com

John Haynsworth

214-559-3700

Sally Larroca

214-363-2598
www.sallylarrocaphotography.com

Jennifer Lipshy Photography

214-358-6822

www.lipshy.com

Milburn's PortraitArt

817-882-0811

www.milburnsportraitart.com

Morgan Studio

214-821-0811

www.morganphotography.com

Debra O'Brien Portraiture

214-373-1703

www.debraobrien.com

Poetic Portraits by Charla

972-407-9382

www.colormehappy.com

Stacy Sims Photography

214-684-4648

www.stacysimsphotography.com

Nichole Capatino Stephens Photography

214-542-2051

www.nicholestephens.com

Amy Twomey Photography

214-435-9763

www.amytwomeyphotography.com

Angela Weedon Photography

972-496-6696

www.weedonphoto.com

Kimberly Wylie Photography

214-219-7003

www.wyliephotography.com

PHOTOGRAPHERS (CHAIN PORTRAIT STUDIOS)

Fetal Fotos

214-387-9966

www.fetalfotosusa.com

Kiddie Kandids

www.kiddiekandids.com

The Picture People

Collin Creek Mall
972-422-4711

Town East Mall
972-270-6686

Valley View Center
972-385-7055

Vista Ridge
972-315-7553

www.picturepeople.com

The Studio at Target

888-887-8994

www.target.com

POISON CONTROL

Texas Poison Control Network

800-222-1222

www.poisoncontrol.org

R

RESTAURANTS

BAKERIES

Bread Winner's Bakery & Café

Dallas/McKinney Avenue
214-754-4940

Dallas/Lovers Lane
214-351-3339

www.breadwinnerscafe.com

Celebrity Café & Bakery

Dallas/Highland Park Village
214-528-6612

BARBECUE

Dickey's BBQ Pit

www.dickeys.com

Peggy Sue BBQ

214-987-9188

BREAKFAST/BRUNCH

Café Brazil

Dallas/University Park
214-691-7791
www.cafebrazil.com

Dream Café

Addison
972-503-7326

Dallas
214-954-0486

Lucky's

Addsion
972-447-0624

Dallas
214-522-3500

BURGERS

Ball's Hamburgers

Dallas/Snider Plaza
214-373-1717

Dallas/Northwest Highway
214-352-2525

Burger House

214-361-0370

Chip's Old Fashioned Hamburgers

Dallas/Cole Avenue
214-526-1092

Dallas/Lovers Lane
214-691-2447

Gazebo Burger

214-368-3387

Who's Who Burgers

214-522-1980

CASUAL

Café Express

www.café-express.com

Chili's Grill and Bar

www.chilis.com

Einstein Bros.

www.einsteinbros.com

Highland Park Pharmacy

214-521-2126

Luby's

www.lubys.com

McAlister's

972-248-8288
www.mcalisters.com

Mermaid Bar

214-363-8311
www.neimanmarcus.com

The Purple Cow

Dallas/Preston Royal Village
214-373-0037

Dallas/Preston Road
972-473-6100

Fort Worth
817-737-7177

Slider & Blues

Dallas
214-696-8632

Plano
972-867-8666

Snuffer's Restaurant and Bar

Addison
972-991-8811

Dallas/Greenville Avenue
214-826-6850

Dallas/Preston Road
214-265-9911

Plano
469-467-9911

www.snuffers.com

Wild About Harry's

Dallas/Knox Street
214-520-3113

Dallas/Preston Road
214-378-5000

CHINESE

Pei Wei Asian Diner

www.peiwei.com

P.F. Chang's China Bistro

Dallas/NorthPark
214-265-8669

Dallas/Dallas Parkway
972-818-3336

Grapevine
817-421-6658

www.pfchangs.com

GOURMET TO GO

Central Market

Dallas
214-234-7000

Fort Worth
817-989-4700

Plano
469-241-8300

www.centralmarket.com

Eatzi's

214-526-1515

www.eatzis.com

La Madeleine

www.lamadeleine.com

Whole Foods

214-520-7993

www.wholefoods.com

ITALIAN

California Pizza Kitchen

Dallas
214-750-7067

Frisco
972-712-0884

Plano
469-366-0060

Grapevine
817-481-4255

www.cpk.com

Campisi's Egyptian Restaurant

Dallas/East Mockingbird Lane
214-827-0355

Dallas/Elm Street
214-752-0141

www.campisis.com

Carrabba's Italian Grill

Dallas /Luther Lane
214-361-2255

Dallas/Lakewood
214-823-8678

Dallas/Dallas Parkway
972-732-7752

Plano
972-516-9900

Grapevine
817-410-8461

www.carrabbas.com

Pasta Plus

214-373-3999

Patrizzio's

Plano
972-964-2200

Dallas
214-522-7878

Romano's Macaroni Grill

www.macaronigrill.com

Sal's Pizza Restaurant

Dallas
214-522-1828

Plano
972-943-8600

www.salspizzadallas.com

JAPANESE

Blue Fish

Dallas/Dallas Parkway
972-250-3473

Dallas/Greenville Avenue
214-824-3474

Las Colinas
972-385-3474

Sushi on McKinney

214-521-0969

LATIN

Gloria's

Dallas/Greenville Avenue
214-874-0088

Addison
972-387-8842

Dallas/Lemmon Avenue
214-521-7576

www.gloriasrestaurants.com

La Duni Latin Kitchen & Baking Studio

214-520-6888
www.laduni.com

MEXICAN

Cantina Laredo

Dallas/Inwood Village
214-350-5227

Dallas/Lakewood
214-821-5785

www.cantinalaredo.com

Joe T. Garcia's Mexican Restaurant

817-626-4356
www.joets.com

Luna de Noche

972-233-1880

Mi Cocina

Dallas/Highland Park Village
214-521-6426

Plano
972-473-8777

www.mcrowd.com

Rafa's Café Mexico

214-357-2080

Taco Diner

Dallas/Villanova Street
214-363-3111
www.mcrowd.com

SEAFOOD

Fish City Grill

Flower Mound
972-899-1630

Dallas
214-891-9979

www.fishcitygrill.com

Half Shells Oyster Bar & Grill

Dallas
214-691-8165

Plano
469-241-1300

www.fishcitygrill.com

Picardy's Shrimp Shop

214-373-4099

UPSCALE FOR SPECIAL OCCASIONS

Bob's Steak & Chop House

Dallas
214-528-9446

Plano
972-608-2627

www.bobs-steakandchop.com

Café Pacific

214-526-1170

Capital Grille

214-303-0500
www.thecapitalgrille.com

Javier's Restaurant

214-521-4211
www.javiers.net

Roy's

972-473-6263
www.roysrestaurant.com

S

SAFETY (HOME)

Dr. Babyproofer

972-380-1116

Little Bird Babyproofer

972-712-3312 (Office)
214-228-8518 (Cell)

SAFETY (POOL)

Durafence

972-720-9977
www.guardianpoolfence.com

Katchakid

972-221-6605
www.advanced-pool-covers.com

Leslie's Swimming Pool Supplies

800-537-5437
www.lesliespool.com

Poolguard Pool Alarm

800-242-7163
www.poolguard.com

Protect-A-Child Pool Fence

972.681-7171 or 800-992-2206
www.protectachild.com

Protect 1 by Elite/SonarGuard

214-222-7233
www.sonarguard.com

SAFETY (TOY)

The Juvenile Products Manufacturers Association (JPMA)

856-638-0420
www.jpma.org

US Consumer Product Safety Commission (CPSC)

800-638-2772
www.cpsc.gov

SCRAPBOOKING

Creative Memories

800-341-5275
www.creativememories.com

Jo-Ann Fabric and Crafts

Dallas/Preston Forest Shopping Center
214-369-9699

Dallas/East Mockingbird Lane
214-821-4520

Fort Worth
817-485-6048

Frisco
972-712-4009

Plano
972-424-0011

Nationwide 888-739-4120
www.jo-ann.com

Michaels

Dallas/Greenville Avenue
214-461-9491

Dallas/Alpha Road
972-239-2800

Plano/West Plano Parkway
972-473-7313

Plano/West 15th Street
972-691-1355

Fort Worth
817-423-1727

Southlake
817-749-2300

www.michaels.com

Recollections . . . The Scrapbook Experience

Dallas
214-572-1112

Frisco
972-377-4069

www.recollectionsonline.com

Scrapbook Barn

972-418-8600
www.thescrapbookbarn.com

Scrapbook Page

817-346-2100 or 888-682-6685
www.scrapbookpage.com

Scrapbook Supercenter

Plano/Custer Road
972-673-0641

Plano/West Park
972-673-0690

www.scapbooksupercenteronline.com

Scrapbook Warehouse

Colleyville
817-656-4905

Lewisville
214-488-1700

www.scrap-bookwarehouse.com

Scrappin' Memories

972-874-2767

SHOES

Dillard's

Dallas/Preston Road
972-386-4595

Dallas/NorthPark Center
214-373-7000

Hurst
817-284-4566

Irving
972-258-4968

Plano
972-202-4730

www.dillards.com

Kid's Shoe Cottage

972-691-8474
www.kidsshoecottage.com

Kidzfeet

972-398-0860

Naturino

214-363-7757
www.naturino.com

Nordstrom

Dallas
972-702-0055

Frisco
972-712-3794

www.nordstrom.com

Stride Rite

Dallas
214-373-1182

Mesquite
972-270-6487

Dallas
972-661-8948

Plano
972-202-8453

Southlake
817-481-9992

Lewisville
972-459-9163

Arlington
817-467-7676

Frisco
469-633-1282

www.striderite.com

SPECIALTY HEALTH RESOURCES

Early Childhood Intervention

800-250-2246
www.eci.state.tx.us

Lakewood Pediatric Therapy, Inc.

The Sensory Integration Center of Dallas
214-821-9083

The Sensory Integration Center of Coppell
972-745-8087

www.sensoryintegration.com

The Language, Speech, and Hearing Clinic

972-774-1772
www.shelton.org

STATIONERY

Bow Tied, Too!

817-732-4595

Carté

214-559-6168

Cheekie Designs
214-691-5328

Extravaganza
972-899-3550

Finestationery.com
888-808-FINE
www.finestationery.com

French Blue
888-474-5585
www.frenchblueonline.com

JLD Greetings (Junior League of Dallas)
214-357-8822

Needle in a Haystack
214-528-2850

The Paper Lion
972-540-5966

Polka Dots
214-739-2107

Pretty Girl Events
214-929-5510

The Social Bee
972-781-0151

Socially Write
469-241-0059

The Write Invite
214-956-9966

Write Selection
214-750-0531
www.writeselectiononline.com

SUPPORT GROUPS

Allen/McKinney Area Mothers of Multiples
972-260-9330
www.amamom.org

American Cancer Society
800-ACS-2345
www.cancer.org

At-Home Dads of Greater Dallas
972-267-7699
www.slowlane.com/groups/ahddallas

At-Home Dads of Greater Fort Worth
817-475-9963
www.slowlane.com/groups/fwahd

Autism Society of America
Collin County
214-925-2722

Denton County
866-407-6593

Tarrant County
817-390-2829

www.autism-society.org

Bereaved Parents USA
North Texas
940-387-5767

National
708-748-7866

www.bereavedparentsusa.org

Candlelighters Support Group

972-566-7367 or 972-566-4987

Caring Hearts

214-345-2613

Compassionate Friends of Carrollton-Farmers Branch

972-245-9773

Dallas Epilepsy Foundation Support Group

214-823-8809

Depression after Delivery

800-944-4773
www.depressionafterdelivery.com

DMOTTC (Dallas Mothers of Twins and Triplets Club)

www.dallastwins.org

Down Syndrome Guild

214-267-1374

Down Syndrome Partnership of Tarrant County

www.dsptc.org

Early Childhood Intervention

800-250-2246
www.eci.state.tx.us

Easter Seals

Dallas
214-366-4201
www.dallas.easterseals.org

Fort Worth
817-536-8693
www.easterseals-fw.org

Infant and Toddler Intervention Program

972-599-7722
www.itipnt.org

Leukemia Society of America

North Texas Chapter
972-239-0959 or 800-955-4572
www.leukemia.org

MEND (Mommies Enduring Neonatal Death)

972-459-2396

Muscular Dystrophy Association

800-572-1717
www.mdausa.org

National Down Syndrome Society

800-221-4602
www.ndss.org

New Moms Support Group

214-345-8568

North Dallas Mothers of Twins Club

214-890-5965

Parents Without Partners

214-676-3553
www.parentswithoutpartners.com

Plano Area Mothers of Multiples

214-890-5966

www.pamom.org

Postpartum Depression Support Group

972-699-0420

www.dallasparents.org

Postpartum Resource Center of Texas

877-472-1002

www.texaspostpartum.org

Spina Bifida Association of Dallas

972-238-8755

www.sbad.gpcreative.com

WARM (What About Remembering Me) Place

817-870-2722

TOYSTORES

Babies "R" Us

Lewisville
972-459-9333

Arlington
817-784-2229

Plano
972-735-1229

Addison
972-247-4229

Fort Worth
817-423-8829

www.babiesrus.com

Bebe Grand

214-887-9224

www.bebegrand.com

Collectible Trains & Toys

214-373-9469 or 800-462-4902

www.trainsandtoys.com

Designs for Children

817-732-6711

Discovery Toys

800-341-TOYS or 214-821-7688

www.discoverytoys.com

Lakeshore Learning Center

972-934-8866

www.lakeshorelearning.com

Learning Express

Dallas
214-696-4876

Frisco
214-387-8697

Plano
972-473-8697

McKinney
972-542-8697

www.learningexpress.com

Sensational Beginnings

800-444-2147

www.sb-kids.com

Target and Super Target

www.target.com

Toys "R" Us

Dallas
214-363-3192

Mesquite
972-270-6164

Irving
972-252-5959

Dallas
972-296-5936

Plano
972-422-0408

Lewisville
972-315-6210

Frisco
972-712-0054

Arlington
817-784-0843

Hurst
817-589-7181

www.toysrus.com

Toys Unique!

214-956-8697

Toy Works

817-737-8697

Whole Earth Provisions

214-824-7444

WoodenToys-And-More

888-213-8278
www.woodentoys-and-more.com

Zebra Hall

800-834-9165
www.zebrahall.com

U

UNIQUE GIFTS

American Forests

202-737-1944
www.americanforests.org

Arm Hole

214-824-9544

Art by Anne Hines

214-207-1196

Baby Rags Company

214-868-3452
www.babyragscompany.com

Belly Casts by Mara Black

214-327-8863

Bunnies and Bows

972-317-2962
www.bunniesandbows.com

Burdick Baby

Frisco
972-712-1377

Grapevine
817-310-3358

www.burdickbaby.com

Calyx and Corolla

800-800-7788
www.calyxandcorolla.com

Cheekie Designs

214-691-5328

Chiffoniers

817-731-8545

The China Belle

972-231-0355

The Copper Lamp

214-369-5166 or 800-765-6519
www.copperlamp.com

EmbroidMe

972-668-8530
www.embroidme-frisco.com

Exposures

800-222-4947
www.exposuresonline.com

For Goodness Sake!

214-691-9411
www.forgoodnesssake.net

GoToBaby

866-510-baby
www.gotobaby.com

Keep-U-N-Stiches

214-321-0505

Kelco Designs, Inc.

405-341-9425
www.Kelcodesignsokc.com

Kidoodle

972-596-5456

Korshak Kids at Stanley Korshak

214-871-3668

Lavish

415-565-0540
www.shoplavish.com

Judith Leiber

866-542-7167
www.judithleiber.com

little words one-of-a-kind stories for children

214-208-4052
www.littlewordscreations.com

The Monogram Shop

East Hampton, New York
631-329-3379

Locust Valley, New York
516-676-5411

www.themonogramshops.com

Paper Doll

817-738-8500

Personalized Railcars for the Trains at NorthPark

214-361-7354
www.rmhdallas.com

Red Llama Studio

214-215-3049
www.redllamastudio.com

Rue1

214-265-0900

St. Michael's Woman's Exchange

214-521-3862

Sew Write Embroidery

972-874-1150

Spilled Milk Kid Couture

214-566-2610
www.spilledmilk.biz

Spiritual Garden

972-458-9229
www.myspiritualgarden.com

Sweet Classic Baking Co.

Sue Whiteside: 214-349-9780
Ann West: 214-342-2536

TuTu Cute Creations

214-707-6123

Unmistakably Molly

214-696-8686

The Well Appointed House

888-WELL-APP
www.wellappointedhouse.com

The Write Invite

214-956-9966

Yo My Booties

310-717-4912
www.yomybooties.com

V

VOLUNTEER ORGANIZATIONS (NONPROFIT)

Boys and Girls Clubs of Greater Dallas

214-821-2950
www.bgcdallas.org

Bryan's House

214-559-3946
www.bryanshouse.org

ChildCareGroup

214-630-7911
www.ChildCareGroup.org

Dallas Children's Advocacy Center

214-818-2600
www.dcac.org

The Family Place

214-559-2170
www.familyplace.org

Genesis Women's Shelter

214-559-2050
www.genesisshelter.org

Junior League

Junior League of Arlington
817-277-9481
www.jlarlington.org

Junior League of Dallas
214-357-8822
www.jld.net

Junior League of Fort Worth
817-332-7500
www.juniorleaguefw.org

Junior League of Plano
972-769-0557
www.jlplano.org

Junior League of Richardson
972-644-5979
www.jlrtx.com

Love for Children, Inc.

Contact: Monica Hinkle, 214-662-0130
www.love4children.org

Ronald McDonald House Charities Greater North Texas

214-520-5614
www.rmhcntx.com

Volunteers of America, Texas

817-529-7300
www.voatx.org

Volunteer Center of North Texas

Dallas County
214-826-6767

Collin County
972-422-1050

Tarrant County
817-926-9001

www.volunteernorthtexas.org

Women's Auxiliary of Children's Medical Center Dallas

214-456-8360
www.childrens.com

ABOUT THE AUTHORS

Kim Radtke Bannister and Kelli Strobel Chabria met during graduate school at Southern Methodist University in Dallas, Texas, where both studied TV/Radio/Film. Their careers in the field of journalism took them in different directions, but they developed skills and relationships that would one day lead them to work together.

Upon receiving her M.A., Bannister went to work writing the authorized biography of world-renowned restaurateur Phil Romano, founder of Fuddrucker's and Macaroni Grill, while freelancing for *The Dallas Morning News, WHERE Dallas, Dallas Family* and *Dallas Child*. Chabria's passion was behind the television camera as assignment editor at CNN's Dallas bureau. She covered both local and national stories, such as the tragedy in Columbine.

Bannister and her husband Nevin were one of the first couples in their circle of friends to have a baby, their daughter Sawyer. Soon after, Chabria and her husband A.J. welcomed their son, Joshua. They both considered themselves very in-the-know about things to do, where to shop, eat, exercise, etc., in Dallas, but parenthood changed everything! Two years later when Bannister's son Ford was born, she and Chabria decided it was time to pool resources, share experiences, talk to others, and gather research—thus, the birth of *littleDallas: The Definitive Guide to Life with Little Ones in the Dallas Area.*

Originally from Lake Forest, Illinois, Bannister moved to Dallas to attend SMU and received her B.A. in journalism with a minor in art history in 1992. Prior to earning her masters degree, she did public relations for a local art gallery, worked as assistant producer for *Today's Family* on KDTV-Channel 11/CBS and as the public relations assistant for Neiman Marcus downtown. Most recently, Bannister created l i t t l e w o r d s, one-of-a-kind stories for children (www.littlewordscreations.com). Her community volunteerism includes: ArtReach Dallas, Board of Directors, 1995; SMU Student Member of the Board of Trustees; SMU Young Alumni Association, Board Member at Large; Dallas Museum of Art; Dallas Children's Advocacy Center; the Women's Auxiliary of Children's Medical Center Dallas; Lakewood Early Childhood PTA; and The Parish Episcopal School.

Chabria was born and bred in southern California. She attended the University of the Pacific where she received a B.A. in communications in 1991. Chabria worked in sports marketing before moving to Dallas in 1996 to attend graduate school at SMU. While attending graduate school she was hired by CNN where she worked for five years. Chabria is actively involved with her church, Lakewood Early Childhood PTA, Women's Auxiliary of Children's Medical Center Dallas, and The Learning Tree.

Kim Radtke Bannister and Kelli Strobel Chabria are available for speaking engagements, interviews, and book signings per request. Please visit www.littledallas.com for more information or call 214-208-4052 to arrange an interview.

CONTACTS:
KIM RADTKE BANNISTER, 214-208-4052
KELLI STROBEL CHABRIA, 214-232-3759
WWW.LITTLEDALLAS.COM